ADVANCE PRAISE FOR
Go to the Sources

"Lucy Maynard Salmon was a leading professional historian long before many other women could claim the same. Her ideas about the nature of historical inquiry and knowledge, as Professor Bohan persuasively argues in this interesting and informed intellectual biography, are as fresh today in many ways as they were innovative in hers."

Michael Whelan, Associate Professor of History,
Montclair State University

"Dr. Bohan's deeply researched and well-written study on Lucy Maynard Salmon brings new attention to the work of a true pioneer in the use of original sources to teach history."

Don Carleton, Director, Center for American History,
University of Texas at Austin

"Lucy Maynard Salmon was in the vanguard of historians and social educators concerned with expanding both the form and substance of history education as well as women's place in the world. Dr. Bohan's book offers fresh insights into this neglected yet important intellectual and feminist figure."

Margaret Crocco, Associate Professor, Program in Social Studies,
Teachers College, Columbia University

Go to the Sources

Alan R. Sadovnik and Susan F. Semel
General Editors

Vol. 20

PETER LANG
New York • Washington, D.C./Baltimore • Bern
Frankfurt am Main • Berlin • Brussels • Vienna • Oxford

Chara Haeussler Bohan

Go to the Sources

Lucy Maynard Salmon
and the Teaching of History

PETER LANG
New York • Washington, D.C./Baltimore • Bern
Frankfurt am Main • Berlin • Brussels • Vienna • Oxford

Library of Congress Cataloging-in-Publication Data
Bohan, Chara Haeussler.
Go to the sources: Lucy Maynard Salmon and the teaching
of history / Chara Haeussler Bohan.
p. cm. — (History of schools and schooling; vol. 20)
Includes bibliographical references (p.) and index.
1. Salmon, Lucy Maynard, 1853–1927. 2. Vassar College—
Faculty—Biography. 3. History teachers—United States—
Biography. I. Title. II. Series.
LD7182.8.S3 B64   907'.202—dc21 [B]   00-067533
ISBN 0-8204-5504-0
ISSN 1089-0678

Bibliographic information published by **Die Deutsche Bibliothek**.
Die Deutsche Bibliothek lists this publication in the "Deutsche
Nationalbibliografie"; detailed bibliographic data is available
on the Internet at http://dnb.ddb.de/.

Cover design by Lisa Barfield

© 2004 Peter Lang Publishing, Inc., New York
275 Seventh Avenue, 28th Floor, New York, NY 10001
www.peterlangusa.com

All rights reserved.
Reprint or reproduction, even partially, in all forms such as microfilm,
xerography, microfiche, microcard, and offset strictly prohibited.

Contents

List of Illustrations xi

Acknowledgments xiii

Foreword by O. L. Davis, Jr. xvii

1 Introduction—Lucy Maynard Salmon (1853–1927) 1
    Significance of Salmon's Work 3
    Salmon's Current Relevance 6

2 Formative Experiences and Early Career 9
    Lucy Salmon's Collegiate Education at Michigan 10
    The Start of a Professional and Scholarly Career: Principal, Graduate
        Student, Instructor 15
    Salmon and Professor Woodrow Wilson at Bryn Mawr 18
    Salmon's Early Vassar College Career 23

3 Salmon's Leadership in Historical, Academic, and
    Suffrage Associations 25
    Local, Regional, and National Historical Associations: The American
        Historical Association 26
    The Dinner Affair 28
    Vassar College Historical Association 32
    Association of History Teachers of the Middle States and Maryland 32

Academic Organizations: American Association of University Women and American Association of University Professors 33
Suffrage Activities 34
Vassar College Suffrage Movement 37

4 Democratic Ideals, Life, and Relationships at Vassar College 41
Vassar's Environment and Salmon's Desire for Democratic Governance 42
Collegial Relations and Salmon's Personality 45
Relations with Students 49
Relationship with Adelaide Underhill 52

5 The Nature of History 55
The New Social History 56
On the Nature of History: Definition and Indefiniteness of History 57
History in the Round 59
History: Past with Respect to the Present 60
Value of Facts 60
History Rewritten 61
Domestic Service 63
Salmon's Writings on Newspapers 68

6 Educational Philosophy and History Courses 73
Philosophical Perspective: Age-Appropriate Historical Study 74
Sources, Judgment, and the Committee of Seven 76
Salmon's Philosophical Perspective: Progressive Methods of History Instruction 81
Courses Taught During a Forty-Year Career at Vassar College 84
Salmon's Course on Historical Material 87
Salmon's Course on American History 90

7 Lucy Salmon's Pedagogical Practices and Mentoring of Students 93
The "Long Table," Discussion, and Other Teaching Methods 96
Mentoring of Students 99
Examinations 102

The Legacy of Salmon's Students: Their Work
   in Her Classes 106
Criticism of Salmon's Methods 108

8 Lucy Salmon's Legacy 111
World War I 112
Close of Salmon's Professional Career 113
Salmon's Significance to Education 116

Photographs 119

Notes 129

Bibliography 151

Index 161

Author Information 165

*Dedicated to my husband, Thomas Eugene Bohan,
son, Thomas Caleb Bohan, and daughter, Chloë Adele Bohan.*

*Dedicated also to the zany and loyal family I was born into
on the first day of January, 1966, and
to all the teachers who inspired my desire to learn.*

Illustrations

Adelaide Underhill 119

Vassar Suffrage Parade 120

Salmon's Classroom 121

Salmon's Childhood home 122

Salmon with college students 123

The "Long Table" 124

Salmon's kitchen 125

Examination in History S 126

Salmon as a student 127

Salmon as Vassar professor 128

Acknowledgments

Lucy Maynard Salmon was unknown to me when I began the research for this book. I first learned about Salmon from Michael Whelan, my former professor at Teachers College, Columbia University. Professor Whelan wrote his dissertation on Albert Bushnell Hart, who, along with Salmon and several other prominent historians, served on the American Historical Association's Committee of Seven during the late 1800s. Whelan thought Salmon's life and contributions would be an interesting topic for research. He was correct.

I soon became fascinated with the possibility of researching her life. Her numerous papers were housed, in a fairly well organized manner, at Special Collections, Vassar College Libraries. Salmon's papers turned out to be a gold mine of information. To her credit, Salmon saved everything—laundry lists, invitations, letters from students, colleagues, friends, and family, wills, course syllabi, student work, photographs, publications, organizational information, newspaper clippings, contracts, accounting documents. The assistance of the Vassar College archivist, Nancy MacKechnie, and her assistants, Gita Nàdas and Dean Rogers, proved invaluable. They directed me to other collections within Vassar Libraries, all of which proved tremendously helpful in my development of a fuller picture of Salmon's life at Vassar. Nancy MacKechnie's vast knowledge of Vassar and its history also provided me with a network of individuals who had direct and indirect knowledge of Salmon. Considering that Salmon died in 1927, meeting anyone in the 1997–1999 period who knew Salmon was astonishing. I had assumed that she was safely dead! However, Professor Evalyn Clark, the former Vassar College history department chair, had been a student at Vassar toward the end of Salmon's career. She graciously spent an afternoon recalling her memories of Lucy Salmon. Two other Vassar alumni, E-tu Zen Sun and Jeanette Hopkins, whose mothers had been students in Salmon's classes, volunteered their knowledge of Salmon. At Vassar, a tight-knit community exists, and it made me feel extremely welcome.

Collections at several other institutions proved helpful, as well. Further, the assistance of the several archivists who mailed numerous photocopies or directed me to particular collections was beneficial. These other collections included the Bentley Historical Library at the University of Michigan, the university that Salmon attended as an undergraduate and graduate student, the Yale University Library, the Milton S. Eisenhower Library, and the Library of Congress.

O. L. Davis, Jr., at the University of Texas at Austin, and his wife, Joan Davis, assisted in numerous ways. I know that I can never properly express my gratitude to Dr. Davis. He introduced me to fellow leaders in the field of education and carefully edited thousands of pages of my work, and both he and his wife demonstrated sincere concern for my well-being. I count my lucky stars, for I could not have found a better mentor anywhere in the country. Dr. Davis's loyal following of students—his extended family—reminded me of the relationships that Lucy Salmon formed with her students.

Finally, I must thank family, friends, and professional colleagues. Jennifer Deets, Catherine Martinez, and Linda Badal listened contentedly to stories of Lucy Salmon for quite some time, and Jennifer also lent her editorial pen. Wesley Null encouraged me to finish (in the form of friendly competition mixed with sincere support) when it seemed at times that the project might be stalled permanently. Wayne Urban, a well-respected historian at Georgia State University, generously offered editorial suggestions. My parents, Fred and Liz Haeussler, provided a loving and boisterous home in which education was heralded as an ultimate priority. My siblings, Melina and Ric, affectionately known as Auntie and Uncle Ric, and Melina's spouse, Don Byers, became the extended Texas branch of the Haeussler clan. And, last but certainly not least, my husband, Tom, son, Caleb, and daughter, Chloë, taught and continue to teach me every day about the joy of living. They inspire me to be the best mother, wife, teacher, researcher, and author that I can be. The balancing act was not always easy, but I learned to juggle the demands of family and profession. Women in Lucy Salmon's era were not able to enjoy the benefits of both family and career. I am sincerely grateful for the pioneering women of her time who sacrificed in order to forge opportunities for women who followed.

An abbreviated chapter about Lucy Salmon's career was published in 1999 in *"Bending the Future to their Will": Civic Women, Social Education, and Democracy*, a book edited by Margaret Smith Crocco and O. L. Davis, Jr.

This biography, I hope, will serve as a beginning of inquiry, not only into Lucy

Salmon's career but also into the broader fields of women's studies, education, and history. Much research about Salmon remains to be unearthed in the vast archives throughout the United States. Many of Salmon's papers remain untouched. Of course, although I tried to be as accurate as possible throughout my research, I must accept any errors of fact or analysis as my responsibility alone.

Foreword

In the teaching of history in contemporary American schools, one feature appears to be central: students' use of original source materials in their studies. Students in real classrooms actually may use few or none of these sources, but the advocacy of their use is widespread and pervasive. This idea is fresh and different or it appears to be. Indeed, many teachers sense that students' study of history would be improved by their focused attention, at least some of the time, on original sources. Students' thinking with original sources, they note, can be featured in class discussions, teacher presentations, and writing tasks. A growing number of researchers, moreover, are mounting serious inquiries into dimensions of students' development of historical thinking. Even so, a number of history teachers wonder how such reasonable ideas only recently have gained prominent attention.

This wonder, of course, betrays the unfortunate ahistoricism of the field of education generally and the teaching of history specifically. Most American educators simply possess superficial, if any, awareness of the origins of commonplace practices and ideas.

Actually, the idea of using original sources in history instruction in American schools is not new. Neither is the actual use in teaching practice. Nevertheless, memory in the field of history teaching is extremely shallow. The use of sources is only an example of this failed understanding. A bit of good news is that this specific condition need not exist.

The actual origins of the uses of sources in history teaching reasonably may be of only arcane interest. However, for history educators to know about major contributors to this practice can only raise their professional insights.

This prospect is one of the several contributions of Chara Haeussler Bohan's superb biography of Lucy Maynard Salmon, a long-time Vassar College professor of history. To be sure, it was only one of Professor Salmon's interests, but it was important. Indeed, her advice to students was as simple as it was direct, "Go to the sources."

For Salmon, sources included—but were never limited to—paper documents, letters, and diaries. She insisted that her students recognize their value, of course, but she also called their attention to elements of commonplace material culture— kitchen implements, for example, and the clothing worn by ordinary people. Integral to her teaching was her emphasis on students becoming increasingly aware of the great range of possible sources for making historical meanings.

She did not neglect facts or stories or interpretations. Instead, she encouraged her students to think about the kinds of sources that would have enabled historians to infer relationships and to develop interpretations. She was much more than an enthusiast; she followed her intellectual and professional commitments through her teaching and other activities. For example, she collected sources for her Vassar undergraduates and also for high school students. Her books of source documents were used in schools across the United States.

Salmon became as widely an acknowledged authority in history as she was in the teaching of history. A notable historian, she helped launch the field of social history with her important books about domestic service and newspapers. She founded the Association of History Teachers of the Middle States and Maryland, the oldest regional group of history teachers in the nation. She was the first woman to be elected to the American Historical Association's Executive Committee. Later, she served as a member of that Association's Committee of Seven whose recommendations influenced the school history curriculum so powerfully that their traces continue to be known today. She was a founding member of the forerunner of the American Association of University Women. More than a historian and an inspiring, innovative teacher, Salmon was a leader in the movement to secure for women the right to vote.

In the preparation of this truly outstanding biography, Chara Haeussler Bohan faithfully followed Salmon's basic advice to historians. She went to the sources, which were extensive, and she returned again and again to the sources. Salmon's records at Vassar were extensive; she seemed to have saved all manner of things, from lecture notes to student papers, correspondence with individuals of little renown as well as with those whose names most people might know, "to do" lists as well as grocery receipts, class rosters and examination papers. Professor Bohan, during repeated archival trips, read them all. As important, she thought about the facts that they revealed. She also sought Salmon material in the collections of other historians and in the archives of the American Historical Association. Constructed from her scholarly mastery of the sources, she wrote the story of Lucy Maynard Salmon's life and career with great sensitivity and insight.

Professor Bohan's personal development as historian has been a delight to witness. I recall her excitement as she told me about her discovery of Lucy Maynard Salmon during a Spring seminar on curriculum history. This intense interest never faltered; it only grew. That she would write her dissertation about historian Salmon became an easy choice. Throughout the process of her research and writing, she enjoyed sharing her newly found bits and wonderments after each archival visit. We conversed about problems of interpretation, but we almost always emphasized the sound, considered judgments that she had brought with her. She wrote invited book chapters and articles from her research even as she moved deliberately to complete her dissertation. After its completion, she received the meritorious 2000 Distinguished Dissertation Award from Kappa Delta Pi, the international honor society in education.

With the publication of this biography, I invite American educators, particularly teachers of history, to Chara Bohan's deft portrayal of Lucy Maynard Salmon. They will come to know a prominent historian and history educator who, by her own teaching and scholarship, advanced both history and education. Additionally, they will develop an enriched understanding of the early and effective use of sources in the school history program. They will add a measure, at least, to their vessel of memory. Joining Professor Bohan and others of us who have been influenced by Lucy Maynard Salmon, they may be encouraged to expand the use of sources in the teaching of history to American children and youth.

O. L. Davis, Jr.
Catherine Mae Parker Centennial
    Professor of Curriculum and Instruction
The University of Texas at Austin

CHAPTER 1
Introduction—Lucy Maynard Salmon (1853–1927)

> *All experience is the product of both the features of the world and the biography of the individual. Our experience is influenced by our past as it interacts with our present.*
> ELLIOT W. EISNER,
> Learning and Teaching the Ways of Knowing, *1985, pp. 25–26*

Lucy Maynard Salmon, a pioneer in American education, is a name not commonly recognized today. As has been the case with other notable early female pioneers in education, Lucy Salmon's life unfortunately has been marginalized and largely forgotten in the pages of history.[1] An exploration of her life and career can answer fundamental and important questions about the nature of education in general. An inspiring, progressive educator, an advocate of suffrage and women's rights, a scholarly researcher and prolific author, Salmon pushed the boundaries of human understanding. Much can be learned about her that is particularly relevant today. Indeed, a number of lessons contained in Salmon's writings about the teaching of history can help to improve education, particularly history and social education.

Only one biography of Salmon was ever written. A friend and former colleague of Salmon, Louise Fargo Brown, published *Apostle of Democracy: The Life of Lucy Maynard Salmon,* in 1943. Although informative, this work follows a strictly chronological framework, tends to be celebratory and anecdotally descriptive without referencing sources, and does not explore in depth the central ideas about teaching history that Salmon expressed in her writings. Perhaps, too, Brown's account lacked a suitable level of historical detachment.

In the late nineteenth century, Salmon's early career in education was influenced by study under many highly regarded historians, including the young Woodrow Wilson. Ultimately, her vocation spanned a forty-year tenure at Vassar College, in Poughkeepsie, New York. Since her death in 1927, Salmon has remained a presence on the Vassar campus. Indeed, while the research for this biography was undertaken, a collection of Salmon's essays was compiled and published by historians connected to Vassar College.[2] An endowed professorial chair and a fund for research at Vassar College endure in her name. Clearly, this biography and the selected compilation of her essays demonstrate that Salmon warrants renewed national attention and a contemporary, or "rewritten," historical narrative. A thorough exploration of Salmon's groundbreaking ideas, especially with regard to the nature and teaching of history, is the primary objective of this book.

An exploration of Salmon's life and career will add to a larger body of knowledge in the field of biography, history, education, and women's studies.[3] She was a prolific author, with more than a dozen books and a hundred essays and public lectures to her credit. Among her many areas of research, she is primarily remembered for her work on the history of domestic science, the history of the newspaper, and the teaching of history.

Much can be learned from an examination of Lucy Salmon's career about the evolution of history and social education. Salmon's career spanned a time period when American higher education underwent tremendous transformation in its organization, administration, curriculum, mission, and place in public life.

The earliest institutions of higher education in the United States had been small, liberal arts colleges for the education of men of privilege, but the late 1800s witnessed the growth of large research universities.[4] New universities such as Johns Hopkins symbolized the new ideal of research in America.[5] Indeed, the 1890s had realized a basic turning point in American higher education.[6] Many small colleges had been transformed into large research institutions. Salmon graduated from one of America's early eminent research universities, the University of Michigan, in only the second class to admit women. At Michigan, Salmon found a love and a commitment to historical investigation that grew throughout her career.

In 1887, she became a professor of history at Vassar College, one of the historic "Seven Sister" colleges. Vassar College, a single-sex institution, had been established in the mid-1800s to provide collegiate education to women at a time when most institutions of higher learning were not open to women. Salmon began her career during a time when history was just beginning to become part of the standard school curriculum. Most of the nation's colleges of education and teachers colleges had not been established; hence, the teaching of courses in schools at the lower levels remained areas of concern, interest, and investigation for professors in the various disciplines. Salmon also was qualified to write about history and social education at the elementary and secondary levels because her professional experience included work in schools. A secondary school teacher, principal, and normal school instructor before she became a history professor, Salmon developed an interest in educational issues at various levels early in her career.

Salmon maintained a concern for the teaching of history throughout her life, but her academic writings on history education became decidedly more prolific toward the end of her career. Salmon's extensive research about domestic service and the history of the newspaper turned out to be pioneering works of historical scholarship at the turn of the twentieth century; nonetheless, her writings on education in general constitute a more relevant legacy to current questions and problems.

An intellectual progressive, Salmon spent her career working to improve education through her teaching, writing, and speaking. Her innovative methods of teaching remain as inspiring and interesting today as they were one hundred years ago. Certainly, contemporary teachers and students would benefit from introduction to Salmon's many recommendations about the teaching of history. An advocate of the new social history, Salmon believed that in order to be relevant, history must speak to the present. Therefore, history must be rewritten continuously. Indeed, the last work Salmon completed before her death, *Why Is History Rewritten?*, provided a rationale and legitimation of the need for history to be reinterpreted by succeeding generations.

Significance of Salmon's Work

Lucy Maynard Salmon (1853–1927) articulated a distinctive vision of education in America. For early twentieth-century America, Salmon's views were unconventional, progressive, democratic, and pluralistic. Undoubtedly, her vision was shaped by her status as a woman in a time when few women were afforded higher-education opportunities, even fewer pursued postgraduate degrees, and most were disenfranchised. Aware of her own exceptional educational background and standing in academia, Salmon assiduously worked to improve education. Salmon not only developed innovative teaching methods for her classroom but also lectured and wrote about such practices, thereby earning national recognition as an educator.

Although she experienced many successes in advancing knowledge about teaching and history in general, she also encountered sharp professional criticism. For example, her work in the 1890s on the American Historical Association's Committee of Seven, which examined the secondary school history curriculum nationwide, helped expand and standardize secondary-school course offerings in history. Composed of prominent historians, the Committee of Seven included Salmon as its only female member. Still, Salmon's first major historical work on domestic service met an unenthusiastic reception by the community of historians. Indeed, some critics deemed the study of domestic roles, a predominantly female arena of interest and employment, to be unworthy of academic pursuit.

Salmon's recommendations for the teaching of school history were progressive. Notions of improving society through education, cooperation, community works, and social activism were essential components of the Progressive era legacy. The hallmark of progressive era educational change with respect to history and social education was the development of new social science methods of research and investigation, expanded course sequences, innovative and experiential teaching methods, social studies curricula designed for younger children, and, ultimately, new community civics courses that "completely ignored formal politics and government in favor of themes of cooperation and community."[7] By emphasizing broadened notions of history, groups such as women, blacks, children, immigrants, and servants that had been neglected in traditional histories and that had not possessed political rights ultimately came to be included in the new social education curricula. Not only was Salmon at the forefront of advocating progressive educational reform, but also her beliefs and pedagogy were so novel that she occasionally faced strong opposition.[8]

Rejecting the transmission model of learning, Salmon favored instructional methods that encouraged independent thinking and judgment. She encouraged students to embrace history in a pluralistic sense, as a subject that encompassed all aspects of human endeavors, rather than as one limited only to military and political events. In her own scholarship, she wrote about the history of ordinary elements of life, such as domestic service, the newspaper, the kitchen, the backyard, and the main street. Indeed, her modern approach to historical studies was object based, as well, and included trips to museums to examine rocks, tools, and other artifacts. Such nontraditional subjects often were dismissed as insignificant by leading historians in the late nineteenth and early twentieth centuries.

Moreover, Lucy Salmon advocated and implemented innovative methods of teaching history. She believed that students should learn history not only through texts but also by thoughtfully experiencing and carefully examining their own communities. Although she promoted a balanced approach to teaching secondary school history that included textbooks, source documents, lectures, and independent research, she especially encouraged students' use of source documents in the classroom. She believed that this latter approach routinely was neglected in history courses. Indeed, one of her prominent legacies at Vassar is her reputation as the professor who urged her students "to go to the sources."[9] Furthermore, Salmon urged students to become involved in community endeavors; she practiced these beliefs herself. Active in the civic community at the national and local levels, Salmon held leadership roles in suffrage organizations, historical associations, and community improvement groups.

Salmon's work and career, however, have heretofore been largely ignored. Perhaps her ideas were too innovative and inclusive for a society that had not realized participatory democracy and that in practice did not support equal education for all of its citizenry, especially women. Indeed, many people with whom she worked and communicated opposed women's education, suffrage, and professional pursuits. Although Salmon was somewhat tepid in her initial support of the women's movement, she eventually became not only an advocate of suffrage but a leader in the national movement.

From a current perspective, Salmon would be viewed as an early feminist leader. During Lucy Salmon's life and career in the mid-nineteenth century, "feminism" as a term came into the English language.[10] However, the term was not popularly employed until the mid-twentieth century, so Salmon did not categorize herself as a feminist. Typically, women in nineteenth-century American society shouldered distinct feminine roles and responsibilities.[11] Women occupied the sphere of domesticity, while men fulfilled public roles. Salmon, in many ways, defied these conventional, traditional roles. Salmon was a *New Woman*. The concept of the New Woman, which gradually replaced the cult of domesticity and the doctrine of separate spheres, included females who were "professionally trained, career and role conscious, and usually self-supporting."[12] Like Salmon, many of these career-minded women did not marry. The second generation of the New Woman blazed the path toward reconciling career and marriage.

Recent scholarship has uncovered a previously lost dimension of history—the world as seen from a distinctly female perspective, which included work, family, values, relationships, and politics.[13] Women educators, such as Salmon, are an integral part of the narrative in women's history. Nancy Cott and Elizabeth Pleck credit the intensification of research in women's history not only to modern feminist thought but also to the rise of "new social history."[14] Paradoxically, Lucy Salmon was one of the first advocates of the "new social history," preceding the work of the three earliest female social historians, Mary Sumner Benson, Elisabeth Anthony Dexter, and Julia Cherry Spruill. Working at an all-female college, Salmon occupied a "separate sphere"[15] that did not limit her activities but became a source of creative inspiration.

Indeed, this single-sex environment enabled the routine establishment of strong emotional bonds between women[16] and provided advantages for women that promoted gender equity.[17] Some modern historians believe that women should not be viewed separately but should be considered as part of a larger narrative of education history. Yet, Salmon worked in a time period when opportunities for women were limited. Because she worked at a distinct campus for women, Salmon's observations preserve a historic record of female higher education during a time when mainstream research was male dominated.

Clearly, Lucy Salmon's career must be considered in the context of the times during which she worked. She taught throughout the Progressive era, at a time when women's colleges began to flourish, yet she remained disenfranchised for all but the last seven years of her life. Her world was filled with complexities, such as increased industrialization, massive immigration, technological innovation, and, ultimately, world war. Nonetheless, she remained committed to a belief in human progress. Accordingly, progress was possible through education. Toward the end of her life, she must have been amazed at the remarkable changes she had witnessed since her birth.

Salmon's Current Relevance

Lucy Salmon's career is truly relevant to current educational issues. Examining Salmon's role as an educator from a broad perspective is necessary to understand her current importance. Her legacy highlights the questions "What is education?" and, more particularly, "What constitutes social studies or history education?" Is history education telling students what they should know? Many current educators are dismayed by the lack of factual information current students possess. For example, Diane Ravitch's report *What Do Our 17-Year-Olds Know?*[18] noted significant gaps in students' content knowledge. More recently, the national history report card reflected a similar lack in students' understanding of historical events. Perhaps knowing the names of the U.S. presidents and state capitals is an important part of being an informed citizen. Lectures in history can be an expedient form of disseminating factual knowledge and of valuing teacher expertise.

Salmon's emphasis on the new social history, however, reminds educators to address the issue of how subject matter in history can be broadened to include all aspects of society. How can the everyday, ordinary aspects of life be included in social education? Indeed, if every fact cannot be taught (for facts are as numerous as sands by the sea), how do teachers engage the selection process? After such selection, what pedagogical practices are appropriate for students to learn history? Salmon considered a variety of methods to confront these questions that included discussions at the long table, informal lectures, essay examinations, and experiential learning. Should history education emphasize process or content? Salmon decidedly emphasized process but never dismissed content. She believed that students quickly would forget memorized material but that they would remember the methods learned about how to research and write long after they had left the classroom. Salmon's favorite quotation, and one that she repeatedly employed on examinations and in her writings, expressed her notion about the importance of methods. The author noted, "The ideal college education seems to me to be the one where a student learns things he is not going to use in after life by methods that he is going to use. The former element gives the breadth, the latter element gives the training."[19]

Salmon's emphasis on independent research and critical thinking sounds remarkably familiar to recently announced state and national social studies standards, which stress student development of these skills. Salmon did not simply pronounce lofty educational slogans. Indeed, she put into practice the educational goals she wanted teachers to attain. Her students' examinations and research projects validate that critical thinking was a vital aspect of her curriculum.

Salmon's work also expanded notions of how and where primary sources could be located. She naturally recognized the Declaration of Independence, the Federalist Papers, the Gettysburg Address, and the Versailles Treaty as critical original source documents. Nevertheless, she insisted that primary historical sources could also be found on Main Street, in the backyard, in the kitchen, and in the family cookbook.

Some of the changes Salmon worked to bring about in education, particularly history and social studies education, have been revisited several times in the contemporary era. Recent literature reveals that much has been learned about young students' capacity for historical understanding. Descriptions of students' capacity for historical understanding abound, and recommendations for enhancing historical studies begin with elementary students and continue for secondary and collegiate level students. Certainly, some of Salmon's recommendations about age-appropriate materials and learning seem antiquated by comparison to this recent research; however, many of Salmon's recommendations for experiential, hands-on historical learning appear current and remarkably similar to recent research.

Finally, an examination of Salmon's career leads to an examination of how the study of history can have practical applications. In studying a hometown, a student can learn about city planning. Also, a student might become involved in a political cause, as did Salmon with the suffrage movement, and contribute to making a difference, all the while learning about the democratic process. A student might start a local historical association or work for a historical museum. The possibilities for practical applications of history learning remain endless. Salmon would be satisfied to know that her life and work continue to stimulate thought about the purpose and methods of education.

More important, Salmon's life speaks to the importance in the teaching profession of close human relations. In a society in which violence is perpetrated in schools and where lawyers for educational organizations recommend that teachers never touch students for fear of resultant lawsuits, a nurturing, caring quality to teaching has eroded or been lost in education. Imagine what a wonderful place America's schools would be if more teachers were as dedicated and loving toward their students as Salmon was to hers. Her life story serves as a testament to the importance of innovative teaching coupled with caring human relationships in the education profession. A century later, Salmon's work suggests ways in which social education, citizenship education, and history education can be reconceptualized to encompass a pluralistic and democratic society for the education of all Americans.

In addition to Salmon's current relevance, a book-length biography addresses the paucity of scholarship on women educators. In *Founding Mothers and Others: Women Educational Leaders During the Progressive Era,* Sadovnik and Semel argue that little has been written about female educators, especially teachers and professors. While Horace Mann and John Dewey are familiar, few women educators are as well known. Given the fact that teaching has been a predominantly female profession for the past one and one-half centuries, certainly women have made profound contributions to modern education in America. Indeed, Sadovnik and Semel wrote that one of the objectives of their book was "to document the contributions of women to the Progressive Education Movement."[20] Their book, and the work of Solomon, Antler, Eisenmann, Crocco, Weiler, Reynolds, Blount, Bordin, Miller-Bernal, Dzuback, and others, is part of the growing literature on female educators. Despite these historians' efforts to expand the body of work on education during the past two decades, Eisenmann claims that the women's educational history literature has not influenced intellectual and institutional history as much as it has shaped social history. A reworking of the story of American higher education has not yet evolved.[21] Women continue to be treated as the "other." Dzuback recently argued that gender is central to the story of American higher education.[22] A book-length biography of Lucy Maynard Salmon adds to this growing body of knowledge, which will be critical to a "fuller story that blends the variety of populations, institutions, and purposes of U.S. higher education."[23] This blending, Eisenmann asserts, will reduce the separatism while honoring the work of women and others in academe. Certainly, there are multitudinous lessons to be learned by examining the teaching careers of these early female pioneers in education.

CHAPTER 2
Formative Experiences and Early Career

A Woman's college! maddest folly going!
What can girls learn within its walls worth knowing?
FLORIAN IN GILBERT AND SULLIVAN'S Princess Ida

In Fulton, New York, Lucy Maynard Salmon began life on July 27, 1853, before the American Civil War during a historical time when rural living was typical.[1] Indeed, Fulton was a small community along the banks of the Oswego River in upstate New York. River trade and farming were common modes of living in this region throughout the nineteenth century. Lucy Salmon's grandfather initially had settled on a farm in Fulton, but her father decided to venture away from agriculture and established what became a prosperous tannery in the area.

Lucy Salmon lived her formative years in the latter half of the nineteenth century, and her childhood memories included much time spent sewing clothes to wear, a chore she grew to dislike.[2] Her preference for playing outdoors conflicted with the late-Victorian-era custom for girls. Although she was outwardly shy, her break with some existing social conventions eventually became more familiar and foreshadowed her determination to succeed in a male-dominated society. In her later years, for example, she created a stir at Vassar by riding her bicycle around the campus. At the time, such physical exertion was deemed inappropriate for ladies.

Lucy Salmon was born to a family of English and French descent that had been a part of the early immigration to North America.[3] Records of Salmon's Puritan ancestors in Salem, Massachusetts, date back to 1654. Salmon was one of two children and the only daughter of George and Maria Clara Maynard Salmon. She had straight brown hair, pale ivory skin, and sparkling blue eyes. George Salmon also had three sons with his first wife, who had died when the boys were young.

Lucy Salmon's mother, Maria, died when Lucy was just seven years old. One year later, George Salmon remarried for a third time. Salmon's stepmother, Caroline Page, helped rear George Salmon's children who remained in the house. Death remained hauntingly familiar in the Salmon household and undoubtedly contributed to Lucy Salmon's lifelong struggle with depression.

Salmon's natural mother, Maria Maynard Salmon, had studied under Mary Lyon at Ipswich Seminary in the mid-nineteenth century. Later, Maria Maynard became the principal of Fulton Female Seminary (later renamed Fulton Falley Seminary). The seminary's reputation grew stronger under Maynard's leadership.[4] Salmon's mother was extremely well-educated for the period, and Lucy Salmon's decision to pursue a university education, although unusual in the mid-1870s, was possible in part because of family support. Lucy Salmon attended Fulton for two years and continued her secondary education in Ann Arbor, Michigan, close to relatives, in order to obtain the necessary preparation to enter the University of Michigan. The university ran a preparatory program to help students get ready for college studies. Salmon began her preparatory year in 1871, and upon acceptance to the University of Michigan, she entered her freshman year in 1872. The university had been in operation for more than twenty-five years.[5] Nevertheless, Salmon entered Michigan in only the second class to admit women.[6]

Lucy Salmon's Collegiate Education at Michigan

American higher education experienced tremendous transformation in the late nineteenth century during the period that Salmon was a student, and these changes continued throughout her years as a teacher. Although the Yale Report of 1828 had maintained the steadfastness of a prescribed college curriculum dominated by the study of literature, Latin, and Greek, by the 1850s many American academics who had attended German universities began to push for changes in higher education.[7] Henry Tappan, who in 1851 was elected the first president of the University of Michigan, was a "devotee of the German system of higher learning," and in his office he pressed not only for expansion of the curriculum but for elevation of the level of scholarship.[8] Yet, Tappan also warned against overcrowding the curriculum and cramming too many courses into the four years of study.[9] Although he left the presidency in 1863, Tappan set into motion irrevocable changes at the Ann Arbor campus. Eventually, similar reforms swept across college campuses throughout the country, led most notably by Charles Eliot, who became president of Harvard in 1869 at the age of thirty-five.[10] Eliot was a forceful and convincing proponent of the elective system. Electives offered students choice in studies, incorporation of new fields of knowledge such as science and modern languages, and the opportunity to concentrate in a particular field of knowledge.

In 1871, when Salmon began her preparatory year at the University of Michigan, James B. Angell assumed its presidency. In his inaugural address, Angell remarked,

> The public mind is now in a plastic, impressionable state, and every vigorous college, nay, every capable worker, may help to shape its decisions upon education. . . . In this day of unparalleled activity in college life, the institution which is not steadily advancing is certainly falling behind.[11]

Angell, profoundly aware of the transformation in American higher education, wanted to ensure that his university progressed at a pace equal to that of other prominent institutions. However, Angell's progressivism was tempered with a conservative side that, albeit to a lesser extent, promoted the university's existing utilitarian program of study and fostered a Christian spirit.[12] Salmon came to know Angell during her Michigan days and maintained her relationship with him long afterward in occasional exchanges of correspondence.[13] Generally, in these letters they discussed educational issues or expressed congratulatory sentiments about the other's professional accomplishments.

The post–Civil War era was a time when American institutions of higher learning were reevaluating their basic purposes and goals and many academic leaders were beginning to realize that the "dawning of a new era" in higher education was at hand.[14] Brubaker attributes the changes and the growth of universities during this period to several factors, including

> the rationalism and empiricism of the Enlightenment, the impact of the American and French Revolutions, the influence of the resurgent German universities of the nineteenth century, and the utilitarian need for incorporating new fields of knowledge . . . to serve the requirements of an expanding society.[15]

Numbers alone demonstrate the magnitude of the changes that were occurring in higher education. In 1870, approximately 62,000 students were enrolled in colleges; by 1890, that number had grown to 157,000 students, and by 1910, it exceeded 355,000 students.[16] The number of colleges also increased immensely over the course of time, and one of the greatest periods of expansion occurred in the late 1800s, after the Civil War. In 1776, just prior to the American Revolution, nine colleges existed in the American colonies. By 1876, the United States had 311 colleges and, in 1960, 2,026.[17]

When Salmon chose to attend college, few options for women were available in higher education. In 1870, two years before Salmon entered the University of Michigan, approximately 60 percent of the colleges in the United States offered degrees exclusively to men, while only 12 percent of all colleges were single-sex institutions for women. At the remaining coeducational institutions, men overwhelmingly outnumbered women.[18] In fact, 1870 was the first year that Michigan admitted women to its student body.[19] Among the general population, only a small percentage of both genders entered college; moreover, fewer than 1 percent of all women ages eighteen to twenty-one attended college.[20] Salmon was one of twelve women, along with sixty men, who enrolled in the Michigan class of 1876. In addition to Salmon, Alice Freeman Palmer, later president of Wellesley College and the first dean of the University of Chicago, and Angie Chapin and Mary Marstin, later teachers at new women's colleges, were among the twelve female students in Michigan's class of 1876.[21] These women characterized the first generation of middle-class, educated, professional women.

Once at college, however, many women students still faced difficulties. For example, not all professors at institutions of higher learning favored women's education. At Michigan and later as a postgraduate student at Bryn Mawr, Salmon encountered a culture of male chauvinism regarding women's capabilities. In *Education for Equality*, Patricia Butcher remarked,

> Increasingly fearful that educated women would forsake their traditional domestic duties and encroach upon the male sphere, the popular presses of the nineteenth and early twentieth centuries publicized the notion that women's unique mental and physiological traits rendered them incapable of education and destined them solely for the world confined by parlor, nursery, and kitchen. Opposition to women's education took many guises over the decades. The most gripping arguments were those laden with scientific findings derived from biology, physiology, medicine and, later, eugenics. All focused around three issues: women's health would suffer if they pursued intellectual endeavors; women were incapable of learning because their brains were too small; and education would deter them from marital and maternal responsibilities.[22]

Indeed, the issue of education of women was debated vigorously during this time period. One author of a popular woman's journal argued that women were "intellectual inferiors and should be submissive to the superior sex."[23] Many articles in the women's rights press, however, advocated an entirely different perspective on the purposes of female education. In fact, articles in the women's rights press reflected a diversity of opinion about the benefits of women's education ranging from the ideal of republican motherhood to the promotion of independent workers and trained professionals. Of course, the issue of coeducation was even more complex and contested. In 1854, *Una*, a women's rights periodical, criticized the University of Michigan for its policy of refusing to admit women.[24] After the Civil War, partly for the economic reason that it would have been too costly to establish separate colleges for women, the number of coeducational institutions of higher education increased.

Nonetheless, women did not enter coeducational institutions without struggle.[25] In many colleges, women faced intolerance and discrimination. For example, male students at Dickinson College refused to participate in an oratory contest because women had entered.[26] Details of the ongoing women's campaign to gain admittance to the University of Michigan, which lasted throughout the 1850s and 1860s, were featured in the *Revolution,* a popular feminist periodical. The regents of the state ultimately admitted women on the basis that future mothers and teachers needed a good education but denied that "women's rights" activists had influenced the decision.[27]

At the University of Michigan, Salmon studied under Charles Kendall Adams, the prominent professor of history who later became president of Cornell University and, subsequently, the University of Wisconsin.[28] Adams was not an ardent champion of the vast changes occurring within academia, nor was he a strong proponent of coeducation. He admitted that, "In all parts of the country, the sad fact stares us in the face that the training which has long been considered essential to finished scholarship has been losing ground from year to year in favor of the people."[29] As a historian, Adams believed that social or intellectual change should be reached slowly, and he believed that prescribed studies should remain part of the undergraduate curriculum.[30] However, he realized, somewhat to his dismay, that the college curriculum was changing in large part because of the increasing U.S. population and the resultant demands for a more practical course of study. Adams sentiments might not have boded well for Lucy Salmon as one of the first women to attend the University of Michigan. Nonetheless, Salmon proved that she was academically superior and merited college education.

Indeed, Lucy Salmon's Michigan undergraduate transcript revealed that she was largely a product of a traditional curriculum, with the majority of her classes in Latin and Greek. Mathematics was also part of the prescribed curriculum for her freshman and sophomore years.[31] Beginning in the second semester of her sophomore year, Salmon was able to take only one course in history each semester. In fact, in the 1890s, Michigan was one of the few midwestern or western state universities that maintained required freshman and sophomore classes.[32]

Salmon clearly was a gifted and dedicated student at Michigan. During her senior year, she returned early from vacation in order to study. Salmon wrote to her brother Pomeroy, "The professors are all very good to me, I think I must have got into their good graces by coming back and studying through the vacation."[33] Evidently, she sometimes labored until she fell asleep dreaming about her homework. She explained to family,

> I dozed over the constitutional changes introduced by the Norman conquest until I was at a loss to know whether William conquered the Normans in England or the Constitution or whether the constitution didn't conquer him, and was it the English

or the Norman or his own constitution? I thought I would dream it out, but I haven't quite straightened it out yet. This is the first time since September that I haven't had one of those dreadful theses to worry over.[34]

Salmon's assiduous efforts earned excellent grades. She received pluses (+) (a numbered or lettered grading system did not then exist) in all but one course over her entire four years of undergraduate study.[35] Moreover, Salmon appreciated that it was a privilege to attend Michigan and expressed guilt to her brother, Pomeroy, feeling that it was "selfish" of her to be there.[36] Her strong sense of family obligation made Salmon keenly aware that her absence from home was felt. Had she been at home in upstate New York, she surely would have been assisting in the running of the household. Indeed, Salmon wrote to Pomeroy in 1876, during her senior year, that she "was just about to pack up my trunk and go home myself—I think of you and mother so often."[37] Furthermore, Salmon understood that most women her age did not have the benefit of a college education.

While at Michigan, Salmon also engaged in a variety of social and intellectual extracurricular activities. She was a member of the Students' Christian Association and the President of Q.C.[38] Q.C. was a local women's society at Michigan that Salmon helped to found. It met once a week, and members engaged in intellectual debate and conversation. Organizing this group was the beginning of her lifelong interest and commitment to founding intellectual organizations. At one meeting, the members debated the merits of higher education for men and women. Q.C. provided a sense of community and sisterhood for Salmon.[39] Its members, who included Alice Freeman Palmer, were all pioneers in higher education for women. Many of Salmon's ideas and principles about higher education can be traced to her undergraduate experience at Michigan.[40]

In 1876, the University of Michigan awarded Salmon an A.B. in history. When later asked about what she had learned during her four years at Michigan, Salmon responded indirectly by identifying three important influences on her education. First was the conscious effort by the faculty and students to expand the boundaries of knowledge. Second were the great teachers who demonstrated activity, enthusiasm, and patience. Third was the intellectual atmosphere in which learning was its own reward, for there existed no grading system, honors, or prizes.[41] These experiences helped to form Salmon's ideas about education, which Salmon carried throughout her professional career.

Most early female graduates of college believed that they needed to choose between marriage and a career. For many of these women, especially those from the upper socioeconomic classes, the choice of paid work brought social disapproval. However, higher education provided many women with a heightened sense of independence, and teaching became the most common field of employment for these women. Like other educated women of the time, Salmon chose teaching as her profession and never married. She believed, however, that women should not enter teaching unless they had a true sense of vocation.[42] Salmon, who subsequently taught at Vassar College for forty years, firmly believed that teaching was her vocation. The field in which she chose to teach—history—was dominated by men. Indeed, most of her colleagues in professional historical associations were men. Rather than take an unassuming posture in deference to her gender, Lucy Salmon diplomatically and politely expressed her convictions and made her imprint on American education at the turn of the twentieth century.

The Start of a Professional and Scholarly Career: Principal, Graduate Student, Instructor

Following her graduation from the University of Michigan, Salmon accepted a job as assistant principal of a newly established high school in McGregor, Iowa. In many ways, Salmon simply followed a career path similar to that of her mother prior to marriage. For Salmon, her first position was her entrance into a lifelong career in education, and her experience at McGregor was filled with challenges and achievements. In this small-town community school, Salmon began to form ideas about education that were based upon actual practice. Initially, as an inexperienced teacher, she faced the common problem of how to discipline unruly children. One former student recalled,

> What tricks we big boys in the High School tried to play on her! She was oh, so young, to be so highly educated and so modest and blushing in her unpretentious efficiency. She won us all by pretending never to see our rudeness, and violations of her regulations.[43]

Although Salmon managed discipline problems with some trepidation but apparent adeptness, she did not enjoy handling these problems. She wrote to her brother, Pomeroy, "Discipline in the High School is below par and things in my department seem to be going to destruction, in the opinion of others as well as my own, but I don't feel disposed to stop them."[44] Yet, on the whole, her first year's performance was commendable, and she was asked to return the following year as principal at a salary of $75 a month.[45] For the next four years, Salmon worked extremely hard as principal and teacher, and she was generally well liked by the parents and students. Students at McGregor High School were active. During Salmon's tenure, they held literary society entertainment, student artwork shows, and high school concerts.[46] While Salmon was principal, McGregor achieved a rank of second in the state.[47]

Despite Salmon's accomplishments and her warm reception in McGregor, she felt intellectually isolated and was plagued by feelings of inadequacy. McGregor, located in rural Iowa, was distant from any large cities, and Salmon continually faced the challenge of teaching classes for which she believed she was ill prepared. Perhaps she came to realize that she would prefer teaching college-level students, who presumably would be more motivated and require less disciplinary intervention. At any rate, after the 1880–1881 school year, she resigned her position and took a year off from paid employment in order to stave off a nervous breakdown.[48] Salmon had worked tireless long hours for four years at McGregor. The isolation and the loss of family members during her young career caused greater emotional strain than the physical and intellectual demands of her job. In order to obtain much-needed rest, Salmon spent the year in the homes of various relatives.[49] The following year, she returned to the University of Michigan's classrooms as a graduate student in order to pursue further studies in political science and history. The return to a stimulating, intellectual atmosphere renewed Salmon's emotional health.

Salmon's archival papers contain few records of her year as a graduate student at Michigan. Presumably she studied diligently, because her transcript reveals that she matriculated in courses in history, pedagogy, political economy, and international law.[50] In addition, she wrote a master's thesis entitled, "A History of the Appointing Power of the President." This paper was so well received that she later gave presentations at historical conferences about this work, and the thesis was published in 1886 in the first volume of the American Historical Association's papers.[51] Salmon's adviser, Professor Charles Kendall Adams, described Salmon's thesis as "the most conspicuous success of his efforts in training students in original research."[52] Interestingly, Salmon's first historical research investigated a conventional political topic. She had not yet become acquainted with social history. Later works explored less conventional topics.

After earning an A.M. in 1883 from the School of Political Science at the University of Michigan,[53] Salmon accepted a job teaching history at the State Normal School in Terre Haute, Indiana. Normal schools were the precursors of teacher's colleges. Established in January 1870, the State Normal School began with fewer than twelve students.[54] During Salmon's tenure, however, the student body grew tremendously, although the number of faculty remained relatively small. Including the president and vice president, there were nineteen instructors in 1886.[55] Ten, including Lucy Salmon, held faculty positions in distinct departments, and seven individuals served as assistants. In addition, five teachers, referred to as critics, administered and supervised practice teachers. Conversely, by 1886 the student body comprised 769 students: 315 men and 454 women.[56] Salmon's classes must have been fairly large, making teaching a challenging task.

The stated purpose of the State Normal School was "to prepare those who wished to teach in the common schools of the country" and to instruct college and university graduates aiming "to be superintendents and principals of high schools."⁵⁷ Graduates who were residents of Indiana had to promise to teach in the common schools of the state for a period of time equal to twice that spent in the Normal School. Salmon provided the sole instruction in history. Although she enjoyed teaching a subject in which she had earned her degree and for which she felt comfortably prepared, she found that she had philosophical differences with the mission and administration of the school. Indiana State Normal School was considered not a high school, academy, or college but a technical school to prepare teachers. Salmon wrote,

> I enjoyed my work with the students immensely. . . . But I was a mis-fit in the administration,—it seemed to me that, in a homely phrase, it always put the cart before the horse and encouraged the students to believe it was possible to learn how to teach a subject without knowing anything about the subject itself.⁵⁸

Although Salmon remained interested in education throughout her life, her experience at the Terre Haute Normal School tainted her perspective about all normal schools. She did not think that a role existed for normal schools in the American educational system. However, her experience at Indiana also fostered a lifelong concern with educational issues.

During vacations from Indiana, Salmon attended educational meetings and wrote about educational issues. For example, she published "Education in Michigan During the Territorial Period" while she taught at Terre Haute.⁵⁹ This paper was a carefully documented investigation into state legislation and practical experiments in education prior to Michigan's gaining statehood.⁶⁰ Toward the end of the article, Salmon addressed the fundamental issue of the importance of studying the history of education. She wrote that no question was more important than the education of the working classes. Furthermore,

> If an examination of the period means anything, it means that we may often save ourselves from serious mistakes by a better acquaintance with what has been done by our predecessors. . . . It does not seem too much to hope that at no distant day a knowledge of the principles of education, and the history of its progressive steps, will be considered as essential to every citizen as a familiarity with the principles of political economy and with the leading events in English and American history.⁶¹

While teaching at Terre Haute, she also joined the American Historical Association (AHA), in 1885. She was one of the first women to be accepted as an AHA member, having been sponsored by Charles Kendall Adams, her mentor at Michigan.

Salmon searched for educational and career options while she taught at Terre Haute. In March 1885, she wrote to Professor Herbert Baxter Adams, of Johns Hopkins University, indicating that she wished to continue her studies in history.⁶²

She requested an exception to Johns Hopkins's policy of not admitting women, asking "whether there are any conditions, and if so what under which I could receive the same advantage of instruction and study in the department of history as are given to gentlemen."[63] Salmon also noted that half of the students she taught at Indiana State Normal School were men. Nonetheless, graduate study at Johns Hopkins did not become an option for Salmon. Johns Hopkins did not admit women students.

In March 1886, while Salmon was still in Terre Haute, Alice E. Freeman (Palmer), her friend and former classmate at Michigan and now president of Wellesley College, extended her an offer to teach history and political science at the college.[64] She offered Salmon $1,000 per year plus board and washing. Although Freeman acknowledged that she was unable to offer Salmon a better salary, Salmon considered it an extremely enticing offer. Certainly, Salmon carefully considered the invitation. She had not enjoyed teaching at Indiana State Normal School. Still, for unknown reasons, she had reservations about accepting the Wellesley offer, and, in the end, she declined it. Salmon later explained to a friend,

> At one time years ago I was teaching for a very brief period in a school whose policy I had no sympathy whatever and the conditions seemed intolerable. Like the traditional clap of thunder from a clear sky came an offer of a position at Wellesley. . . . I had many friends in the faculty, Alice Freeman had been a classmate in college. The one thing was *I didn't want to go!* Why I didn't want to go I couldn't explain very clearly,- it was simply a feeling that I couldn't be happy at Wellesley.[65]

As luck (or perhaps misfortune) would have it, she instead elected to study history with a future president of the United States, Woodrow Wilson, at Bryn Mawr College. Perhaps Michigan President James B. Angell's advice was influential, for he wrote to Salmon that she had more to gain by going to Bryn Mawr than by going to Wellesley.[66] Fortunately, Salmon's rejection of the Wellesley position did not seem to affect her relationship with Freeman, because they maintained correspondence and occasionally met for Michigan alumni events in Boston.[67]

Salmon and Professor Woodrow Wilson at Bryn Mawr

When the chance for Salmon to become a fellow in American history at Bryn Mawr College, in Pennsylvania, arose in 1886, she accepted the opportunity to study under Woodrow Wilson, then a young professor.[68] At age thirty, Wilson was a seemingly self-confident "moving orator."[69] He favored the German lecture method and tended to write works of political history. From all outward appearances, Wilson was not a proponent of women's higher education. Thus, his first teaching assignment at Bryn Mawr, a woman's college, became a distinctly unhappy experience.[70] In the position of professor of political economy and public law, he taught Lucy Salmon. Interestingly, Salmon was three years senior to Wilson in age. Charles Kendall Adams, Salmon's mentor at the University of Michigan, wrote to Salmon, "That Mr. Wilson will be able to help you much you must not anticipate. Indeed I shall be very much surprised if you find that he knows nearly so much history as you do."[71]

Bryn Mawr was in only its second year of operation when Salmon matriculated. It was one of the group of institutions of higher education that later became known as the Seven Sister colleges (the others were Wellesley, Radcliffe, Barnard, Mount Holyoke, Smith, and Vassar, at which Salmon later taught).[72] These colleges were private, selective, all-female institutions of higher learning that offered opportunities for women at a time when many elite private colleges, such as Harvard, Princeton, and Yale, accepted only men.[73]

Women's colleges were strongest in the eastern and southern sections of the United States. Although the early women's colleges struggled for academic prestige, by the end of the nineteenth century many had become as academically rigorous as corresponding male and coeducational institutions.[74] The founders of the Seven Sister colleges promised to develop women's minds without sacrificing their femininity. They offered leadership opportunities typically not available to women at coeducational institutions. In general, the curriculum offered at women's schools emphasized classical studies in Latin and Greek but permitted some elective studies in the sciences and fine arts.[75] The curriculum also tended to be modeled after that at the older private men's institutions. Bryn Mawr, which was founded in 1884, slightly later than the other eastern women's colleges, adopted a more innovative curriculum than did other women's colleges. The curriculum was based upon the Johns Hopkins model, which "permitted a judicious use of electives."[76]

Prior to his arrival at Bryn Mawr, Wilson reviewed a version of Salmon's master's thesis, "The History of the Appointing Power in the United States," which she presented at the Seminary of Historical and Political Science in 1885.[77] Thus, he was familiar with her work. Wilson wrote to her that Bryn Mawr had too few teachers and graduate students to hold separate formal courses for advanced pupils.[78] In fact, in its first year of operation, only seven graduate students enrolled at Bryn Mawr.

Although Wilson came to characterize his first teaching job at Bryn Mawr as unpleasant, he worked diligently in preparation for class, struck out in new directions, and did not let the textbook dictate the scope and sequence of his courses. Wilson taught Greek and Roman history, English and American history, a course that included French history, the Renaissance, and the German Reformation, and political economy and politics.[79] One unusual method that Wilson implemented was to teach Greek and Roman history concurrently. Consequently, he devoted one week to Greek history and the next to Roman history, so that students could make comparisons reasonably. Wilson also wanted students to perceive connections between history and contemporary affairs. In order to emphasize this point, he developed a curriculum in which he taught the history of England in reverse chronological order.[80]

Wilson's pedagogical approach relied primarily on lectures. He defended this teaching method vigorously, commenting,

> Some of the subtlest and most lasting effects of genuine oratory have gone forth from secluded lecture desks into the hearts of quiet groups of students; and it would seem to be good policy to endure much indifferent lecturing for the sake of leaving places open for the men who have in them the inestimable force of chastened eloquence.[81]

At Bryn Mawr, Wilson developed the habit of talking generally about a topic; while he spoke, students were not permitted to take notes. There followed fifteen to twenty minutes of dictation during which students were required to take notes. Wilson continued this practice at Wesleyan and later at Princeton. According to former students and subsequent biographers, Wilson was a polished and eloquent lecturer from the beginning. One student remarked that Wilson's speeches were fascinating and held her "spellbound."[82] Despite his success as a lecturer, this teaching method was not completely favorable to all students. One author said that he "did not seem to welcome questions and preferred to carry on the main discussion himself. He lectured too much and expected very little from students."[83] Wilson himself was aware of some of the problems with lecturing. In fact, he remarked,

> Lecturing to young women of the present generation on the history and principles of politics is about as appropriate and profitable as would be lecturing to stone masons on the evolution of fashion in dress.[84]

Such sentiments, however, reveal that Wilson found flaws with his audience, rather than his pedagogy.

Salmon and Wilson met three times a week for seminars, and Salmon recalled that these conferences were "absolutely informal."[85] Still, during the academic year, Salmon grew secretly to disdain Wilson's sense of self-importance, as well as his teaching methods. She realized that Wilson had limited regard for women's academic potential. In 1887, Wilson explained that his new fellow in History, Cora Agnes Benneson, "was a pleasant small person of mind which it will be very hard, but I trust not impossible, to impress."[86] Benneson, who succeeded Salmon as Wilson's third fellow, had earned an A.B., 1878; LL.B., 1880; and A.M., 1883, all from the University of Michigan. Benneson's achievements belie Wilson's disdainful and clearly inaccurate assessment.

Indeed, at Bryn Mawr, Woodrow Wilson appeared to be uncomfortable teaching women. When Wilson joined the faculty in 1885, he noted, "I should, of course, prefer to teach young men, and if I find that teaching at Bryn Mawr stands in the way of my teaching afterward in some men's college, I shall, of course, withdraw."[87] In a letter Wilson later wrote to his wife during his third year at Bryn Mawr, he confided,

> When I think of you, my little wife, I love this "College for Women," because *you* are a woman: but when I think only of myself, I hate the place very cordially: for you are the *only* woman hereabouts of your genuine, perfect sort- the only woman anywhere of your perfect title to be worshipped by men.[88]

As for Salmon, Wilson wrote that she "needed only constant encouragement—but that amounted to carrying her on my shoulders. I'm *tired* of carrying female Fellows on my shoulders!"[89]

Salmon certainly was aware of Wilson's sentiments with regard to women's education. Indeed, in a letter to her former mentor, Charles Kendall Adams, Salmon noted,

> I am quite sure that he [Wilson] never wholeheartedly believed in college education for women. He once said to me that a woman who had married an intellectual, educated man was often better educated than a woman who had college training. All of this used to amuse me, and I never presented any other side of the subject to him, or stated my own views- it would have been useless to do so.[90]

Not only did Wilson assume that women's intellectual abilities were inferior; his teaching methodology failed to impress Salmon. While he was an exceedingly gifted lecturer, Salmon said, "he never liked teaching as differentiated from lecturing."[91] Although Lucy Salmon was the only student in Wilson's graduate seminar, he tended to dominate the conversation and frequently lectured to her.[92]

Even at such an early point in her career, Salmon's teaching methodology differed significantly from Wilson's. Generally, she did not favor the German lecture method but believed that the teacher's role at the university level was to encourage thinking and independent research. Salmon had little regard for Wilson's pedagogy. In 1919, while he was president of the United States, Salmon wrote that "President Wilson has never been a teacher. No man belongs to any occupation so long as he lacks the essential characteristics of that class."[93] Ironically, at her public memorial, one of the historians who paid tribute to Salmon, aware of pedagogical separation between Wilson and Salmon, remarked,

> But it may interest her friends to know that her views on the guidance of a class too large to conduct by the seminary method closely resembled those of Woodrow Wilson. Many years ago, while he was President of Princeton, he told me that the lecture

should be relegated to a secondary position, not entirely eliminated, for it still had value as synthesis, as an opportunity to expound a point of view and to exhibit to the students a model of historical method- but made secondary to, or co-ordinate with, class discussion. . . . This is the method which, I understand, was introduced at Vassar by Miss Salmon, and which is still successfully practiced at Vassar.[94]

Although Salmon and Wilson's methodological approaches to teaching differed, the distinctions were writ not in black and white but in shades of gray.

Still, even when Wilson became governor of New Jersey and later president of the United States, Salmon never completely revised her early opinion of him. In an article written in *The Nation* under the pen name "A Neutral" during Wilson's term as U.S. president, Salmon wrote that Wilson "has always been intensely interested in his own career. . . . He is thus inherently a self-centered man."[95]

After Bryn Mawr, Wilson became a professor of history at Wesleyan University and, later, at Princeton University. Wilson spent twelve years as a professor at Princeton (1890–1902) before being promoted to president of the university.[96] During his tenure as professor, he was tremendously popular. In fact, he was nominated seven times as the undergraduates' favorite professor. At Princeton, he taught upper-division courses in political economy, public law, and politics. Because of his popularity, Wilson's classes were large, and, often, students had standing room only. One former student recalled that if someone wanted to skip one of his classes, another student eagerly took the vacant seat.

Lectures remained the core of Wilson's classes and, often, "a student could get by, or even achieve an honor grade, simply by memorizing the dictated material."[97] Aware of the weaknesses of the lecture method, Wilson searched for ways to encourage more active learning. Indeed, as president of the university, he later introduced a preceptorial system, in which students met in less formal settings and in smaller groups with "tutors" who typically had recently earned graduate degrees and hoped to obtain university appointments.[98] During his academic career, Wilson published several books that generally covered topics in political history, such as his study of congressional government and his biography of George Washington.[99] Yet, Wilson, like Salmon, was an advocate of the new social history.

Salmon claimed never to have met Wilson again after she completed her work at Bryn Mawr, other than to have seen him in a Boston restaurant and heard him address the National Equal Suffrage Association in Atlantic City in 1916.[100] However, Wilson visited the Vassar campus on December 9, 1892, to lecture on democracy and again on May 3, 1902, to give the Founder's Day address.[101] Perhaps Salmon forgot about these lectures when recalling her Wilson memories twenty-five years later, or perhaps she purposefully avoided attending Wilson's Vassar speeches. Either way, the discrepancy is indicative of the poor relations between the two. One Wilson biographer labeled Salmon's recollections "acid."[102] Having to work with disapproving male professors such as Woodrow Wilson surely constituted a serious challenge for women like Lucy Salmon in the 1870s. Regrettably, such challenges continued after graduate school, because professional opportunities for educated women were limited.

Salmon's Early Vassar College Career

After completing her year as a fellow in History at Bryn Mawr in 1887, Salmon was appointed an associate professor of history at Vassar College in Poughkeepsie, New York. Matthew Vassar established the college in 1865. As an institution, Vassar had as its stated mission to provide an education intellectually equal to that provided elsewhere to men. Indeed, Matthew Vassar communicated to the Board of Trustees, "It occurred to me that woman, having received from her Creator the same intellectual constitution as man, has the same right as man to intellectual culture and development."[103] Such sentiments were extremely progressive for the mid-1800s, a time when universal public education did not exist and women, for the most part, were not permitted to study at the same institutions as men.[104]

Vassar established a rigorous curriculum similar to the studies at corresponding male institutions. Quickly, Vassar became an institution that provided an academically challenging and first-rate education. Indeed, some of Vassar's earliest graduates established themselves as intellectual and progressive leaders throughout the United States. These notable early graduates included Harriot Stanton Blatch '78, a leader of the New York suffrage movement and daughter of Elizabeth Cady Stanton; Julia Lathrop '80, a settlement house leader at Hull House, in Chicago, along with Jane Addams, who in 1916 became the first chief of the U.S. Children's Bureau; Dr. Emma Culbertson '77, vice president and first female member of the American Academy of Medicine; and Annie Howes Barnes '74 and Helen Hiscock Baskus '73, Association of Collegiate Alumnae presidents; several other alumnae went on to teaching careers at Wellesley, Smith, Vassar, and other notable institutions.[105]

By national standards, the quality of the faculty at Vassar was superb. However, scholars have not achieved consensus as to the quality of the education many of the early women's institutions provided. Liva Baker claimed that "First-rate faculty was difficult to hire and keep—then as now."[106] However, Leslie Miller-Bernal argues that single-sex female colleges promote gender equity, provide educational advantages to women, and serve as a means of redressing deep rooted aspects of sexism.[107] Clearly, leadership opportunities for women in education were limited, even though "the nineteenth century witnessed a dramatic shift in the teaching force."[108] At women's colleges, female faculty members were guaranteed to be welcome, and, in fact, Wellesley at its founding was committed to an all-female faculty and president.[109] Vassar president Henry Noble MacCracken found that his predecessor, James Monroe Taylor, had recruited professors whose teaching ability was better than that which he had known at Harvard or Yale.

Remarkably, at Vassar, the majority of the faculty was female. For example, in 1911–1912, during Salmon's career, only 17 of the 108 faculty were male.[110] One of the most prominent faculty members, then and ever, was Maria Mitchell, an astronomy professor (1865–1888). Mitchell established the orbit of a newly discovered comet and for this accomplishment became the first woman elected to the American Academy of Arts and Sciences (1847).[111] At Vassar, Mitchell lived in the Observatory, rather than in the residence halls, and devoted herself not only to scientific pursuits but also to the advancement of women.

When Salmon came to Vassar in 1887, she was the only history professor at the college, but the department quickly expanded. Salmon developed a long and distinguished career as the chair of the history department at Vassar College (1887–1927). She became an acknowledged expert on domestic service and on the role of the newspaper in historical studies. She published comprehensive books: *Domestic Service* (1897), *Progress in the Household* (1906), *The Newspaper and the Historian* (1923), and, *The Newspaper and the Authority* (1923). Her teaching and writings also focused on general history and history education.[112]

In addition to her research contributions, Salmon led a distinguished career as a teacher and as a member of national history and education associations. She served as a member of the Executive Council of the American Historical Association (AHA) and several prominent AHA committees, founded the Association of History Teachers of the Middle States and Maryland, the oldest extant council devoted to history education, and worked on the Executive Council of the American Association of University Professors. Salmon's leadership in these and other prominent education organizations earned her national recognition.

Salmon's leadership roles in these organizations are the focus of the next chapter, and the remainder of this book is devoted to exploration of Salmon's life at Vassar and her ideas about the nature and teaching of history. Although entirely separate chapters could be devoted to Salmon's work on domestic service or the newspaper, for the purpose of this writing Salmon's major works serve to illustrate her conceptions of history and illuminate how she encouraged students to implement similar historical research methods in her classroom.

CHAPTER 3

Salmon's Leadership in Historical, Academic, and Suffrage Associations

> *Once women are the center of attention,*
> *history has a different script.*
> NANCY WOLOCH,
> Women and the American Experience, *p. v*

Lucy Salmon was one of the first and most prominent female leaders in the historical profession. Indeed, she joined the American Historical Association in its beginning as others formed it. As a scholar, she developed pioneering forms of historical research and an unsurpassed "modern writing style."[1] Still, her leadership was not confined to the historical profession. Her impressive influence in other arenas, such as suffrage, education, and the community, extended her commitment and faithful dedication to history, to democratic principles, and to Progressive movement causes. Certainly, as a woman in the male-dominated field of history, Salmon found that her gender profoundly shaped her beliefs and affected her leadership abilities in multifaceted ways.

Salmon became a leader in the field of higher education at the beginning of a time that Jackie M. Blount has characterized as "a golden age for women school leaders."[2] Although Blount's analysis targets female superintendents, the Progressive era witnessed the early blossoming of opportunities for women in the field of education in a variety of venues. By assuming leadership positions in several academic organizations, community groups, and Progressive era political causes, Salmon served as a role model to other women. Furthermore, Salmon promoted other women to positions of responsibility.

Salmon was among the early Progressive era female leaders in higher education. Salmon, and others such as Alice Freeman Palmer, president of Wellesley College, M. Carey Thomas, president of Bryn Mawr College, and Mary E. Woolley, president of Mount Holyoke, sought advances for women in institutions of higher learning. During the same time period, other female leaders in education, described as "Founding Mothers," included Caroline Pratt, Helen Parkhurst, Flora J. Cooke, and Ella Flagg Young. The latter group of women leaders promoted progressive educational ideals in the elementary and secondary levels of education. Despite the growth of opportunities, all of these women faced challenges due to gender. Because Salmon was the first to occupy leadership positions in historical associations, she faced many challenges. Nonetheless, she succeeded in promoting innovative approaches to the study of history and in advancing women to roles in historical and educational organizations through the many administrative and elected positions that she held throughout her career.

Local, Regional, and National Historical Associations: The American Historical Association

Significantly, Salmon became one of a very small number of women who enrolled in the American Historical Association, and, during its early years, she was its most influential female member. Herbert B. Adams, a professor of history, had founded the AHA in 1884 at Johns Hopkins University.[3] In the first year, three women joined the Association. Salmon joined the AHA with ten other women the following year, in 1885.[4] At the time Salmon joined the AHA, its membership totaled 375.[5] In 1889, the American Historical Association received special incorporation from Congress. Without a doubt, Salmon's participation in some of the Association's activities was difficult. Although the AHA accepted women members from its inception, some of its activities were closed to women.[6] Yet, throughout her life Salmon remained committed to the work of the American Historical Association. Indeed, only two years after she joined its ranks, she became a life member.[7]

In 1895, after ten years of membership, Salmon must have been aware of changes within the American Historical Association. Several members who believed that the methods of electing AHA officers were autocratic pressed for democratic changes within the administration of the organization. These members led a revolt against the AHA founder Herbert Baxter Adams's "virtual one-man rule and limited view of the AHA's structure and function."[8] Against Adams's wishes, the Association agreed to the National Education Association's request to form a committee to recommend the history curriculum for the nation's secondary schools. Subsequently, in 1897, the AHA established the Committee of Seven.

The Association's Executive Committee invited Salmon to join the AHA's Committee of Seven to consider the scope and sequence of history offerings in secondary schools and to recommend college entrance examinations. Salmon was the only woman to serve on the Committee of Seven, and she contributed to its highly influential final report. Salmon suggested the addition of another woman to membership on the Committee of Seven, but the Association rebuffed her request. In a letter to George Burton Adams dismissing Salmon's request, Herbert Baxter Adams, a fellow Committee member, wrote, "I am inclined to think that one woman is enough!"[9] Salmon's work on the Committee of Seven is treated extensively later in this book, because her work on it served as a foundation for her beliefs about the teaching of history. Salmon's service on the Committee of Seven also contributed to her prominence as a nationally recognized authority in education.

Still, early in the AHA's history, few women broke "the glass ceiling" to serve on the Association's Executive Council. Only slowly did the AHA recognize women for leadership roles. By 1920, for example, approximately 19 percent of the AHA members were women; nevertheless, before 1933, only five women were among the ninety-six members who had been elected to the Association's Executive Council.[10] Salmon, who served on the Executive Council from 1915 to 1919, was the first woman to gain a position as an officer of the American Historical Association.[11] More remarkably, Salmon was elected to the Executive Council at a time when women remained disenfranchised nationally. Salmon's election to the AHA Executive Council highlights the membership's support for a broadened conception of citizenship. Had election been reserved only to those with the legal right to vote, Salmon could not have served on the AHA Executive Council.

Upon Salmon's nomination to the Executive Council, Louise Fargo Brown, a colleague and later a dean at the University of Nevada, wrote that she was glad to see Salmon receive the recognition she had so long deserved.[12] A. C. McLaughlin, a professor of history at the University of Chicago, who also held positions as chair of the Committee of Seven and managing editor of the *American Historical Review*, wrote to Salmon to express his pleasure at her election.[13] In 1915, AHA members elected Salmon to the Executive Council along with Eugene C. Barker, Guy Stanton Ford, Charles H. Haskins, Ulrich B. Philips, and Samuel B. Harding.[14] Election to office, however, did not end Salmon's difficulties as a leader of the AHA. In many of her leadership roles within the Association, Salmon endured gender discrimination. In particular, her position as the only woman on the Executive Council created tremendous controversy when her presence threatened to displace the 1916 annual banquet at the exclusive, all-male Metropolitan Club in New York City. In some ways, Salmon's experience was similar to the problems faced by Martha Burk, of the National Organization for Women (NOW), in her effort, in 2002, to compel the Augusta National Golf Club, home of the Masters Tournament, to accept female members.[15] While Burk enjoyed tremendous media attention and caused national controversy, Salmon endured gender discrimination without fanfare. Despite the nearly one hundred years that separate these events and their differing circumstances, both women confronted the basic challenge of discrimination against women.

The Dinner Affair

The conflict about the dinner began in 1916 during Salmon's first year on the Executive Council. Clarence Bowen, treasurer of the AHA, explained to her that each year, on the day after Thanksgiving, a few officers of the Association (including the AHA president) hosted a dinner for Council members at the Metropolitan Club. He continued,

> There is a Ladies' Annex to the Metropolitan Club so that if you come to the dinner, we can have the dinner in the Ladies' Annex instead of the club where no women are allowed. If you come to the dinner you would be the only woman present. . . . We have never had a woman at our dinner or at our Council meeting but if you will kindly come, rest assured it will be a pleasure to all of us to meet you.[16]

Of course, Salmon found the letter disturbing. Initially, she was uncertain as to the appropriate manner in which to respond to Bowen. She sought the advice of a Council colleague, Columbia University professor William Dunning. From Salmon's perspective, she understood that she had not been invited to the dinner or the luncheon the next day at the Metropolitan Club because she was expressly informed that no woman had ever attended either one.[17] She added, "I am sure the writer must have drafted a dozen letters before achieving one so eminently successful in conveying to me the information that my presence would be somewhat superfluous."[18] Believing that she was unwelcome at these events, Salmon initially declined the invitations. However, Evarts B. Greene, secretary of the Council, later wrote to her and intimated that she should attend the AHA Council meeting. Hence, Salmon's perplexity grew. She not only wondered how she should proceed; she also wondered about Dunning's opinion in the matter.

Unbeknownst to Salmon, Dunning had begun correspondence with Greene about Salmon's possible presence at the dinner.[19] Dunning confessed to Greene that he did not feel well satisfied with the handling of this matter, but perhaps "we may do better next year."[20] Apparently, not all officers truly desired Salmon's presence at the Metropolitan Club dinner. Dunning replied to Salmon's inquiry that the following day's luncheon was a purely business function and that it had been rescheduled for Columbia University's faculty club, which had always been open to women, and, furthermore, that he had arranged for her to attend. He added, "If, as you guess, 'the presence of a woman on the board is not particularly agreeable to a few of the members,' I venture to guess that those few are going to have a lot of disagreeable facts to confront in the ensuing years."[21] In the end, notwithstanding the correspondence, Salmon apparently did not attend the dinner function at the Metropolitan Club. She attended the luncheon and meeting at Columbia the next day, however.

The next year, 1917, the simmering controversy about a woman's attendance at the Executive Council dinner escalated. This problem became entwined, as well, with other differences over the nature of the dinner. During 1917, at a meeting in Cincinnati, the Council had voted to hold a subscription dinner at which all members paid their own way, rather than the traditional arrangement in which the president and one or two other members hosted and paid for the dinner.[22] Many Council members believed that a subscription arrangement would be more democratic and would not prevent a poor man from assuming the presidency of the AHA.[23] Bancroft and his followers claimed in 1915 that the AHA's power structure was elitist. Council members were sensitive to such obviously undemocratic practices. In addition, some members did not want a formal dinner at all in light of the existing war conditions. George Burr, Cornell University professor and president of the AHA in 1916, wrote to Evarts B. Greene,

> The plan of a subscription dinner did not, as you know, have its origin with me; but I have earnestly supported it, not alone because of what seems to me the country's great and growing need for such economies, and because of the Association's own poverty, but also because of what I fear is the discourtesy to Miss Salmon in our holding a meeting any sort of place to which she can hardly come. When last year, during an intermission of the Council's session, I mentioned to her the dinner (as, being host, I felt bound to do) I discerned at once that she did not understand the matter as did Mr. Bowen.... Perhaps, I am no expert in such things, there is no way, while the Council includes but one woman, to provide for her presence with us; but I wish that could be made to appear to her as well as to us, or else that something might be substituted for our time-honored dinner at the Club.[24]

Nonetheless, a majority of Council members voted to suspend the subscription dinner, because Worthington C. Ford, the AHA president in 1917, and Clarence Bowen, the AHA treasurer, offered to host the dinner at the Metropolitan Club and pressed members to accept.[25] Bowen informed Salmon that if she chose to attend the meeting, the Council could hold the dinner at the Ladies Annex of the Metropolitan Club. Salmon initially indicated her willingness to attend the Council subscription dinner if held earlier as originally proposed, rather than the day after Thanksgiving, which conflicted with a previous engagement at Vassar.[26] When the idea of a subscription dinner was abandoned in favor of the traditional

Metropolitan Club banquet, Salmon declined the invitation. Once again, the AHA Executive Council held its annual dinner without the presence of its only female member.

Although some men on the Executive Council acted surprised that Salmon did not attend more dinners or speak more often at the meetings,[27] in the face of discrimination and rejection, Salmon's ability to participate and to influence others was limited. Nonetheless, Salmon continued her charge to increase female leadership positions in the AHA. She subtly insisted that women should be considered for AHA positions. For example, one year after her election to the AHA Executive Council, Salmon wrote to Secretary Evarts B. Greene,

> My embarrassment comes largely from the fact that the membership of the Association is about two-thirds men and one-third women. For the most part, however, all appointments have been made from the men members. I have no desire whatever to suggest any radical change of policy. All of the women that I know are ready and glad to do everything that they are asked to do and yet they have no desire to claim appointments or elections as their due. Yet, when you suggest "names of promising scholars who have not yet been brought into close relationship with the actual work of the Association," those that most naturally occur to me are the names of women. We have, for example, at least two dozen brilliant women who are graduates of Vassar College who have taken their doctor's degree in history at Cornell, Columbia, Wisconsin, Chicago and Yale. At least a dozen other women who have not been connected with Vassar have done most acceptable work in the field of history. These are the names that naturally suggest themselves to me and yet I hesitate to name them as to do so may seem a radical change of policy.[28]

Subsequently, Salmon wrote to Greene, "I do not wish to seem to press the names of women for membership on any of these committees; and yet, as I think I have written more than once before, I can but feel that the Association has by self-denying ordinance been deprived of the services of a good many able women."[29] Clearly, Salmon wanted to advance women to AHA leadership roles. As a member of the AHA Committee on Appointments, one of her primary duties was to suggest names for various committees. However, she never recommended all women with whom she was acquainted. Salmon was discriminating in her recommendations. For example, Salmon confidentially expressed to Greene that she did not have much faith in the judgment of Miss A. B. Thompson.[30] Yet, Salmon continued to believe in the importance of promoting women to leadership roles. In order that her efforts might be successful, however, Salmon realized that she could not be perceived as overbearing or "radical," notwithstanding her later claims to have been a "revolutionist all her life."[31]

Despite the limited nature of Salmon's power within the AHA, Salmon continued active membership throughout her career. She sporadically presented at AHA annual conferences.[32] She served on the AHA's prominent Committee of Seven. In 1917, Salmon was asked to preside over the AHA dinner for women.[33] She also worked on arrangements for annual conferences and served on the AHA General Committee in the 1910s. Nonetheless, Salmon never became the chair of an AHA committee and, therefore, was not listed on the agenda for AHA Executive Council business meetings. Salmon's efforts within the AHA usually took place behind the scenes, rather than in the limelight, in her dealings with other members and in her attempts to promote women to various positions.

Salmon worked to advance women for leadership positions in other groups, as well. For example, when the presidency of Vassar College became vacant in 1913, Salmon endorsed two women candidates, one of whom was Amy L. Reed.[34] Although neither was offered the Vassar presidency, Salmon never stopped her crusade to help women obtain leadership roles and viewed colleges for women as central to these possibilities. In fact, in 1906, she wrote to a former student, "The discouraging feature is the indifference of the public to needs of the woman's college, while pouring out with lavish hand for the man's college. But perhaps we shall come into our own in time."[35]

In the early 1900s, Salmon also suggested to the Vassar trustees that the faculty govern itself until it appointed a new president.[36] Although she recommended women candidates, the trustees did not choose any of them. Their selection, Henry Noble MacCracken, the fifth president of Vassar College, nevertheless was ideologically and educationally progressive. Throughout Salmon's career, she promoted many women's careers and especially supported her former female students in their professional careers. Salmon's skillful advancement of women characterized myriad endeavors that she pursued.

Salmon was astute about the manner in which she conducted her professional relationships. She maintained extensive correspondence with fellow historians and frequently invited them to speak at Vassar[37] or to share meals with her when she attended scholarly conferences. In addition, she frequently mailed to colleagues copies of her publications.[38] In fact, she even attempted to garner support for a new AHA magazine devoted to literary history that would appeal to general readers, but several colleagues, including William Roscoe Thayer and Frederick Jackson Turner, rebuffed her effort.[39] Salmon believed that "literary history," with its attention to prose, was written in a more interesting manner than "traditional or academic history" and would be popular with a wider audience of readers. Once again, her democratic principles were apparent, and her interest presaged by some forty years the commercial success of *American Heritage* magazine.[40] Salmon's connections, however, enabled her to garner enough support to establish regional and local organizations dedicated to the study of history. Salmon continued to hope that smaller, both town and state, historical associations would affiliate with the larger American Historical Association.

Vassar College Historical Association

Salmon tirelessly promoted progressive methods of history teaching, particularly through her leadership in local and national organizations. In 1896, she founded the Vassar Historical Association, composed of Vassar alumnae who were interested in increasing acquisitions for the Department of History, preserving historical material, and introducing scientific methodologies into local historical societies.[41]

Initially, the organization grew out of Salmon's arrangements for a reunion to be held close to Washington's birthday for graduates at Vassar College. She was interested in reports from her former students about the opportunities for graduate work in history at various colleges.[42] Salmon could relay this information to current students. The group's official founding date is recorded as February 22, 1896, and Vassar College credits Salmon's historical association with the donation of many books to the Vassar library.[43]

True to her intent, Salmon was able to secure affiliation of the Vassar Alumnae Historical Association with the American Historical Association. The Vassar group met annually until 1913, at which its meeting date conflicted with another campus activity that the Vassar president declined to change. Sensing official, although tacit, criticism of her organization, Salmon never called another meeting of the Vassar Alumnae Historical Association, and hence the organization disbanded. At this time, however, Salmon had become much more involved with state and national historical associations and certainly lacked the time to devote to this small organization of her former students.

Association of History Teachers of the Middle States and Maryland

Hoping to broaden her efforts to connect history teachers to the American Historical Association and the larger historical community, Salmon solicited support around the turn of the century for a regional historical association that would include both teachers and academics. She invited Herbert B. Adams, AHA secretary, to a Philadelphia meeting of history teachers of the Middle States and Maryland to be held in 1900.[44] Salmon desired to connect the work of state and local historical societies to the larger national organization. With regard to this pursuit, Salmon achieved modest success. For example, Henry Bourne, of the AHA General Committee, wrote Salmon in 1904 to inform her that the next AHA session would be devoted to state and local historical societies in order to bring the work of the Association into closer contact with state and local organizations.[45]

Nonetheless, Salmon continued to solicit support for an organization that welcomed both historians and history teachers in schools. She wrote, for example, to

James Harvey Robinson at Columbia University to ask him if he would assist with the contemplated organization. Robinson assented and suggested some others who also might be willing to become involved.[46] Salmon wrote to other historians, as well, hoping to garner support for her organization.[47]

Salmon's idea for the organization came to fruition at the annual conference of the Association of Colleges and Preparatory Schools of the Middle States and Maryland held in Syracuse, during Thanksgiving recess, 1901. Members interested in the teaching of history met and decided to form an organization known as the Historical Association of the Middle States and Maryland. The name was later changed to the Association of History Teachers of the Middle States and Maryland. An Executive Committee that included Professor James Harvey Robinson, of Columbia University; Professor E. H. Castle, of Teachers College, Columbia University; Professor Julius Sachs; Lucy M. Salmon; Jane Brownell; Professor D. C. Munro; and Dr. Eugene W. Lyttle was appointed to draw up a constitution and by-laws.[48]

The Executive Committee met in New York on February 8, 1902, and drafted and later submitted a constitution. The stated purpose of the Association was "to advance the study and teaching of history and government through discussion and publication" and to "promote personal acquaintance among teachers and students of history."[49] The organization's first program was held at Teachers College, Columbia University, on Friday and Saturday, March 13–14, 1903. At the first meeting, Salmon, along with several others, addressed the question "What may reasonably be expected of the high school teacher of history?" Salmon was also elected president at this meeting.[50] F. S. Edmonds, of Central High School, in Philadelphia, was elected vice president, and Professor E. H. Castle, of Teachers College, Columbia University, became secretary-treasurer.

By 1903, Salmon officially had founded and then become president of the Association of History Teachers of the Middle States and Maryland.[51] Still extant in 2003 (it is currently named the Middle States Council for the Social Studies), it is the oldest regional council dedicated to history education, preceding by twenty years the formation of the National Council for the Social Studies.

Academic Organizations: American Association of University Women and American Association of University Professors

Salmon was also involved in the founding of two prominent academic organizations, the American Association of University Women (AAUW) and the American Association of University Professors (AAUP). The former organization was an outgrowth of the Western Association of Collegiate Alumni, which Jane Bancroft, the first fellow in history at Bryn Mawr College, had founded, in December 1883.[52] Salmon was one of the original members present at the first meeting. Bancroft's advice and assistance led to the union of the Western Association of Collegiate Alumnae with the Association of Collegiate Alumnae in 1889. The later organization ultimately became the American Association of University Women.

Apparently, Salmon was more involved with the American Association of University Professors than she was with the AAUW. The idea of forming the AAUP began at a conference attended by representatives of eight universities in November 1913. Two years later, more than 250 individuals attended the association's first official organizational meeting, held in New York City on January 1-2, 1915.[53] AAUP activities in the early years involved investigations of a number of alleged violations of academic freedom, but the group's stated purpose was to handle the entire field of professional problems. Salmon became a member of the AAUP Council in 1917[54] and in 1919 was elected to the Executive Committee of the AAUP.[55] Salmon dedicated her efforts to actively soliciting academics to join the organization. In addition, she served on AAUP committees that created organizational policies and participated in AAUP investigations in disputes between professors and academic institutions.[56] The AAUP investigatory work was sensitive in nature, so Salmon's correspondence alludes to particular cases but omits specific details and names. Disputes often involved issues of contracts, academic freedom, and governance. Because Salmon was involved with the AAUP in its early formation, much of her worked involved recruiting members to increase the size and power of the organization.

Salmon frequently emerged as a leader in many organizations to which she belonged, and in several cases, she helped found groups that had no antecedent. Through her work in these associations, Salmon hoped to foster progress in historical study, in particular, and educational institutions, in general. Her involvement in the suffrage movement, described in the next section, is indicative of her pioneering leadership to bring about progressive social change in American society.

Suffrage Activities

Salmon paved the way for increased numbers of women to participate in leadership roles, not only in historical associations but also in the American political arena. In the early 1900s, for example, Salmon accepted prominent positions in the burgeoning national suffrage movement and assisted with the effort to enfranchise women throughout the United States. Not only did she head the suffrage movement at Vassar College, she also became an officer of the National College Equal Suffrage League (NCESL), an auxiliary of the National American Woman Suffrage Association (NAWSA). She served, additionally, on the Executive Advisory Council of the Congressional Union for Woman Suffrage, led by Alice Paul. Undoubtedly, Salmon's work for suffrage was not only an extension of her efforts to promote women in leadership roles but also part of her broad vision to bring about a truly democratic society in which all citizens, women and men, were part of the civic community and contributed to its history.

The suffrage movement in the United States was precipitated by women's participation in the antislavery movement in the early to mid-1800s. At the World Anti-Slavery Convention in London in 1848, both Lucretia Mott and Elizabeth Cady Stanton, prominent American activists, were denied the right to sit on the convention floor with their male colleagues.[57] This insult prompted Mott and Stanton to issue a call for American women to meet in Seneca Falls, New York. At that meeting, in 1848, delegates formulated a Declaration of Sentiments. This manifesto, modeled after the Declaration of Independence, proclaimed the self-evident truth that "all men and women are created equal."[58] The women who participated in the Seneca Falls Convention, however, clearly lacked mainstream popular support. Nancy Woloch, for example, characterized the antebellum women's rights advocates as "an extremely small and marginal group."[59] Indeed, Salmon delayed her own identification as a women's rights advocate until the early 1900s. Moreover, Salmon wrote to her friend Adelaide Underhill in 1897 that she had been reading *The Outlook,* a feminist periodical, because a Wellesley woman with whom she had been sharing quarters in Zurich received it. Salmon wrote that she had been reading *The Outlook*'s

> latest twaddle on the woman question, coeducation, politics for women, clubs, etc., and long to edit for a few weeks a woman's paper and give the editors of the O—a little advice; not that they would take it, but it would be a satisfaction to free one's mind.[60]

Only when woman's suffrage became a national movement during the Progressive era did Salmon slowly add her support to the effort.

In 1906, however, she spoke to the Thirty-Eighth Annual Convention of the National American Woman Suffrage Association, in Baltimore, that honored the eighty-sixth birthday of Susan B. Anthony. In her address, Salmon recalled having attended, in 1863, at the tender age of ten, her first suffrage meeting and one at which Anthony spoke.[61] As a child, Salmon grew up in the Finger Lakes region of New York, near Seneca Falls. Still, Salmon confessed that many years had passed before she became committed to the fight for suffrage. By 1911, Salmon not only was interested in suffrage activities in New York but also became involved at the national level.

Conflicts within the suffrage movement had hampered its initial progress. However, the length of the fight to achieve the vote also helped secure a large base of support.[62] Networks of women's causes developed political arenas and fostered a feminist context for diverse kinds of women's work. After 1900, the Progressive movement aided the suffrage cause; by then, many Americans no longer viewed it as "outlandish and bizarre."[63] Moreover, in several western states, women already had been granted the right to vote. Although these western women constituted only a small minority of the overall female population, they proved, at least on a symbolic level, that women's votes contributed to the political process. The National American Woman Suffrage Association became the successor movement to Mott's and Stanton's women's organization. From 1905 to 1915, Dr. Anna Howard Shaw served as president of NAWSA, and this organization developed a large base of support.

In the early years of the new century, Salmon tended to align herself with Anna Howard Shaw and the more conservative wing of the suffrage movement, despite Salmon's long acquaintance with Harriot Stanton Blatch, Vassar College '78, the daughter of Elizabeth Cady Stanton. Stanton headed the more radical New York suffrage movement.[64] Although they differed on issues of suffrage, Blatch and Salmon maintained cordial correspondence throughout Salmon's Vassar career. Even before Salmon became actively involved in the national suffrage movement, she and Blatch shared ideas. Blatch read Salmon's *Domestic Service* and "found it scholarly and convincing,"[65] although she sarcastically noted that a reviewer referred to Salmon as "'Lucious,' and apparently thinks you must be a man. Any display of authority must connote male."[66] Respecting each other's intellect, both women extended invitations to the other to give lectures; they also shared social time when visiting one another.[67] For example, Blatch spoke at Vassar about suffrage on several occasions and enjoyed meals with Salmon. In addition, Blatch invited Salmon to go to Albany to speak at a hearing before the Judiciary Committee of the Senate and Assembly on a proposed amendment that would give women the right to vote.[68]

Both Blatch and Alice Paul, who led the Congressional Union for Woman Suffrage (later known as the National Women's Party), had been influenced by the confrontational activities of the Pankhursts, prominent English suffragists. The Congressional Union attracted much public attention by staging suffrage parades. Indeed, many Americans considered such political tactics to be shocking. Although Salmon attended the first meeting of the Congressional Union's Advisory Council at Alice Paul's personal invitation, she must have been an apprehensive participant. Certainly, she developed ideological differences with the policies of the Congressional Union. After two and one-half years, Salmon requested that her name be removed from the files of the New York Congressional Union's Advisory Council.[69] Salmon subsequently agreed to Anna Shaw's request that she devote all of her efforts on behalf of suffrage to the National American Woman Suffrage Association.

Although the women's movement increasingly gained popular acceptance after the turn of the century, particularly among educated women, many women perceived the tactics of the Union to be radical and began to oppose them, even within the walls of academia. For example, Henry Holt, publisher and editor of *The Unpopular Review,* a journal in which Salmon published a few articles, wrote that it was unfortunate that Salmon had written about suffrage because "from some points of view my mind is made up regarding woman suffrage. So I am mighty sorry that the article yu [*sic*] offer me is on that. But I should like to see it anyhow. There is no knowing that but yu [*sic*] may convert me!"70 Even among educated women, there were many who opposed suffrage. Caroline Atwater, the wife of a Vassar College trustee, in a letter to Salmon, revealed class bias as a reason for her opposition to suffrage. Atwater explained,

> And I by no means understand, yet, the future value of woman's suffrage. If it were a campaign for suffrage governed by educational and property-holding powers, I would be with you heart and soul. But your movement asks for the admission to rights many millions more of uneducated, ignorant foreigners, most of them under the rule of force and the fear of their men.71

Clearly, academia was not united in its support for the suffrage movement, even in the early 1900s.

Vassar College Suffrage Movement

Salmon matured into the role of a staunch advocate in the college movement to support woman suffrage. Indeed, her increasingly passionate commitment to the women's suffrage movement ultimately contributed to a conflict with Vassar president James Monroe Taylor. In the early 1900s, Taylor prohibited suffrage movement activities on the Vassar campus.72 In fact, Salmon wrote to Frances Davenport in 1906 that suffrage "has always been a tabooed question here,—has never been debated in the college since I have been here as far as I know, but there seems to be some interest in the subject now."73

Salmon and other faculty members who participated in suffrage movement activities therefore were compelled to go off-campus for their activities. Despite the continuing prohibition of suffrage activities on the Vassar campus, Salmon was elected vice president of the National College Equal Suffrage League. That same year, as "presiding officer" of the Vassar suffrage movement, she entertained Anna Howard Shaw at her Poughkeepsie home before Shaw gave a public lecture.74

At the local level in Poughkeepsie, in no small measure because of Salmon's efforts, the suffrage movement gained popularity among Vassar students. Salmon helped recruit members to the student suffrage organization. In addition, Salmon invited prominent suffragists such as Charlotte Perkins Gillman, Anna Howard

Shaw, and Harriot Stanton Blatch to come to Vassar to speak about the movement. In order to avoid the campus ban on suffrage activities, one meeting was held in the cemetery across the street from Vassar. Salmon and Abby Leach, a Vassar professor, although avowed suffragists, acceded to President Taylor's wishes that they keep away from the cemetery meeting. Nonetheless, the meeting, attended by forty undergraduates and by the prominent suffragists Harriot Stanton Blatch and Charlotte Perkins Gillman, was featured in several New York newspapers.[75]

President Taylor was quite upset by the publicity generated by this "graveyard rally." Nevertheless, suffrage activities at Vassar continued, despite his disapproval. Indeed, a year later, Vassar women debated suffrage *on* the campus. When Taylor learned that Vassar faculty had participated in the debate, he criticized them for controverting his policy against discussion of controversial subjects on campus.[76] Salmon and other politically active faculty members believed that his policy limited their academic freedom of speech. Consequently, they objected not only to the policy but also to Taylor's exclusion of the faculty in matters of governance. Salmon's stated beliefs and actions in the midst of this controversy reflected her continued commitment to democracy. In the wake of faculty criticism, Taylor decided, at age sixty-five, that he would retire from the Vassar presidency. Despite these end-of-career difficulties, Taylor's tenure remains properly credited with generally furthering women's education. He added nearly a half a million dollars to Vassar's endowment, offered most faculty positions to women, and encouraged students to find satisfying work after college.[77]

Ironically, M. Carey Thomas, president of Bryn Mawr College and later president of the National College Equal Suffrage League, directly solicited Salmon's support for the college suffrage movement. Thomas invited Salmon to speak at the Women Suffrage Convention in Baltimore, at which the main featured speaker was Jane Addams. Thomas wrote, "I feel that women's colleges and we as college women owe a very great deal to the pioneers. . . . There has been, it seems to me, a great change in public sentiment during the past few years and such recognition would, I think, do good."[78] In 1907, Salmon bought a life membership in the College Suffrage League and increased her suffrage activities at Vassar.[79]

The College Suffrage League's successor, the National College Equal Suffrage League, officially was founded in 1908. Two years later, M. Carey Thomas notified Salmon of her election as an NCESL vice president. Later, Salmon happily reported how widespread the interest in suffrage was among Vassar alumnae.[80] Salmon's work on behalf of suffrage prompted an invitation from the Congressional Union in 1915 to visit the White House when President Woodrow Wilson received envoys of the Woman's Voters Convention.[81] She may not have attended this prominent event. Salmon's papers do not indicate whether she accepted or declined the invitation; however, she later claimed to have seen Wilson only in Boston and Atlantic City after completing her graduate work under his tutelage.

By 1916, the National College Equal Suffrage League experienced severe financial difficulties. The league needed $5,000 for its annual operations but lacked these necessary resources.[82] Several vice presidents of the organization, including Salmon, had been unable to attend meetings. Because the American Historical Association meeting fell near the meeting time of the College Suffrage League, Salmon was one who had not been present at some meetings of the suffrage group. Therefore, Thomas thought Salmon would want to discontinue her service as an officer. Salmon, however, chose to remain on the organization's letterhead even when M. Carey Thomas notified the membership of the College Suffrage League that the group would cease to exist.[83] Thomas indicated several reasons for the disbandment of the NCESL. These included (1) a lack of need for the organization because all of the members of faculties and most of the students were already committed suffragists (2) a desire to shift focus to the ratification of a federal amendment to the Constitution, and (3) the financial instability of the League. Thomas, with remarkable foresight, concluded that Anna Howard Shaw and Carrie Chapman Catt "assure us that if every suffragist does her whole duty during the next two years all the women in the United States will be enfranchised in 1920."[84] Despite the dissolution of NCESL, by 1918 many suffragists recognized that efforts by women such as Lucy Salmon would result in the enfranchisement of all American women.

Salmon became a national leader in both historical and academic associations and in suffrage organizations. Her challenges and successes led to increased options for the women who followed her. No longer would female leaders confront the embarrassment of "dinner affairs" and be forced to devise "graveyard rallies" when banned from public discussion of enfranchisement. Ultimately, women gained the right to vote and the support to head historical organizations. Salmon's commitment to these professional and her communal activities were a straightforward extension of her progressive, democratic principles, which profoundly affected how she taught history.

CHAPTER 4

Democratic Ideals, Life, and Relationships at Vassar College

> *Her education . . . has merely allowed her*
> *to get all dressed up with no place to go.*
> EUNICE FULLER BARNARD *in*
> *the* New York Times, *May 1, 1932*

Lucy Salmon's everyday life and relationships at Vassar College affected both her teaching methods and her persona. As a progressive educator, Salmon generally found support on the Vassar campus for her broad-minded approach to teaching. Salmon fostered many close friendships among those who agreed with her methods. Lasting enmities, however, developed with a few colleagues who disagreed with her pedagogical practices. Nonetheless, Salmon modeled democratic principles in class and on campus and ardently urged the college administration to adopt similar ideals. In contrast with her democratic goals, the turn-of-the-century Vassar community was close knit and predominantly female, with severe regulations on personal conduct.

Nonetheless, Vassar College offered its students an elite education. Following its founding in 1865, the college developed a strong liberal education and fostered at the same time a spirit of investigation. This tradition was maintained even as other universities became large, research-oriented institutions in the second half of the nineteenth century. The aims and methods of instruction delineated in Vassar president John H. Raymond's sketch of the institution that he submitted to the U.S. Commissioner of Education in 1873 accorded conveniently with Salmon's personal philosophy of education. Indeed, Raymond stated that the object of instruction was "not simply to charge memory with facts, but to teach the methods and cultivate a habit of independent research."[1] In addition, the limited size of Vassar's student enrollment, which hovered around 350 when the school was established and which the trustees capped at 1,000 in 1905,[2] fostered strong personal relationships among faculty and students. Certainly, Salmon developed many close connections with students and her colleagues at the college.

Vassar's Environment and Salmon's Desire for Democratic Governance

At the turn of the twentieth century, Vassar was not unique in the type of education it offered to young women. However, having been one of the first female colleges established in the United States, it served as a prototype for others that followed. As the number of colleges increased in the United States, prospective female students and parents encountered an increase in available educational choices. In fact, former Wellesley College president Alice Freeman Palmer, who had attended the University of Michigan with Salmon, noted the nature of some of these choices in her 1889 article.[3] Palmer placed institutions into three categories. The first—coeducational universities—included institutions dominant in the western part of the United States. These schools educated women and men together, established the same requirements for degrees, and generally permitted women to find their own living arrangements. In the late 1800s, most coeducational institutions did not provide dormitories for women.

Vassar was one of the second types of institution that Palmer described—the women's college. Unlike coeducational universities, women's colleges aimed to develop the social and moral aspects of women, as well as their intellectual capabilities.[4] Colleges for women explicitly acted *in loco parentis* and therefore not only provided living quarters, meals, physicians, and social and religious activities but also carefully monitored student conduct. Faculty members lived among the students and were chosen not only for their teaching qualifications but also for their social graces. Palmer, who as Wellesley's president had recruited and hired numerous faculty members, held that a teacher at a woman's college

> must be also a lady of unobjectionable manners and influential character; she should have amiability and a discreet temper, for she is to be a guiding force in a complex community, continually in the presence of her students, an officer of administration and government no less than of instruction.... Learning alone is not enough for women.[5]

The third category of women's colleges Palmer described as the "annex." This category included women's institutions that were affiliated with large, research-oriented universities; examples included Barnard College and Columbia University and Radcliffe College and Harvard University. In the late 1800s, these kinds of arrangements were in their infancy. At the time, these schools offered no degrees, no dormitories, and no female instructors, and their staffs were composed of volunteers from the neighboring institution.[6] Because these colleges were established only shortly before Palmer's article was written, she could not accurately assess their educational worth.[7] Interestingly, in the spring of 1999, Radcliffe merged completely into Harvard and no longer retained an independent educational identity; however, Barnard has chosen to maintain some separation from Columbia.[8]

Clearly, Vassar operated in a fashion like that of Palmer's typical women's college. Located in upstate New York, on a farm near the bucolic Hudson River, the college constructed as its first on-campus building the mammoth Main Hall.[9] For several years, Main Hall, completed in 1864, housed every resident with the exception of the astronomy professor Maria Mitchell, who lived in the observatory. Main Hall also served all instructional, education, residential, social, and religious needs. According to the Reverend John H. Raymond, Vassar's second president (but the school's first functioning president),[10] Matthew Vassar's intent was to found an institution for women equal to those established for men.[11] One notable difference from comparable male institutions, however, was that Vassar officials, like faculty at other women's colleges, took strict measures to ensure a system of housing and living regulations that served as social safeguards for the students.

Having graduated from the University of Michigan, a coeducational institution with few regulations on living, Salmon disliked the unfamiliar and burdensome restrictions commonplace at Vassar. Salmon preferred that students have more freedom than they had, but the time of Vassar College students was carefully controlled.

> Students rose at 6 A.M., said morning prayers at 6:45, breakfasted at 7:00, then arranged their rooms and observed a twenty-minute "silent time"; had morning study hours and recitations from 9:00 to 12:40; dinner at 1:00; recreation from 2:00 to 2:40; afternoon study from 2:45 to 5:45; supper at 6:00, evening prayers and another "silent time"; then evening study hours from 8:00 to 9:00, and required lights out at 10:00 P.M.[12]

When Salmon arrived at Vassar in 1887, she was given a list of students' names with times noted next to each. She learned that the purpose of the list was to aid her supervision of the times of students' baths. Salmon refused to regulate such chores.[13] Although she initially enjoyed the built-in social life provided by the communal living arrangements, Salmon viewed the restrictions as oppressive for both students and faculty. She worked to curtail of the regulations on student life and to institute increased democratic governance. According to Lynn Gordon, "Campaigning for the relaxation of social rules was part of Salmon's effort to create a self-governing community of equals. Salmon wanted students to have a greater voice in their course selection. Most important, she believed Vassar women should practice democracy and cooperation."[14]

Salmon even published her strongly held ideas about the restrictiveness of Vassar College life in *The Vassar Miscellany*.[15] She claimed that the faculty and other resident officers of Vassar College were disenfranchised with respect to residential regulations because they did not have a voice in or the ability to change the rules governing their living conditions.[16] According to Salmon, these rules had come from various sources and were generally antiquated. She suggested "rearrangement of the government of the Vassar Association" and "the enfranchisement of all persons resident in the community."[17] Ultimately, Salmon thought that the greatest beneficiary of such reorganization would be the students, who would benefit from democratic governance. Indeed, Salmon believed that faculty would model democratic principles that would encourage students to abandon their passivity and to engage actively in learning. To Salmon, an advocate of experiential learning, self-government should be part of students' total educational process.

Later in her Vassar career, Salmon found other opportunities to cultivate democratic principles and to empower the faculty and students in matters of governance. She initiated clubs for students to organize and manage. In the classroom, Salmon also granted students various freedoms and choices, such as the freedom to select writing assignments or essay questions on examinations.

The most poignant evidence of Salmon's cultivation of democratic ideals occurred in 1914, during the interim period following the retirement of Vassar's president, James Monroe Taylor. While the Board of Trustees searched for a replacement, Salmon and other prominent faculty members began to implement changes in the system of governance at the college. They believed that faculty members should have a greater role in making policy decisions. For example, she suggested that Vassar adopt an open forum for the discussion of public affairs.[18] In another letter, she expressed hope that Vassar would "make a permanent contribution to educational theory and practice in the form of a plan of academic government that would truly represent all the elements included in a college."[19] Salmon pressed to implement her vision of a more democratic community. In addition, Salmon offered several suggestions for the choice of president in which she stressed the need for reorganization of the administration.[20] Indeed, Salmon, using the pseudonym "A Near Professor," earlier had published her ideas about the pitfalls of college governance and its need for revision in an article titled, "The Next College President."[21] In essence, Salmon's article indicted the authoritarian system of governance that prevailed on college campuses.[22]

In a letter to the college trustees, Salmon described several candidates that she favored for the vacant presidency, two of whom were women and graduates of Vassar College. None of the people Salmon recommended became Vassar's next president. The new president, Henry Noble MacCracken, however, was much more progressive than his predecessor in his views of education. Consequently, he was much more amenable to Salmon and other faculty members who wanted to bring about progressive change on the Vassar campus. Salmon and MacCracken worked together and were responsible, in large part, for the adoption, in 1923, of *The Vassar College Statute of Instruction,* which became an acknowledged model for college constitutions in the United States.[23]

Salmon's ardent commitment to democratic principles and progressive educational reform on the Vassar campus certainly influenced, both positively and negatively, her relations with colleagues. Many of the faculty who agreed with Salmon's ideas cultivated fruitful relationships with her. However, individuals who disagreed with Salmon's ideology or methods unfortunately often developed adversarial relations with her.

Collegial Relations and Salmon's Personality

Salmon's quite complex personality influenced the bonds she formed with other people. Louise Fargo Brown's biography of Salmon portrays her as shy, at times docile, intelligent, and, above all else, tremendously dedicated to her profession. Yet, on the cover of Brown's biography of Salmon, she calls Salmon a "stormy petrel in the field of education."[24] Theodore Clarke Smith furnished a different picture in his review of the Brown biography in *The American Historical Review.* Smith wrote, "Miss Salmon's numerous oddities, to which the biographer scarcely alludes, made her a source of endless tales and anecdotes, usually friendly, often affectionate, but always the outcome of her selfless pursuit of historical or social truth and justice."[25] Evidently, Salmon's personality offered contrasting impressions to those who encountered her.

Patricia Palmieri claimed in her work *In Adamless Eden* that Salmon was the ringleader of the faculty insurrection against Vassar president James Taylor, an action that forced him to resign.[26] Participation in such an activity is hardly typical of a shy, docile person. Certainly, Salmon had strong differences and, at times, a contentious relationship with President Taylor. Yet, claiming Salmon was a "ringleader" who led "an insurrection" suggests a callousness that neglects the complexities of Salmon's personality and disregards Salmon's longstanding spirited relationship with Taylor. During her career, Salmon had differed with President Taylor over his creation of a separate economics department, his attempt to give the history department chairmanship to Salmon's rival, James Baldwin, his banning of suffrage activities on the campus, and his autocratic style of governance. Depicting Vassar as a place of contentious faculty relationships between men and women supports Palmieri's argument that Wellesley's all-female environment in the Victorian era was a flowering Eden. This distinctly separate female college was a pioneer that she claims was critical to the women's rights movement. While Palmieri's assessment is generally valid, Salmon was not a ruthless revolutionist.

Indeed, Salmon felt she was an inwardly shy person. Her letters, especially those to her family and to Adelaide Underhill, reveal many insecurities. She was not always socially comfortable. Nevertheless, over the years, she became a strong presence on the Vassar campus, and she certainly made her opinions known. Elizabeth Daniels wrote that some faculty members "had sharp daily differences with Salmon and her modus operandi and even those who were in accord with her views of modernization and the need for change, found her to be a bit bossy and somewhat outrageous in her ways."[27]

Despite her confident willingness to express her opinions on the Vassar campus, Salmon at times revealed a lack of self-confidence to her close friends. For example, during the 1906–07 school year, after twenty years of service at Vassar as the history department chair, Salmon wrote to Frances Davenport that her position was "uncertain and insecure."[28] Salmon was referring to her differences with James Baldwin, a colleague who had earned a Harvard Ph.D. in European history and who had come to Vassar in 1897. Initially unbeknownst to Salmon, Baldwin, with the tacit approval of President Taylor, had secretly attempted to oust Salmon from the chairmanship of the history department.[29] When Salmon learned of Baldwin's maneuvers, however, she displayed remarkable savvy and garnered support from trustees, faculty, and friends. As a result, Baldwin's and Taylor's effort to replace Salmon as the chair proved unsuccessful.

During this incident, Salmon's assertiveness and her determination to save her job became obvious to all. In defense of her chairmanship, she claimed to let it be known that she was "in the market" and would send in her resignation if Baldwin was promoted to chair the history department. Nor would she accept a department divided into separate European and American history departments, with Baldwin heading the former and Salmon the latter.[30] Of course, she realized that her ultimatum would put President Taylor in the disturbing position of having to choose between Baldwin and Salmon. When her strong-arm tactics proved ineffective, Salmon backtracked and wrote to President Taylor that if anything she said had been viewed as an implied ultimatum, it was accidental and not intentional.[31]

Baldwin's effort ultimately was unsuccessful, as the Board of Trustees voted to keep Salmon as head of the department while promoting Baldwin to Professor of History. Salmon's management of the crisis not only shed light on her strong personality but also revealed fundamental differences between Salmon and Baldwin about the nature of history and how it should be taught. "Salmon sent her students to primary sources to learn history . . . she rarely used textbooks. . . . Her classroom was informal and unconventional, but rigorous."[32] Baldwin, on the other hand, was a more traditional history professor who advocated teaching history in a dogmatic manner in which the teacher disseminated facts and tested students' recall. Demonstrating that their disagreement ran far deeper than a clash of academic interests, Salmon, in commenting on the ultimate resolution of her dispute with Baldwin, viewed her victory as just "short of dispensing with Baldwin altogether."[33]

Clearly, Salmon was convinced of the correctness of her methodology and disdained what she perceived as Baldwin's arrogant lecture approach to teaching history. Such sentiments were resoundingly similar to her opinion of Woodrow Wilson. Yet, both Baldwin and Salmon continued to work as colleagues at Vassar for twenty more years. Salmon's dislike of Baldwin was vividly remembered by a former Vassar history department chair, Evalyn Clark. Clark had been a student at Vassar toward the end of Salmon's career in the early 1920s and returned to Vassar as a history professor in 1939, toward the end of Baldwin's career. Clark recalled that Baldwin was a "real problem . . . who thought he should be running everything . . . [and who] was impressed with his own importance."[34] Clark evidently sided with Salmon.

Salmon's dispute with Baldwin was not the first instance in which she differed sharply with a male professor whom she believed threatened her authority in the history department. The popularity among the students of Herbert Mills, a professor of economics, was second only to that of Lucy Salmon.[35] Still, Salmon and Mills refused to speak with each other for years. Mills had joined the Vassar history department as an economist in 1890, but, in 1893, he supported a separation of history and economics into two departments. Apparently, "Mills did not approve of Salmon's iconoclastic teaching methods, did not want to be associated with them, and moved as soon as possible for the division."[36] Salmon viewed the suggested division as a threatened act of treason. Ironically, in 1915, Marjorie Dodd MacCracken, the wife of Vassar's new president, Henry Noble MacCracken, unknowingly seated Mills and Salmon together at dinner. Apparently embarrassed by the situation, they began to talk to each other. Fundamentally, the differences between Mills and Salmon stemmed from their disparate pedagogical practices.

Most of Salmon's Vassar colleagues, however, respected Salmon's pedagogy and cherished her empathetic, yet serious personality. Salmon's most enduring relationship developed with a former student, Adelaide Underhill, who returned to Vassar and eventually became the college's librarian. Their relationship is explored more fully later in this chapter.

Salmon became a close associate of many members of her department. Over time, she became a respected elder colleague. Furthermore, as department chair, she encouraged faculty to work together, particularly in team teaching the introductory European history course. In this class of approximately 300 students, members of the department taught sections of twenty-five students. Instructors met with their sections three times each week. Salmon coordinated the course, and six times a year the entire class met together for a general lecture, which was generally illustrated with slides.[37] Members of the department shared the lecturing responsibility, and occasionally a guest speaker was invited.

During her forty-year Vassar tenure, Salmon became particularly close with two younger members of her department, Louise Fargo Brown and Eloise Ellery. Salmon corresponded with these women much more frequently than she did with others. For example, Salmon's papers contain only twelve letters from James Baldwin, although he was a colleague for thirty years.[38] Approximately 120 letters, however, exist from Brown to Salmon and 150 letters from Ellery to Salmon, even though neither women spent as many years in the department with Salmon as did Baldwin.[39]

The custom and etiquette of the era was to communicate through letters, even though faculty offices were in close proximity. Faculty members might pass each other in the halls, but they sent letters to one another to express ideas or needs. According to Elizabeth Daniels, such practices constituted "yesterday's email."[40] Salmon also corresponded with the department members Ida C. Thallon, C. Mildred Thompson, and Lucy E. Textor, but less frequently than she did with Brown and Ellery. Thompson, a Vassar graduate of 1903, earned a doctorate in American history from Columbia University and began her teaching career at Vassar in 1909 under Salmon's guidance. By 1923, Thompson became college dean, a position she retained until her retirement in 1948.[41]

Louise Fargo Brown came to the Vassar history department in the early 1900s but left for a few years to serve as dean of women at the University of Nevada.[42] Despite the vast distance in miles between them, Salmon and Brown maintained their close personal friendship. After leaving the University of Nevada, Brown worked with John Franklin Jameson (a founder of the American Historical Association and of the Division of Manuscripts of the Library of Congress) in Washington, D.C., and lived with Salmon's friend and former student Frances Davenport (Vassar 1891).[43] When Brown rejoined the Vassar community in the fall of 1919, Salmon invited Brown to live with her.[44] Ultimately, Brown honored Salmon and their friendship by writing Salmon's biography and by dedicating the book to Salmon's lifelong companion, Adelaide Underhill.

Eloise Ellery, a fellow professor, was also close to Salmon. They vacationed together in Williamstown, Massachusetts, during the summer of 1921, and Ellery sent Salmon several letters describing her travels when she visited Asia two years later.[45] Ellery eventually succeeded Salmon as chair of the Vassar history department in 1925. After Salmon resigned her position as chair, she continued to teach one course each semester. As chair, Ellery often sought Salmon's advice or opinion on departmental matters. For example, when a new professor of history was hired, Ellery wrote that she kept wondering whether or not Salmon would like the man. Ellery was comforted with the thought that Salmon would approve.[46]

Salmon linked herself professionally to both Vassar College presidents who held office during her tenure. To both President James Monroe Taylor and President Henry Noble MacCracken, she freely expressed her opinions. Such frankness, however, did not always endear her to these men. The correspondence between President MacCracken and Salmon numbers more than 140 letters, and the correspondence between President Taylor and Salmon exceeds 475.[47] Salmon's voluminous letters to the Vassar College presidents surely must have grown bothersome, especially when she focused on trivial matters. Indeed, in one letter to Taylor, for example, Salmon complained that the college laundry had lost her stockings.

More frequently, Salmon expressed concerns over the administration of the college and sought to improve the environment and education provided. Not surprisingly, she often sought money for the history department or funds to increase the acquisitions of the Vassar library.[48] Salmon acknowledged that she sent frequent requests. As she explained to President MacCracken, she wrote "when anything is on one's mind. . ." but knew it was "impossible to act on all suggestions."[49] Salmon's letters, however, often produced results. Some faculty, perhaps, perceived Salmon as pushy and ill adapted because she embraced too seriously her commitment to education at Vassar. According to Elizabeth Daniels, nevertheless, at the end of Salmon's life she "would be able to count the many ways in which she had been kingmaker of the modern Vassar."[50] Her influence on the college was quite a significant personal accomplishment.

Relations with Students

In general, Salmon was highly regarded on the Vassar campus as an excellent teacher. Indeed, in her book *Gender and Higher Education in the Progressive Era*, Gordon refers to Salmon as popular, inspiring, and a leader among women students.[51] Salmon not only organized the student suffrage organization but also formed eating clubs, discussion groups, and historical societies for students.

The gigantic volume of letters written by Vassar College students and alumnae to Lucy Salmon alone stands as a mountain of supportive evidence about Salmon's popularity as a teacher. Excluding the massive correspondence between Lucy Salmon and Adelaide Underhill (Vassar 1888), student letters written to Salmon fill eight archival boxes and include more than 2,200 letters.[52] Salmon corresponded with hundreds of students but became especially close with ten of them. They include Edith Rickert (1891), Helen Grow Rottschaefer (1915), Sophia Chen Zen (1919), Rebecca Lawrence Lowrie (1913), Mary Berkheimer (1913), Mary Anderson (1889), Beatrice Berle Bishop (1923), Elsie M. Rushmore (1906), Louise M. Seaman (1915), and Elizabeth Updegraff (1895). Several of these women were instrumental in the establishment of Vassar's Lucy Maynard Salmon Fund for Research, which continues to exist today.

Many of the student letters to Salmon exhibit a tone of adoration and sincere gratitude. For example, one student wrote in tribute, "Whatever success I have had I feel I owe to you, both to your training and to the inspiration you were to all of us."[53] Elizabeth Updegraff, chair of the committee that established the research fund in Salmon's name, wrote, in April 1926, "It is right that we should honor her, that she may realize what in her great modesty she would never admit, her inestimable gifts to us during her thirty-nine years at Vassar."[54] Fifty years after she graduated from Vassar, Mrs. William Harrington recalled what it was like to have class with Lucy Salmon:

> I wish I could make you see her as we first saw her, fifty years ago. . . . The first thing you noticed were her very blue eyes. Then there were her shy mannerisms, — the lifted eyebrow, the wave of her hand, — the upward inflection of her voice as she ended a sentence, her attention to the details of her dress. . . .
>
> And for another reason I wish I might take you back fifty years, that you might feel something of the shock that her method of teaching gave us. We had all had some history, but it had been the committing to memory of lists of battles, name of kings, dates, cut and dried facts and probably all taken from one book. Now we had no textbook, she lectured to us, we took notes and then we were told to go to the library and find out for ourselves the answers to such questions as her lecture might have provoked. She would have had put on one of those tables a number of books pertaining to the subject, but the mere fact that there were so many books was appalling. I am sure I was not the only one who had to learn from sad experience that the material she turned in had to come from more than one authority. . .
>
> Then, too, she was the first person who had ever suggested that history was a continuous affair. . . . Also, that the history of one country was intimately related to the history of all other countries.
>
> I know that her real desire was to inspire me with something of her love and enthusiasm for her own vocation, — teaching.[55]

Many times Salmon received gifts from former students. For example, fifteen years after she graduated, Edith Rickert sent Salmon a watercolor painting as a Christmas gift.[56] In addition, Salmon commonly invited former students to visit her at home or to vacation with her.[57] Elsie Rushmore recalled the pleasure of eating in her home and Miss Salmon's remark to her, "My friend, how delightful for us to have a guest for breakfast who wears a pink gingham dress and doesn't read the death list."[58]

Salmon insisted that she be called "Miss Salmon" and never allowed herself to be addressed as Professor Salmon.[59] She preferred "Miss" because it was an ordinary term of respect, rather than a title that differentiated professional rank and status. Although Miss or Mr. were common forms of address for faculty during this time period, Salmon made a specific point to write that letters addressed otherwise would be returned unopened and unanswered to the sender.[60] This action was a symbolic gesture of Salmon's continued commitment to living her democratic principles. Despite insisting on familiar address and having many friends and collegial relationships, Salmon appeared inwardly shy, perhaps a bit awkward, and somewhat reserved.

At times, some students felt uncomfortable in Salmon's presence. Indeed, one particular student, Margaret Shipp (1905), wrote to her sister that she found Miss Salmon difficult to speak to individually. Shipp attended a party at Salmon's house in 1905 and reported that Salmon's house was filled with elegant furniture but that the home seemed a place to study rather than to live. Although Shipp delighted in the party's food, she found both Adelaide Underhill and Salmon socially awkward. She explained,

> Every single remark I or anyone made to Miss S. during the whole evening fell perfectly flat. It was pathetic, and yet so funny, so absolutely absurd. I wish I could do justice to Miss S. and yet tell her lack of tact at the same time, but I'm afraid I can't. . . . She cannot converse, but she talks delightfully—to a group: She doesn't treat you as an individual, only as a member of her class in American History or Nineteenth Century History. She seems to have no power at all to respond to what you attempt to say to her.[61]

Another student, Ruth Adams (1904), daughter of the Yale historian George B. Adams, expressed similar sentiments.

Although her personality may have seemed awkward to some students, Salmon was more interested that her Vassar students follow her example and pursue careers. She had dedicated much effort to the promotion of women to leadership positions and to demonstrating women's intellectual capabilities. Salmon's aspirations for her students included their choosing to start a career over the prospect of marriage, development of their intellectual potential, and their becoming leaders in their chosen professions. She could not hide her disappointment when matrimony intervened and cut short a former student's career.[62]

Clearly, Salmon's teaching was illuminating for most Vassar College students, many of whom communicated with Salmon long after they left the campus. Although not all students understood Salmon's techniques, she certainly gathered a large and loyal following of dedicated, adoring students. In April 1927, 999 students donated more than $33,000 to the Lucy Maynard Salmon Fund for Research.[63] This fund represents a lasting, real, and symbolic legacy of Salmon's career at Vassar.

Relationship with Adelaide Underhill

Lucy Salmon's relationship with her former student Adelaide Underhill (1888) became the most intimate and personal connection in Salmon's life. As a student, Underhill had been one of Salmon's "most ardent admirers," but their relationship became mutually supportive after Underhill returned to Vassar as a member of the library staff.[64] Over time, the strength of their personal and professional bond increased.

When Salmon began her career at Vassar, college authorities insisted that female faculty members live with the students. Salmon grew to dislike life in the dormitories because of the general lack of privacy. After a two-year leave of absence in 1898–1900, during which time she traveled in Europe, studied, and attempted to recover from exhaustion and depression, Salmon returned to Vassar unwilling to resume her dormitory duties. Shortly thereafter, Salmon and Adelaide Underhill decided to share a house together a small distance away from the Vassar campus on Mill Street in Poughkeepsie. They previously had experienced common living arrangements one summer when Salmon traveled with Underhill to Europe. They lived together throughout the remainder of their lives, and neither woman married.[65] Each grew to rely on the other for professional and emotional support.[66]

The nature of Lucy Salmon's sexual orientation has been debated, although little evidence about this aspect of her life exists.[67] Clearly, she was a woman who developed a number of close female friendships. However, the customs of the Victorian era must serve as a context that shapes understanding of Salmon's relationships. Carroll Smith-Rosenberg argued that nineteenth-century American society did not place taboos on female relationships, but the societal structure in which women routinely formed friendships separate from male relations encouraged "homosocial ties."[68] Indeed, Smith-Rosenberg found in her study that the notoriously repressive Victorian sexual ethos may have been in practice more flexible than societal conventions in the twentieth century. Furthermore, at colleges for women, such as Vassar, most relationships, both public and private, necessarily were between women.

Patricia Palmieri found that during the late Victorian, or Progressive, era (1870–1900)[69] academic women at Wellesley similarly forged "deep emotional bonds" with women. Historical debate continues over how to define and treat these exclusively female relationships. Some of these women spoke of themselves as spinsters or as celibate or as having romantic friendships with other women. Such relationships were sometimes called Boston marriages. Victorian-era academic women at female colleges with close ties to other females never employed the term "lesbian" to define themselves. Indeed, the term "lesbian" did not come into use in the English language until Freudian psychology gained currency in the twentieth century. Palmieri prefers to use the term "women-committed women" to describe these relationships because such terminology encompassed the range of emotional, intellectual, social, and perhaps physical support that these women provided one another.[70]

Evalyn Clark recalled a closeness in the Vassar community because faculty and students lived, dined, and worked together. Most women, she explained, remained unmarried because, at that time, a married woman would have been viewed as not being sufficiently dedicated to her profession.[71] In other words, living with other women, choosing not to marry, and engaging in scholarly pursuits constituted the norm for women faculty at Vassar. Despite Salmon's success in the male-dominated historical profession, women were her primary focus throughout her professional and personal life at Vassar.

Although close relationships between women were quite common at Vassar, Salmon clearly was particularly committed to Adelaide Underhill in both professional and emotional terms. The two women lived together for nearly thirty years, and only death ended their relationship. Salmon provided Adelaide Underhill a life estate in her will that, upon Underhill's death, was transferred to Vassar College.[72] In writing to Salmon, friends frequently sent regards to Miss Underhill, and, similarly, Salmon mentioned her housemate in letters to others.[73] Whenever the two women were separated, they corresponded extensively. In their letters, both expressed love and affection for each other. For example, in one letter Salmon wrote to Underhill, "Meantime remember that blue or not blue, I always have a heart full of love for you."[74]

Louise Fargo Brown described Salmon and Underhill's relationship beautifully:

> Between these two shy women there developed a perfect understanding. Miss Salmon respected her friend's judgment, and depended on her for advice on many subjects. Between them there always existed a delicate reserve, which was bridged by deep affection on both sides. Miss Underhill maintained somewhat the attitude of the disciple toward the master; to Miss Salmon she was always "sister," and supplied that deeply felt need in ample measure. In her practically continuous campaigns for reforms within the college, the sympathetic understanding of this colleague was especially precious.[75]

On a professional level, Salmon and Underhill collaborated on increasing the acquisitions of the Vassar library. Because of Salmon's views that history instruction should encourage independent work, the library was a critical resource for Salmon and her students. The women often spent time together after dinner examining catalogs of books, and Salmon even published articles in library journals.[76] In addition, Salmon repeatedly sent requests to the Vassar president to acquire books, newspapers, and journals for the Vassar library and published a plea in *The Vassar Quarterly* that alumni not throw away old materials such as newspapers but remember the library instead.[77] Certainly, in many respects, Salmon's and Underhill's relationship grew to be mutually supportive.

Salmon's life at Vassar College was principled and rich with personal connections. She was committed to the ideal of democracy and to its actualization on the Vassar campus. In addition, she dedicated herself to improving the education offered at Vassar. In the process of ensuring a progressive educational environment, Salmon constructed enduring friendships and, along the way, picked up a few enemies. Although "a born general," Salmon did not relish fighting.[78] Rather, she enjoyed cultivating relationships with colleagues and students. These relationships were the basis of good teaching. Without Salmon's strong personal connections to students, however, her teaching methods would not have been nearly as successful as they were. Because Salmon inspired students, her remarkable pedagogy merits special interest.

CHAPTER 5

The Nature of History

There is a history in all men's lives,
Figuring the nature of times deceas'd,
The which observ'd, a man may prophesy,
With near aim, of the main chance of things
As yet not come to life, which in their seeds
And weak beginnings lie intreasured.
WILLIAM SHAKESPEARE, Henry IV, Part 2

Long before Lucy Salmon lived, England's great playwright, William Shakespeare, noted that every person possesses a history. Although the essence of history might be conveyed to future generations, animated stories are deeply buried by time, with the seeds of truth not having sprouted life. Salmon and other historians of her era surely concurred with Shakespeare's sentiments. They uncovered "intreasured" seeds but never unearthed historical truth. Still, their search for truth inspired continual inquiry. Their perspective was positivist.

For Salmon, another purpose of history was to reveal the story of the diverse lives (Shakespeare's *all*), rather than simply to tell about the lives of prominent people. Salmon's conviction led her to advocate "the new social history" of the late nineteenth and early twentieth centuries. Her complex beliefs about the nature of history and how these ideas influenced her understanding of education and pedagogy are explored in this chapter.

Salmon's educational tenets were influenced by her conception of history and were reflected in her writing and teaching of history. Over time, her conception of history broadened. As a student, Salmon wrote standard political history, but, as a scholar, she decided to write about less traditional historical topics. She intentionally chose to write about ordinary people and objects in history, rather than public figures and well-known events. She became, as a consequence, one of the vanguards of the new social history. Early in her career, she investigated domestic service, primarily in the United States. A second edition of *Domestic Service* included an added section on European domestic employment. Toward the end of her career, Salmon researched the history of the newspaper. Examination of domestic help enabled Salmon to explore the history of ordinary people, both employees and employers, whereas her newspaper inquiry probed a medium widely available to all people and that she believed reflected society as a whole.

As a historian, Salmon adopted an innovative approach to education and teaching. As an active member of the American Historical Association, she was one of the early historians who advocated the new social history, along with prominent contemporaries such as Woodrow Wilson, Frederick Jackson Turner, and James Harvey Robinson. In 1904, at the International Congress of Arts and Science, these historians argued for interpretive history that incorporated all aspects of human life, rather than traditional narrative political histories.[1] Robinson called this approach "the new history," and, in 1912, he published *The New History: Essays Illustrating the Modern Historical Outlook*.[2] His book was extremely popular and influential. Salmon, for example, wrote that Robinson's book and J. T. Shotwell's *Introduction to the History of History* were "the best expositions of the new history."[3] Several years later, in 1921, Salmon wrote to Robinson asking how to procure additional copies.[4] Robinson's book remained popular, and Salmon wanted it for her students.

In the early 1900s, Salmon regularly communicated with and shared ideas about the nature of history with these prominent historians. Indeed, she authored a pamphlet for teachers titled "The Sources of Robinson's *History of Western Europe*," intended to accompany Robinson's text with teaching ideas and a chart.[5] Robinson and Salmon conferred about this project and other topics of historical interest.[6] In 1905, Salmon invited Robinson to visit Vassar College to speak to the Vassar Alumnae Association. In accepting the invitation and discussing his proposed speech, Robinson remarked that "in a recent inquest to determine whether clergymen wished they had happened on another job,—while many bemoaned their fate, all agreed that they never tired of preaching. It would seem that I have the common instinct."[7] Although Robinson confessed to a penchant for preaching, undoubtedly he and Salmon shared many common opinions.

Robinson was only one of several advocates of the new social history with whom Salmon communicated. Among these historians was Frederick Jackson Turner, of the University of Wisconsin and, later, Harvard University. Salmon greatly respected Turner's work. In 1909, Turner accepted Salmon's invitation to breakfast.[8] Salmon viewed Turner's work on the frontier and its significance in American national development as a preeminent contribution to the new social history.[9]

Furthermore, Salmon established extensive, nationwide relationships with other historians. As discussed earlier, Salmon organized and founded the Association of History Teachers of the Mid-States and Maryland and convinced many prominent historians in the northeast to join the group. She was also a leader in the American Historical Association. Other advocates of the new social history with whom she corresponded and visited include J. Franklin Jameson, W. Roscoe Thayer, Charles Beard, Edward Cheyney, Charles H. Haskins, H. Morse Stephens, and Albert Bushnell Hart.[10] These historians attempted to broaden established conceptions of history, even as they struggled to define history.

On the Nature of History: Definition and Indefiniteness of History

To Salmon, history escaped easy definition. In fact, she titled one essay, "On a Certain Indefiniteness in History."[11] Indeed, she never accepted one specific and unambiguous definition of history. Salmon dedicated the first chapter of *Historical Material* to the exploration of several diverse definitions of history.[12] She returned to these ideas in *Why Is History Rewritten?*[13] and explained that the hundreds of definitions of history reveal in their attempts at specificity the very uncertainty even among historians about the nature of history. In *What Is Modern History?* Salmon also discussed these problems of history.[14] Although she acknowledged that a lack of clarity about what constitutes history confused some students, part of the difficulty she attributed to a "poverty of language" in which the finished product was not distinguished from the "raw material from which it is made."[15]

Despite the diversity of meanings, and the opinons of others who denied even the possibility of defining history, Salmon believed that history could be understood by making clear the distinctions among those who write history, the records from which history is drawn, and the methods by which historians construct narratives and advance the boundaries of knowledge. She dedicated *Historical Material,* unfinished at the time of her death, to making such distinctions as clear as possible. For example, in its second chapter, Salmon elucidated the difference between the record and the recorder. She explained that not only are those who have written history not the only recorders of history, "but they have also been the unconscious and impersonal agents that have worked through forces of nature, through language, through institutions and customs, through folklore, through tradition."[16] Salmon continued,

> The record is the original portrayal of events that has been made quite as often unconsciously as consciously; it is the raw material from which the historian constructs history. The historian may in a sense be considered an interpreter or a translator, since he judges in regard to the authenticity of the record, compares different records, and fuses into an organic history the various records that apparently have no relation to each other.[17]

As an example, she explained that Michaelangelo's *Last Judgment* is valuable, not as a historical source about judgment day but because it reveals something of the theology of the Renaissance, and it serves "incidentally as a record of the artist's displeasure at the criticism given the frescoe."[18] After learning of a critic's caviling remarks, Michaelangelo depicted the critic in the painting with a serpent around his waist, among the devils in hell. Salmon added that, occasionally, what is erased is also a record, such as the removal of Jefferson Davis's name from a viaduct in Washington, D.C., even though he was the engineer of the structure; the erasure is a record of sectional hatred during the Reconstruction period.

Succeeding chapters in *Historical Material* detail other types of records that were valuable to the historian. These include marks found in nature, institutions and customs, myths, legends and tradition, archaeological remains, and, of course, oral and written evidence. Salmon sought to make clear to readers that historians constructed history from a variety of materials—not just the obvious written record.

If defining history was problematic, the new social history was even more complex, but, in Salmon's writing, common themes emerge with regard to the nature of this new emphasis. Throughout her work, ideas such as history in the round, the value of history with respect to the present, the relative value of facts, and the notion that history should be rewritten are repeated. According to Salmon, the new history meant a

> radical extension of the base on which the structure of history has been erected. It has grown out of the greatly enlarged conception of the meaning of history and a corresponding expansion of sources from which history is derived. The older school of history was, as regards its content, largely biographical, individualistic, descriptive, militaristic and political. Individuals who had been conspicuous in action and whose activities had largely concerned the state formed the subject matter of the older history. . . . But this narrow individualistic basis has long since ceased to satisfy students of the past. . . . The historian of to-day may rightly claim with Bacon that he has

taken all knowledge to be his province, and he may say with Terence that nothing human is alien to him. Nothing is too humble, nothing is apparently too insignificant or too superficial for the trained eye of the historian to see in it an epitome of the past or the present life around him.[19]

Salmon not only wrote about the new social history but gave public speeches promoting its study and delineating its limitations. For example, she titled one speech given to the Vassar Faculty Club on January 11, 1906, "Some Problems of the New History." Another, given at the New Century Club in Utica, New York, on April 2, 1912, she titled simply "The New History." During the course of Salmon's career, she presented hundreds of speeches about history, such as "On the Nature of History and Methods of Historical Work," many of which detailed her conception of history and in which she incorporated her ideas about the new social history.[20]

History in the Round

For Salmon, the basis of the new history was the concept of "history in the round." This conception meant the presentation of as complete a picture as possible when the telling or writing of history. Circles are round, complete, and unending. Rather than depicting a political portrayal and neglecting other aspects of the story, Salmon believed, historians should illuminate other, often neglected components of historical life. One goal of the historian was to depict a complete, full, "round" picture of historical events. She explained,

> History was once of one dimension, it now has three dimensions; it was long written in the flat, it is now written in the round; it was once a narrative of the marshal deeds of great heroes, it is now a study and interpretation of past life.[21]

Salmon found support from other advocates of the new social history. They agreed that history should be examined and written as a "whole," rather than narrowly confined to the affairs of state. Salmon wrote that the British historian J. R. Green's conception of history in the round encompassed all classes of society, and it also meant that history should be written not only for scholars but also for youth who were participants in the present.[22]

The new social history buttressed her determination to research the history of domestic service and the history of the newspaper. Neither of these topics was standard, political history but instead contributed to development of "history in the round."

History: Past with Respect to the Present

Salmon's perspective on history in the round was a point that she also impressed upon her students. She believed that history was a continuous, evolutionary process, hence the circular quality of history. In addition, the past was important with respect to how it spoke to the present. Although "much that belongs to the present and that seems of overwhelming importance may quickly prove to be ephemeral,"[23] Salmon believed that the present was important as it was brought into relationship with similar conditions of the past.

Indeed, understanding of the past was an important basis on which to build the future. Following this principle, Salmon attempted to demonstrate to students that history was all *around* them, where they lived and breathed. Furthermore, she emphasized that students of history were not the only people who studied the past. Doctors studied a patient's physical history before prescribing treatment. She noted that "history must ever through an evolutionary process reconstruct the life of the past. The study of the past and of the present are not antagonistic, but are ever complementary."[24] Indeed, she reasoned that the further back humanity's knowledge of the past was pushed, the more comprehensive would be human awareness of the present.[25]

Value of Facts

Moreover, Salmon's understanding of the new social history included a belief that facts in and of themselves are valueless. She dissented from the popular notion that teachers should teach only important facts. "Facts of the past are as numerous as sands of the sea,"[26] she noted, and, therefore it is impossible to deal only with important facts. Facts are relative and do not have a fixed value. In former times, she alleged, historians erred in their assumption that

> all facts have always a fixed location and a definite value. Historians were once urged to select only the "important" facts and to discard "unimportant" facts. But no fact is in and of itself either important or unimportant; its importance is due altogether to its association with other facts.[27]

In addition, not only did historians find it difficult to determine "what the facts are" in any given situation; they also found it difficult to decide what was to be considered a fact. Therefore, she reasoned, history is in a process of continuous evolution, rather than being a stagnant body of knowledge made up of unchanging, factual information. Salmon related this newer notion of history to a larger understanding of humanity's process of continual evolution and migration on earth and to the more particular issue of immigration in the United States.

> How can we understand the great question of emigration and immigration unless we know that man has always been a migratory animal, that he has always "moved on" in search of real or fancied improvement in his condition, that *wanderlust* in default of other reasons explains his restless movements? How can we deal with the melting pot in America unless we know that races have always mingled and intermingled through conquest, through intermarriage, through commerce, through exchange of industrial workers, through financial operations, through every reason known to the human mind, and that from the beginning of time purity of the human race has never existed? . . . in the last analysis the human race is one in its hopes, aspirations, and ideals?[28]

In other words, history is part of a continuous evolutionary process, because humans experience continual movement and natural adaptation. Stories are never the same, even if facts remain stagnant, because the relevance and significant emphasis of facts change over time.

For example, the modern revision in the way Christopher Columbus has been viewed historically, for which the five hundredth anniversary of his sailing in 1992 served as impetus, stands as a poignant example of how perspective and significance can evolve over time. Although much had been written previously about Columbus, the shift in historical outlook led to the publication of many new works, such as Kirkpatrick Sale's *The Conquest of Paradise: Christopher Columbus and the Columbian Legacy.*[29] Sale argued that centuries of environmental destruction in the Western hemisphere, attributed to the European colonization begun by Columbus, has tarnished Columbus's image. According to Salmon, such historical transformations necessitate the rewriting of history. Therefore, knowledge of history and historical accounts are never finished and never complete but rather are a continual process.

History Rewritten

The last book Salmon completed before her death, *Why Is History Rewritten?*, published posthumously in 1929, continued her exploration of the nature of history. In this book, Salmon examined why she thought history needed to be rewritten. In many respects, this book was a popular justification for the new social history. In the early 1900s, the historical field clearly was divided about the nature of history. Some historians remained committed to the scientific history that Salmon and her colleagues rejected. "Scientific history" was fact laden, and, Salmon believed, focused on minutiae and irrelevant details. Salmon preferred the new history, and she also believed that history should be written with attention to literary quality. By "literary quality," Salmon focused attention on the narrative style in which history was written. She believed that carefully chosen, eloquent prose was important in the construction of historical accounts. In her letters and essays, she occasionally differentiated between "so-called literary" and "scientific" historians.[30]

In fact, she sought support for a separate historical journal, to be funded by the American Historical Association, that would be devoted exclusively to what she called "literary history." Salmon wrote to several AHA members, including William Roscoe Thayer, Evarts B. Greene, and Frederick Jackson Turner, to solicit their endorsement of her proposal.[31] Her idea never gained widespread support. Turner dismissed Salmon's attempt to start a new journal, for example, by responding that he did not think the Association could fund such an endeavor but that a solution might be that "a department of the present Review *[American Historical Review]* be devoted to papers more interesting to *general readers* of the Review."[32] Thayer, on the other hand, lamented, about one scientific historian,

> Brought up on the motto "to be interesting is to be inaccurate" he would shun Macaulay or Taine or Michelet in order not to injure his "scholarship." . . . For over thirty years I have tried to speed the coming of the higher history [new social history] by means of propaganda, but I now am sure that to have achieved one example of it would have been better than many polemics. I find myself quoting with more and more assent, Matthew Arnold's "Let the long contention cease/Geese are swans and swans are geese."[33]

Thayer was not alone in his concern that no great new social history had yet been written. Salmon, too, expressed such sentiments and acknowledged that nothing was to be found in the new history comparable to the works of Prescott, Macaulay, Carlyle, and Guizot.[34]

Although Salmon persistently advocated the new social history, she also acknowledged the merits of scientific history. She believed accuracy to be important. Still, rewriting history remained a necessity because she thought fallacious the argument that "history deals with facts, these facts do not change, and duplication of work already done means wasted fruitless effort."[35] Salmon noted that, with the birth of historical criticism, an emphasis arose on undiscovered documents and new materials that enabled historians to elaborate earlier historical interpretations. The division among historians she described as

> warring camps, quite unconscious of their mutual interdependence. But as the microscope and the telescope are both essential in extending the boundaries of knowledge and the adherents of neither one are justified in contemptuously rejecting, or in

failing to acknowledge, the services of the other, so it has been made necessary to rewrite history through the theories both schools of historians have worked out.[36]

The purpose of writing history, according to Salmon, was not simply to foster patriotism, good citizenship, or morality. She understood such activities ultimately to "advance the boundaries of knowledge."[37] Salmon believed that writing history was a quest for the truth. The "new historians" had contributed by extending the base upon which history was written. That is, they incorporated large classes of records that had not previously been used by historians in their work.[38] Because history consciously had been used for purposes other than the attainment of truth, historians must rewrite the older accounts. However, she did not conclude that the search for the truth meant that facts had an absolute value; their value was relative.

Ultimately, like many theologians and philosophers before her, Salmon came to the belief that knowledge of the absolute truth could never be attained. "History must always be rewritten because we can only approximate absolute truth, never hope to attain it."[39] Salmon's conception of the nature of history influenced the manner in which she believed that history should be taught. Her approach was both innovative and stimulating. With students, she promoted the notion that history could be found everywhere, even in ordinary life, and she developed experiential methods for students to discover such ideas. For example, one former student recalled that Salmon brought the class to her kitchen in order for them to find history.[40]

Salmon's teaching methods are explored in greater depth in later chapters, but, generally, her approach facilitated student learning of social, as well as political, history. In addition, she fostered students' critical thinking and independent learning. Her work on domestic service, undertaken at the beginning of her career as an historian, had been an initial attempt to "extend the base" upon which history rested. Salmon's book *Domestic Service*,[41] published more than one hundred years ago, in 1897, stands as one of the first modern works of the new social history.

Domestic Service

Salmon began her study of domestic service in the late 1880s, soon after she began teaching at Vassar College. She chose surveys and statistics to collect, analyze, and display data for her research for *Domestic Service*. Although these methods were uncommon forms of historical inquiry at the turn of the twentieth century, they were typical of the work of the new professional social scientists like Florence Kelly, Jane Addams, Carroll Wright, and, later, Mary Beard, who increasingly discussed ideas and methods with one another.[42] In fact, Carroll Wright, the first commissioner of the U.S. Bureau of Labor and later the president of Clark College, assisted

Lucy Salmon in obtaining and calculating census and statistical data for *Domestic Service*. These scholars claimed modern scientific knowledge as the basis of their authority.[43] One of the hallmarks of Progressive-era educational change was the development of these new social science methods of research and investigation. These methods were novel forms of investigation in the late nineteenth century, but their legitimacy was bolstered by a faith in science and a belief in progress.

Salmon used the term "domestic service" to describe household servants, although she did not like the term "servant" because she felt the word connoted social inferiority. The occupations that she studied included cooks, butlers, laundresses, maids, gardeners, general servants, and other household employees. Salmon mailed out 5,000 questionnaires to employers and employees in order to investigate and gain greater knowledge of the conditions and principles of domestic service.[44]

The report of her investigation began with a discussion of the omission of domestic service from general economic and labor theory. She believed that the isolated and personal nature of domestic employment was the cause of its omission in labor considerations. However, in the 1890s, one and one-half million Americans were actively engaged in this line of work, and it consumed $218 million annually.[45] Clearly, Salmon believed domestic service needed to be a part of any consideration of general labor conditions.

In *Domestic Service,* Salmon also examined historical aspects of domestic employment. First, she noted that many eighteenth-century inventions and the development of the factory system caused major changes in household employment. For example, consumers could purchase many items traditionally made in the home, such as soap, candles, and cloth. Thus, many chores left the purview of the home.[46] Second, she examined domestic service during the colonial period, when indentured white servants, black slaves, and Indians performed the majority of work. From 1776 to about 1850, Salmon noted, indentured servants were replaced in the North by free laborers and in the South by an increasing number of slaves. Thus, a great social chasm developed between classes within the South that was not as evident in the northern states.[47] However, the Irish famine of 1846, the German Revolution of 1848, the treaty forging relations between China and the United States in 1844, and the abolition of slavery in 1863 all contributed to the changed nature of domestic employment in the United States. Domestic employees increasingly came from immigrant groups or were former slaves. The aforementioned historical events also fostered different relations between employers and employees in all sections of the nation. Salmon wrote,

> In studying the question of domestic service, therefore, the fact cannot be overlooked that certain historical influences have affected its conditions; that political revolutions have changed its personnel, and industrial development its mobility.[48]

In subsequent chapters, Salmon examined economic aspects of domestic service, such as the average wages for various forms of domestic labor, regional variations in pay, gender differentiation in wages, types of skilled and unskilled labor, and the countries of origin of domestic employees. She included charts to augment her analysis. Salmon concluded that while wages, on average, were fairly high for domestic employees, the wage factor alone did not determine the willingness of people to engage in an occupation.

One of the primary drawbacks of household employment, according to Salmon, was that it offered few opportunities for advancement.[49] Although other advantages existed for the employee, such as the provision of room and board, the industrial and social disadvantages appeared greater than the advantages. For example, hours of work for domestics were often irregular, housework was never completed, opportunities for promotion did not exist, and these positions held low social status. Salmon wondered why society called a woman honorable when she worked in the home as a wife, mother, or daughter without pay, but demeaned the job when it was done in the home of others for pay.[50]

Salmon explored several remedies to the problems of domestic service. Some she categorized as doubtful, but others she found more likely to lead to improvements for both the employer and the employee. Of great importance was the need to eliminate the social stigma and degradation associated with domestic service. Work ought to be judged on its quality, rather than its nature. In addition, she held that household employment ought to be put on a business basis, similar to other occupations, in which principles of division of labor and unconscious cooperation applied. Increasing specialization of employment would benefit domestic service. For example, Salmon listed articles that were made in the home that she thought could be made less expensively and better outside the home. Interestingly, all of the jobs she mentioned, such as making jelly, baking bread, and preparing soup and ice cream, today are produced in large-scale factories.[51] She foresaw with uncanny accuracy that

> It seems inevitable that eventually all articles of food will be prepared out of the house except those requiring the last application of heat, and that scientific skill will reduce to a minimum the labor and expense of this final stage of preparation.[52]

Indeed, Salmon would have loved frozen entrees and the microwave oven!

She addressed potential objections to her proposal, such as the claim that women would be left with little to do. Salmon did not think that all household work for women would be eliminated but believed that the nature of the work would change. The work would become more productive, cost less, and be placed on a business basis. For example, a woman who made delicious pies could sell her pies and hire someone who was better at it than she to do the gardening. Salmon also suggested a profit-sharing system, which had been successful in the business world.[53] Finally, Salmon proposed improvement of education in household affairs. Again, she seems to have predicted the development of colleges of home economics although she advocated "a great professional school, amply equipped for the investigation of all matters pertaining to the household and *open only to graduates of the leading colleges and universities of the country*."[54] *Domestic Service* concluded with a summarization of Salmon's findings and with a clear advocacy on behalf of women who constituted the majority of domestic employees. Her advancement of women in *Domestic Service* recalled her promotion of women in the American Historical Association, her contributions to the suffrage movement, and her work at Vassar College. Salmon noted,

> Women want to work for all the reasons that men want it, but as long as so many of them, when they do work, persistently give their work for nothing, just so long will women's work in general be undervalued.
>
> The readjustment of work and the willingness of larger numbers of women to work for remuneration would be as productive of improvement in all household affairs as division of labor has been elsewhere.[55]

Salmon's comments about women's work being undervalued remain applicable today. Predominantly female professions such as teaching, nursing, secretarial assistance, and household cleaning remain low-paying fields of employment.

A great number of papers in the United States reviewed *Domestic Service* agreeably and recognized the work as pioneering a new field of scientific study. Indeed, the *Chicago Tribune* reported that Salmon's work was a "model of painstaking effort" and the "only work in any language that even professes to discuss the subject in a truly scientific manner."[56] *The Daily Tribune* claimed that "Miss Salmon's work is perhaps the most important, exhaustive and interesting ever prepared on the subject in this country."[57]

Salmon's work on domestic service, however, received some negative criticism in journals such as *New England Magazine* as a work being "beneath the dignity of a historian."[58] Another newspaper commented, "The book is not exactly cheerful reading, and yet it is not unentertaining, and it is of considerable sociologic value."[59] The *New York Communal Advertiser* claimed that Salmon's work "did not receive the attention it merited."[60] In Europe, *Domestic Service* received less favorable commentary. The *London Quarterly Review*[61] did not sanction Salmon's methodology, and the English paper the *Daily Chronicle* claimed that

> Miss Salmon has written a very interesting book about a very unpromising subject.... For all her trouble, however, she could but cover a limited area, and the information supplied has been common knowledge, if not scientifically confirmed, for some years past.... We have not much faith in Mrs. Salmon's suggestions for reform,

but they are ingenious and might answer in America, where relatively little is expected from servants.[62]

Indeed, Salmon was aware of the generally positive reception her book received because the publishers sent her clippings of the reviews from various newspapers. Although the majority were approving reviews and although the book went into a second edition, Salmon still perceived the book as not well received. She complained in a letter to Adelaide Underhill,

> I spent $1500 on domestic service and nobody has cared specially about it—it passed unnoticed at the college except a word from Miss Wood and Dr. Taylor. *The Nation* said the work wasn't worth doing, the American publishers say it is not a financial success, the English publishers that no amount of advertising would ever sell the book, the history people say I have wasted my time on it, the economic people that I don't know about economics—and so it goes.[63]

The criticism of *Domestic Service*, especially from historians and social scientists, clearly pained Lucy Salmon. She had devoted three chapters in the beginning of the book to a discussion of the historical aspects of domestic service. She examined colonial-period conditions for servants and then explored how eighteenth- and nineteenth-century inventions, such as electricity and the development of the factory system, altered working conditions. In three subsequent chapters, she explored the economic implications of domestic service. Perhaps, in examining the social implications of domestic service employment and in suggesting remedies for improvement, Salmon wandered too far afield from traditional history and economic topics.

Still, Salmon's research on domestic service was a seminal work in an emerging "new" field of study, the art and science of homemaking, alternatively called home economics, domestic science, and home arts.[64] Shortly thereafter, by the turn of the twentieth century, this field became an organized effort in the feminization of women's education. Home economics was both traditional and feminist. It included a number of topics related to the "women question,"[65] such as the situation that led to women, whom many Americans thought needed proper training, being destined for employment as domestic servants. No significant prior scholarship had focused on this ancient and predominantly female field of employment prior to Salmon's research. Unwilling to dismiss or to ignore this area of study, Salmon presented her continued work on domestic service in a more easily readable and popular format in *Progress in the Household*, published in 1906.[66]

Salmon's selection of domestic service signified her commitment to broadening established notions of suitable topics for historical study. Certainly, she was not alone in this endeavor. Salmon, in writing about domestic service, created a new social history and also revealed her burgeoning democratic sentiments. She believed that all people contributed to history and that many of their stories needed to be told. Salmon's pluralistic approach was unique, however, in that she wrote about a predominantly female occupation peopled primarily by immigrants and minorities of low socioeconomic status. This history was not a history of great leaders achieving victories on the battlefields of war. Significantly, Salmon not only wrote about a marginalized class of people but also implemented democratic principles by widening the audiences for whom she wrote.

Salmon's Writings on Newspapers

Although Salmon's work on domestic service did not earn appropriate recognition, she received acclaim for her research and writing about newspapers and the teaching of history. During a sabbatical leave in 1921, Salmon worked on her manuscript on newspapers before returning to a more general book on historical material on which she had labored sporadically for years.[67] For nearly three decades at Vassar College, Salmon taught an advanced elective course on historical material, in which students learned about numerous forms of historical evidence, such as the newspaper.[68] In fact, Salmon's course had been so well liked by one former student, Anna Justice, that when Justice died, the family requested donations in memory of Salmon's course. Vassar president Henry Noble MacCracken acknowledged this distinction in a letter to Salmon.[69] Interestingly, the newspaper material research proved to be so vast that Salmon decided to divide the subject into two separate books. They were published as *The Newspaper and the Historian* (1923), the first volume, and *The Newspaper and Authority* (1923), the second volume.

Newspapers held tremendous interest for Salmon because of their increasing importance as a source of information during her lifetime. Unquestionably, newspapers were the preeminent form of mass communication in an era that predated radio, film, and television. During the Civil War, American newspapers first established the practice of printing special Sunday editions with war news,[70] and newspapers remained an important source of war information during World War I. Even though Salmon witnessed the growth of new forms of communication in the early twentieth century, newspapers remained a dominant source of information during her lifetime, as newspaper readership continued its impressive growth. For example, in 1842, one in twenty-six New Yorkers bought a Sunday paper; by 1899, that figure had increased to one in two.[71] Additionally, Salmon's investigation of newspapers revealed her belief in democratic principles because newspapers were widely available and widely read.

In *The Newspaper and the Historian* and *The Newspaper and Authority,* Salmon explored a wealth of information relating to newspapers. She focused, for example, on freedom of the press, regulation and taxation of the press, the law of libel, sources of and bias in the news, the writing of editorials, the influence of newspapers on public opinion, and the value and danger of newspapers as a source of historical information.

In *The Newspaper and the Historian,* Salmon explored the advantages, limitations, and usefulness of the press for historians. Elaborating on ideas published in an earlier article in *The Vassar Quarterly,* Salmon began by tracing the historical development of newspapers.[72] She subsequently examined various facets of newspapers, such as news-collecting agencies, reporters, correspondents, editorials, advertisements, and illustrations, and evaluated their usefulness for the historian. In her conclusion, Salmon probed the extent to which the past could be reconstructed from newspaper accounts.

Whereas contemporary historians understand the value of newspapers in their research, such research was not part of accepted practice by historians during Salmon's lifetime. In fact, she argued, "the belief that the press can not be used to reconstruct the past because of its manifold inaccuracies, is not well founded."[73] Despite the yellow journalism of the 1890s, Salmon contended that reporters and editors generally sought to be accurate. Nonetheless, she acknowledged that some mistakes were inevitable. Salmon believed, however, that newspapers were useful for historians, not as a tool to portray information accurately, but as a means through which the historian could interpret the time period under study.

> In spite of its name, the chief function of the newspaper is not to give the news, it is not even exclusively to reflect public opinion,—important as that is,—but it is to record all contemporaneous human interests, activities, and conditions and thus to serve the future. What the historian wishes from the newspaper is not news,—that always ultimately comes to him from other sources,—but a picture of contemporary life.[74]

Salmon further claimed that editorials, illustrations, and advertisements were of most immediate service to the historian in their reconstructions of the past. For example, she explained that illustrations revealed how women's lives had changed in the early twentieth century. Earlier papers did not portray women outside the fashion magazines or society scenes. However, in the 1910s and 1920s, newspaper illustrations depicted women in various professions, businesses, industry, and even athletics.[75] In her assertion that newspapers were useful for their reflections of society, Salmon advanced the new social history. Rather than examining newspapers for information on political or military history, Salmon argued for their usefulness in illuminating contemporary times. Yet, Salmon did not entirely negate newspapers' usefulness in presenting topics of traditional history. Advertisements and illustrations, for example, revealed "the very real sufferings and privations entailed by war."[76] Salmon believed that the press was the most important source available to the historian for portrayals of life during the past three hundred years. Yet, the manner in which she advocated the portrayal of everyday life differed remarkably from the conventional history of the day. Moreover, her vision was democratic. The newspaper could be used to reflect society as a whole—to show ordinary people engaged in popular activities.

In *The Newspaper and Authority*, Salmon considered "how far the restrictions placed on the newspaper press by external authority have limited its serviceableness for the historian in his attempt to reconstruct the past."[77] In the first chapter, Salmon examined the nature of authority. She claimed that authority, in essence, was conservative, whereas freedom was progressive. Therefore, conflict between the two was inevitable.[78] Historians, she believed, needed to be aware of the restraints placed on the press, sometimes willingly, in many forms and to determine the degree of restraint exerted.

In subsequent chapters, Salmon discussed the theory of censorship, the forms of preventive and punitive censorship, and the impact of censorship of the press. Censorship was not a new idea. In 1501, she wrote, the Pope of the Roman Catholic Church employed censorship in order to protect against heresy.[79] Although many people considered censorship inevitable because of its use for religious, political, or moral purposes, "wherever and whenever found" censorship limited the value of the newspapers affected, "as far as such newspapers are to be used as historical material."[80] Evidently, authorities like the Church and the state found censorship to be advantageous, while the public and the press frequently opposed its use. The costs of censorship were enormous. For example, during World War I, the English government employed fifty censors around the clock to handle press matters.[81] Furthermore, Salmon concluded that the effectiveness of censorship was debatable, its enforcement difficult, and the effect on general morale damaging.

Salmon explored other forms of regulation of the press, such as licensure, control of the supply of printing paper, denial of mail privileges, and taxes on knowledge. In examining this latter point, Salmon discussed English restrictions on the press, which began in 1712 with Parliament's levy of a tax on printed paper, pamphlets, and advertisements.[82] After her discussion of restrictions on the press, Salmon turned to consideration of the concept of freedom of the press.

Although freedom of the press is one of the cornerstones of free government, Salmon found the concept difficult to define, much as it was a challenge to define history. She claimed,

> Censorship of the press is definite, exact, and by its very nature it is subject to exact definition and legal interpretation, but freedom of the press is elusive and inexact, and while it can be consciously felt, it can never be satisfactorily defined.[83]

Nevertheless, Salmon believed that historians should deal with a free press. Not only must the press be a free medium to publish the news, but also it must also be at liberty to interpret, to express opinion, and to circulate the news. If the historian could not deal with a free press, the work of history would suffer. Salmon described restrictions on the press in countries purported to have a free press, such as the limits placed on the press in the United States during World War I (amazingly, she wrote the book shortly after the war ended). She concluded that absolute freedom of the press was an ideal, attainable only in the imagination.

After exploring the problematic question of how libel suits, the press bureau, publicity, advertisements, and propaganda affected the usefulness of the press for the historian, Salmon discussed the very great influence of the press. Historians who simply determined the authoritativeness of a newspaper performed their job insufficiently, for a reporter's selection of facts may be distorted and therefore convey false impressions. Furthermore, a newspaper may be accurate, yet influence little, or it may be notoriously inaccurate, yet tremendously influential. Therefore, the historian must utilize a "microscope" and a "telescope" to determine the character and influence of the press.[84] She concluded that the most frequent charge leveled at the press was that newspapers were filled with inaccuracies.[85] The power to define and enforce higher standards of journalism, however, had to come from within the press itself. "Freedom of the press will not come before the press genuinely believes in freedom of the press, and finds for itself freedom in the mind 'which no chains can bind.' . . . Before genuine freedom of the press comes, before freedom from irksome authority is gained, the impetus towards it must come from the press itself."[86]

Salmon's two exhaustive works on newspapers were generally well received by the academic community. *The American Historical Review* published a highly favorable critique. *The Review* noted that the two volumes were "the most thoroughgoing analysis of newspaper values that has ever been undertaken."[87] Preserved Smith, another reviewer, wrote, "Outside her own college and beyond the memory of the present generation, Miss Salmon's fame will rest on her two volumes on the newspaper."[88] Former student Mary Ross most aptly wrote,

> The most important contribution of *The Newspaper and the Historian* still is the underlying thesis which Miss Salmon's class first illumined to me—that history must be written "in the round," that to be true it must picture the things all sorts of men and women wanted to do, and tried to do, as well as those which the "great men" actually did.[89]

Salmon's exhaustive work on the newspaper constitutes her most consequential offering to history.

CHAPTER 6

Educational Philosophy and History Courses

> *Perhaps most people think and quite naturally that students of history live in the past. As a matter of fact we live in the future!*
> LUCY SALMON TO MRS. JAMES HODGE, JANUARY 4, 1897

Lucy Salmon portrayed her conception of the nature of history in her teaching. A champion of the new social history, she broadened the base of historical study in her courses. Although she cautioned herself and others to implement age-appropriate materials and methods, she strongly emphasized students' use of source materials, independent thinking and judgment, discussion, and hands-on activities, particularly at secondary and collegiate levels of historical study. In addition, she helped facilitate the development of a cohesive, nationwide secondary school history curriculum through her service on the American Historical Association's influential Committee of Seven.

During Salmon's forty-year career at Vassar, she wrote frequently about the teaching of history. She also taught a wide variety of history courses. She taught her favorite offering, "Historical Material," until the end of her life. In this course, Salmon encouraged her students to explore a great variety of historical sources, particularly the less obvious nonwritten records. Salmon's educational philosophy was evident in this course and in the almost twenty others that she taught while at Vassar. Furthermore, Salmon made apparent in writings her philosophical beliefs about teaching history at the elementary and secondary educational levels, gained from her experience as a teacher, secondary school principal, and normal school instructor.

Philosophical Perspective: Age-Appropriate Historical Study

Lucy Salmon reasoned that scientific methods and other forms of research could be applied to the study and teaching of history and, therefore, could assist in the improvement of education. Although she highly valued scientific reasoning, she believed it should not be overemphasized in educational considerations.[1] The historian must "never recognize history [as] a subdivision of physics or biology" and should acknowledge the "individuality of history."[2] In addition, she held that historical study at the elementary, secondary, and university levels should be "age appropriate." Today, she might have employed the term "developmentally appropriate." Furthermore, Salmon thought that the scientific study of education could facilitate the growth of corresponding history curricula and materials. She believed the use of scientific processes could advance knowledge and aid in quests for truth, although she did not hold that historical truth could be ascertained with certitude.

In *The First Yearbook of the National Society for the Scientific Study of Education*, Salmon developed her ideas about the teaching of history at all levels of education.[3] She noted that the object of the study of history differed for readers, students, and historians.[4] When selecting materials for the study of history, teachers should consider not only the variety of history courses offered but also the stages of their students' mental development. Furthermore, Salmon claimed that the study of history had the dual purpose of enhancing students' reasoning skills and providing them information. An advocate of the new social history, she noted the tendency of early writers of history to emphasize military and political affairs, while ignoring other phenomena of society. She thought that social history also should be incorporated into history curricula. Social history was important to teach in schools because it presented a fuller picture of historical phenomenon and included common people to whom the students easily could relate.

Of course, Salmon believed that history should be afforded a prominent place in the school curriculum. She nevertheless agreed that its study must vary according to the mental condition of the child to be educated. Long before Jean Piaget wrote in the 1920s through the 1960s about sensorimotor, preoperational, concrete operational, and formal operational stages of cognitive development, Salmon highlighted five central characteristics that she believed to be pedagogically useful in the teaching of history.[5] The central characteristics Salmon described included imagination, enthusiasm, unification or integration, judgment, and creativity. Salmon wrote,

> The object of the study of history on its educational side is first to train the imagination, to use the phrase in its commonly accepted meaning, during the period that corresponds roughly to the primary grade; it is second, to cultivate enthusiasms during the period that corresponds to the grammar grade; it is third, to secure integra-

tion of facts and ideas during the high school period; it is fourth to train the judgment during the college course; it is fifth, to foster and minister the creative spirit during the university and subsequent periods.[6]

Salmon recommended that teachers have students in the first and second stages of their development learn about history first through mythology and afterward through biography. She believed that such emphases would help cultivate students' imagination, reasoning, and enthusiasm. Salmon believed that elementary school teachers neglected history, a subject that merited greater attention.[7] For the third stage of development, Salmon recommended that students study national interests. American students, therefore, would study United States History, whereas students in other countries would learn about the particular country in which they lived. The objective was for students to learn about the growth and development of their nation. She understood that such study should enhance students' desire for national unity. For college students, who presumably could draw upon a large amount of historical information, Salmon recommended the study of more limited periods in which they could study relationships and comparisons.[8] At the university, the goal of advanced history instruction, according to Salmon, was to encourage students (especially graduate students) to undertake independent work by insisting that they work with original historical source materials.[9]

Salmon's theoretical framework was entirely consistent with her classroom practice of teaching history. At Vassar, she rarely lectured or required formal textbooks. Rather, she requested that her students engage in independent research and thought. Evidence of her general teaching approach is found in the testimonies of Salmon's former students, in her course syllabi, and in copies of examinations that she prepared.[10]

Salmon, according to her understanding of the development of school history instruction, held that history teachers typically emphasized memorization. Toward this end, a textbook was viewed as "infallible and the chief educational purpose served by the teaching of history was that of training the verbal memory."[11] Salmon, on the other hand, insisted that memorization was a poor method of teaching history, but she also disfavored the "source method" in which textbooks were discarded completely and students were taught to reconstruct history from original and all too fragmentary documents. She argued that such a method placed too great a demand on immature students. Rather, at the secondary level, Salmon favored a balanced approach, consistent with the method of teaching history advanced by the Committee of Seven. In this process, teachers should supplement the textbook with illustrative material and original source documents. Salmon did not favor any one method to the exclusion of others. Indeed, she rarely advanced extreme measures in educational endeavors. Instead, she believed that reading textbooks, listening to lectures, and going to the sources were all integral components of students' learning of history. Nevertheless, she ardently advocated the use of sources because she understood that their use in learning history was often neglected. At the university level, in fact, Salmon achieved deserved distinction among academics for her advocacy of the use of sources in history courses.

Sources, Judgment, and the Committee of Seven

Lucy Salmon endorsed developmentally appropriate historical study, and she also favored balanced approaches in the teaching of history. Although she believed that no one method should be used exclusively, she understood that some approaches (e.g., discussion, readings from source documents) were neglected more than were others. Because she knew that many teachers relied predominantly on the traditional lecture method, Salmon encouraged the use of source documents and judgment in the secondary history curriculum. Salmon's prominence in the teaching of school history earned her an invitation to join the American Historical Association's Committee of Seven in 1896.[12] In order to foster more uniformity in the teaching of secondary school history, the AHA appointed the Committee of Seven to consider this burgeoning subject and to recommend college entrance requirements.[13]

Four years earlier, in 1892, the National Education Association (NEA) had created the Committee of Ten to report on the status of secondary education and to recommend standards in the various school subjects. Four years later, the American Historical Association's Committee of Seven evaluated and further developed recommendations for the teaching of historical studies in secondary schools. The work of these committees and several subsequent committees, such as the Committee of Five (1911), the Committee of Eight (1912), and the Commission on the Reorganization of Secondary Education (CRSE, 1918), helped to lay the foundation for the general educational curriculum, and the social studies curriculum in particular, that exists in most American schools today.[14]

The Committee of Seven certainly took into consideration the earlier work of the Committee of Ten, especially inasmuch as Albert Bushnell Hart served on both committees.[15] The National Education Association authorized the Committee of Ten to propose standards for the assorted subjects in the secondary school curriculum.[16] The Committee of Ten consisted of nine separate conferences based upon the academic disciplines of (1) Latin (2) Greek (3) English (4) modern languages (5) mathematics (6) physics, astronomy, and chemistry (7) natural history (8) history, civil government, and political economy, and (9) geography.[17] A distinct conference on geography was held at Cook County Normal school in Illinois and included college and secondary school teachers, a member of the Weather Bureau, and progressive educators such as Francis W. Parker.[18] A special subcommittee on history, civil government, and political economy, meeting in Madison, Wisconsin, developed recommendations to the larger Committee for the teaching of history and social sciences in the schools. Members of the Madison Conference called for a more complete program in history than was commonly practiced, similar to what had been common in Europe for more than fifty years.[19] Although the Report of the Committee of Ten recommended a more comprehensive program of history and social science education, it endorsed only two years of required history and one year of elective history in American high schools.[20]

The Committee of Seven report went further. Concerned about the status of historical studies in secondary education, August F. Nightingale, chairman of the National Education Association's Committee on College Entrance Requirements, had asked historians at the 1896 meeting of the American Historical Association to provide a report detailing the actual practice of teaching history in American schools.[21] In order to make an accurate evaluation, committee members conducted a nationwide survey of the subject of history in schools, analyzed the resultant data, and made appropriate recommendations based upon the social science findings. Indeed, its recommendation had a far greater impact on the development of history education in secondary schools than did the earlier more comprehensive report. The Committee of Seven noted that,

> in spite of all that had been done, and in spite of this awakened interest, there was no recognized consensus of opinion in the country at large, not one generally accepted judgment, not even one well-known point of agreement, which would serve as a beginning for a consideration of the place of history in the high-school curriculum. . . . The task of the committee was, therefore, to discover the actual situation, to see what was doing and what was the prevailing sentiment . . . and having apprehended what was best and most helpful in spirit and tendency among teachers of the country, to seek to give that spirit expression in a report that would be helpful and suggestive, and that would be of service to widening the field of agreement and in laying the foundations for a common understanding.[22]

In other words, the Committee of Seven understood its task to be to evaluate the existing history curriculum and to make suggestions for its reform.

The members of the Committee of Seven included Andrew McLaughlin (chairman), Herbert B. Adams, George L. Fox, Albert Bushnell Hart, Charles H. Haskins, H. Morse Stephens, and, of course, Lucy M. Salmon.[23] Six members were prominent historians. Herbert B. Adams had organized the American Historical Association at its founding in 1884. The Harvard historian Albert Bushnell Hart, a prolific author, had written a popular guide on the study of American history.[24] Hart later was elected president of the American Political Science Association (1912) and the AHA (1909).[25] George L. Fox, headmaster of the Hopkins Grammar School, in New Haven, Connecticut, was the only individual practicing in a secondary school.[26]

After conducting and analyzing the comprehensive nationwide survey of the teaching of history in the nation's schools, the Committee recommended a four-year course sequence consisting of four blocks or periods in the following sequence: (1) ancient history, including Greek and Roman history and the early Middle Ages and closing approximately at 800 A.D.; (2) medieval and modern European history, which would pick up from the close of the ancient history course and continue to the present; (3) English history; and (4) American history and civil government.[27]

Seeking to expand the analysis, the committee also explored the teaching of history in Germany, England, France, and Canada as a means of comparing practices, methods, curricula, teacher preparation, and pedagogy abroad with those employed in the United States.[28] Clearly, the Committee of Seven sought a broad base of comparison, rather than an inward-looking, myopic perspective such as might have resulted from an examination of practices in U.S. schools only. The committee members' belief was that understanding history instruction and history curriculum in other countries could serve to inform and advance the practice of history education in American schools. Nonetheless, the Committee also had to ascertain the common practices of teaching history in American schools, for no nationwide study heretofore had been undertaken.

The Committee of Seven members boldly employed newly developed social science methods to investigate the status of history instruction. Methods such as collecting surveys and analyzing statistical data were rare forms of conducting historical inquiry, particularly in the late 1800s. However, these methods were typical of the work of the new progressive professional social scientists, such as Lester Frank Ward, Florence Kelly, Jane Addams, and Carroll Wright.[29] Clearly, the members of the Committee of Seven were "progressive" in their approach to researching the status of history in schools.

Conducting a survey, or "Circulars of Inquiry," as the members referred to their initial method of gathering data on the status of history education in U.S. schools, was the subject of the very first meeting of the Committee of Seven, held in Cambridge, Massachusetts, on April 16–17, 1897.[30] In later meetings of the Committee of Seven, the discussion regarding pedagogical methods of achieving historical study revealed the Committee's strong divergence of opinion. Some members preferred to use only the textbook in first-year history courses, while others urged a large amount of collateral work.[31] Nonetheless, a consensus held that historical study was not intended to encourage rote memorization of meaningless facts. Clearly, compromise between committee members about the nature of secondary historical study was necessary in order to produce a cohesive published report.

The Committee of Seven's recommendations significantly affected the development of the history curriculum in the nation's schools. Many schools adopted the four-year course sequence. The Committee recognized that it courted criticism for its suggestion of such a comprehensive program but felt that history warranted a prominent place in the curriculum. Furthermore, some schools already offered such a plan, and the Committee decided that it should promulgate an ideal program. Finally, the Committee suggested that if only three years could be devoted to historical study, then three of the four could be chosen and one omitted, or two of the periods could be combined into one year of study.[32]

The Committee believed that the purpose of historical study was for students "to become, not scholastics, but men and women who know their surroundings and have come to a sympathetic knowledge of their environment" and that "the most essential result of secondary education is acquaintance with political and social environment, some appreciation of the nature and state of society, some sense of the duties and responsibilities of citizenship" and "something of the broad and tolerant spirit which is bred by the study of past times and conditions."[33] Furthermore, a consensus held that historical study was not intended to encourage rote memorization of meaningless facts. Instead, historical thinking was to be fostered through textbook and collateral readings, written work, oral reports, map making and reading, notebook preparation, and the appropriate use of original source material.

Evidence of the Committee's long-term significance was apparent more than a decade later when publications in *The History Teacher's Magazine* (later to become *Historical Outlook* and subsequently *The Social Studies*) contained myriad references to the work of the Committee of Seven.[34] The success of the Committee's work in influencing approximate uniformity to the school history curriculum was widely acknowledged. Indeed, the resultant standardization also facilitated consistency in college entrance requirements.

The Committee of Seven did not recommend maintenance of the status quo but suggested moderate progressive reform. These changes included increased support for universal public education, expanded notions of citizenship, extension of subject matter studies to elementary students, curriculum reform, acknowledgement that the purpose of secondary education was not to prepare for college but to prepare for life, development of curricula guidelines that broadened secondary courses of study (antecedent of the comprehensive high school), recommendations of progressive pedagogies rather than reliance on traditional methods such as rote memorization, augmented history course requirements, strengthened social science studies, and a reliance on social science methodologies to gather data and support for the Committee report recommendations.

Salmon's influence on the Committee of Seven's final report certainly included its recommendation that courses employ original sources in order to enhance students' historical study. In fact, the Committee stated, "The use of sources in secondary work is now a matter of so much importance, that it seems to demand special and distinct treatment."[35] The Committee noted that if memorization as an instructional method were to continue to strengthen, retention of history in the curriculum would be jeopardized. The Committee averred, instead, that students should be taught how to read history books, how to think about historical facts, and how to analyze the relationships between evidence and historical statement.

Indeed, many of the Committee of Seven's recommendations related to central tenets of Salmon's beliefs about how history should be taught in the schools. Salmon even believed that elementary school teachers should use sources on a limited basis with young children because documents enabled a child to learn how historians work.[36] She also contributed to the Committee's work by spending the summer of 1897 studying methods of historical instruction in German and Swiss/German schools. Salmon presented the findings of this inquiry in an AHA paper, "History in the German Gymnasia," which the Committee of Seven included as an appendix to its report.[37] Her report revealed the nature of pedagogical methods of historical instruction in Germany. Salmon discussed the German history curriculum, methods of discipline, time allotment for subject matter, and teaching practices. The Committee believed that German methods offered particularly valuable lessons for American schools because, of the foreign instructors studied, German history teachers seemed to have the best understanding of the historical content and of students' psychological development. Furthermore, the uniformity of the German curriculum was noteworthy.[38]

Salmon's research in Europe for her report was not always easy to conduct. She wrote, for example, that one of the directors of a German school "grunted and said in effect that he didn't want any women in his school, but since he apparently had to give permission he would do it."[39] Although many schoolmasters were polite, Salmon reported, "they usually say that a woman in a gymnasium is an unheard of thing."[40]

In addition to the impact of Salmon's study of German history teaching, her ideas about history instruction, such as her advocacy of the use of source documents, clearly influenced the Committee's findings in other ways. In a section of the Committee of Seven's report on methods of teaching history, Salmon's essay "The Teaching of History in Academies and Colleges" was highlighted as one of ten useful articles.[41] With characteristic modesty, however, she took little credit for her work. A decade later, the Committee of Eight, which was the first group to study the conditions of elementary historical studies, thanked Lucy Salmon for her work on the Committee of Seven. The Committee noted that Salmon's study of history in elementary schools had "not received the attention it deserves."[42] Vestiges of her recommendations remain evident in the secondary social studies curriculum today. They include her emphasis on the use of primary source documents and her expansive notion of social history. The historian David Van Tassel wrote that the recommendations made by the Committee of Seven were followed in American secondary schools for more than thirty years.[43] Certainly, the influence of the Committee of Seven is evident today.

Salmon's Philosophical Perspective: Progressive Methods of History Instruction

Lucy Salmon's work on the Committee of Seven also helped her achieve a more mature understanding of progressive methods of history instruction. Progressive education was a part of the larger, multifaceted Progressive era in American history. While controversy surrounds the term "Progressive era," today, historians generally concur that it encompassed the time period from approximately 1890 through 1920. In the arena of education, however, progressivism spanned a greater time period, from the late 1870s through the 1950s.[44] Traditional conceptions of the time period include "Roosevelt and Pinchot, trustbusting, conservation, electoral and civil service reform, the Pure Food and Drug Act, Woodrow Wilson, and yes, the perennial one woman, Jane Addams."[45] Rapid transformation of society was typical of the Progressive era, similar to the changes experienced today due to "changing technology, altered lifestyles and new, massive waves of immigrants."[46]

In the early 1890s, the Progressive movement in the United States was in its infancy. Progressivism was largely conceived as a democratic reform movement that arose in response to the problems and paradoxes evident in the Gilded Age. Pernicious evils of the Industrial Age included rapid urbanization, an increase in factories and resultant pollution, massive poverty, particularly among the immigrants hired to perform routinized work, substandard and crowded living conditions, and enormous economic and social gaps between the wealthy and the poor.[47] Notions of improving society through cooperation, community works, and social activism were essential components of the Progressive era legacy. Those who identified themselves as progressives articulated "their discontents and social visions."[48] Although not a uniform group, progressives sought to correct these insidious evils through increased democracy, regulation of big business, public service, social justice, conservation, and public service.[49]

Salmon plainly was a proponent of progressive education. She hoped to bring positive change to American society by improvement in education. According to Lawrence Cremin, progressive education

> began as part of a vast humanitarian effort to apply the promise of American life—the ideal of government by, of, and for the people—to the puzzling new urban-industrial civilization that came into being during the latter half of the nineteenth century . . . it meant applying in the classroom the pedagogical principles derived from new scientific research in psychology and the social sciences. . . . Finally, Progressivism implied the radical faith that culture could be democratized without being vulgarized.[50]

More recently, William Reese argued that the origins of progressive education "were part of a larger humanitarian movement" that "sought both social stability and social uplift."[51] During the late nineteenth century, in the education arena, important events developed as part of the progressive movement. Progressive educators and citizens sought not only to improve the quality of education but also to increase access to education. This laboratory of democracy began with the school.

William Reese traced the origins of progressivism to a "rising ethos of caring within emergent capitalism, which increased human misery, but also" promoted "empathy, compassion, and social action."[52] He claimed that progressivism had antecedents in Romanticism and in the eighteenth- and nineteenth-century reform movements of the Western world. For example, a growing fascination with the child can be found in the Enlightenment and in the Romantic-era writings of John Locke, Jean-Jacques Rousseau, Ralph Waldo Emerson, Henry David Thoreau, and, more specifically in the arena of education, in the work of Johann Pestalozzi and Freidrich Froebel.[53] The origins of universal American education and romantic ideals of kinder, more active pedagogy date back to Horace Mann's vision of public schooling.

Universal schooling was just one of the reforms associated with the progressive movement. John Dewey (1859–1952), a prominent American philosopher and educator, was one of the leading reformers associated with progressive education.[54] Dewey and other progressives held a profound belief in the possibility of "attainment of a better society through education."[55] In order to integrate the vast numbers of students entering late-nineteenth-century American schools into the democratic society, progressive theory held that education should start with a focus on the child's interests and particular stage of development. The project method, group learning, experiential learning, and students' active participation in class were just some of the reforms Dewey and other progressive educators advocated. Certainly, Lucy Salmon was keenly aware of Dewey's theoretical ideas and advocated progressive educational ideals, as well. Salmon had been a student at Michigan, where Dewey taught prior to his tenure at the University of Chicago and Columbia University. Dewey's family had been friends with the president of the University of Michigan, James B. Angell, and Salmon also included Angell in her professional circle.[56] John Dewey's wife, Alice, like Salmon, had been one of the early female students to graduate from the University of Michigan. Alice welcomed Salmon to her home in the early 1890s when Salmon came to give guest lectures at Michigan.[57] Certainly, Salmon and Dewey shared beliefs about progressive education when they convened.

For Salmon, progressive education meant the application of scientific study to pedagogy. Moreover, she identified herself as a progressive educator and happily reported to Vassar College president Henry MacCracken, "The progressives are everywhere in the saddle!"[58] She also was attracted to progressive methods in the classroom. With regard to pedagogy, Salmon concluded that students' independent research and the use of source materials enhanced their critical thinking skills and constituted a more stimulating process of learning history than rote memorization. In addition, methods such as class discussion enabled students to be active participants, rather than passive learners. Furthermore, Salmon had a strong faith in democratic principles. She understood that sources of historical information were available to anyone, everywhere, even in one's backyard. In fact, she published a pamphlet entitled, "History in a Back Yard."[59] This perspective reflected her democratic philosophy that individuals could undertake historical study about a wide range of topics and that history could appeal to a larger audience than an elite group of academicians.

With small classes at Vassar College, Salmon could also implement the progressive, hands-on, experiential type of history learning she adored writing about and teaching. In "History in a Back Yard," for example, she explored the notion that history was part of the present. She explained that fences, stone walls, and hedges constituted history and revealed not only notions of property ownership but attitudes about privacy and seclusion.[60] Furthermore, a garden revealed history. Plants could be connected to their countries of origin, such as daffodils to Holland or lilacs to Persia. The names of plants, such as narcissus and heliotrope, recalled ancient history. The galvanized metal trashcan in the backyard was a record of sanitation and modern industrial developments.[61] She concluded,

> So our back yard has the records of all the ages within its narrow enclosure. Prehistoric questions of ownership of land lie in our fences, classical mythology blooms in our bulbs, the discovery of a new world rises in our Norway maple.... The advantages of studying history in a back yard are manifold.[62]

In the classroom, Salmon required that her students engage in experiential activities. She brought pupils to her kitchen and her backyard, for example, to discover history. She asked them on examinations what history would be evident in their hometown if all written records perished.

In an essay titled "Main Street," Salmon explored her insistent theme that history was everywhere part of the present.[63] According to Salmon, any town's main street held records that connected it with the beginning of time. From historical records, "it is possible to reconstruct in a measure the history of the past, to interpret the spirit of the present, and even in a measure to anticipate what its future will be."[64] Main Street's foundation of slate and shale was its oldest geological formation, whereas the factories, trolleys, and trucks that lined the street served as evidence of modern industry. The architecture of buildings on Main Street, which included Ionic, Doric, and Corinthian columns and Roman arches, revealed connections to ancient Greek and Roman history. The pedestrians and shop owners suggested the multitudinous ethnicities among the citizenry. Salmon's students engaged in an experiential lesson in which they took a trolley ride along the main street of Poughkeepsie in order to find history.

Another methodological approach considered progressive that Salmon favored was the seminar. She first encountered this method as a student at Michigan.[65] Most history instruction in the late 1800s and early 1900s consisted of a teacher lecturing and rote memorization by the students. Acknowledging the periodic necessity of lecturing, particularly to large groups, Salmon favored the discussion method in her own courses. Discussion required active participation by the learner. Salmon wrote that "Mental dyspepsia [indigestion] is incurred at an early age if the child is allowed to be a mere passive recipient of all that comes from books or instructor."[66] At Vassar, she became well known for the "table long" at which students held many discussions and intellectually digested the subject matter. ("The table long" is discussed in more detail in the next chapter.) Importantly, Salmon's preference for a seminar-style classroom manifested itself early in her career in her difficult relations with Woodrow Wilson and later with James Baldwin, who both preferred to lecture.

Salmon generally was consistent in her practices and beliefs. She employed progressive methods in her classroom. She believed students ought to be participants in the learning process and sought means for actively engaging them in history. Through the history courses that she taught at Vassar College, she found a variety of means by which to involve students in their discovery of history.

Courses Taught During a Forty-Year Career at Vassar College

Lucy Salmon taught numerous history courses during her forty years (1887–1927) as a professor at Vassar College. During her tenure, the nature of the college curriculum changed dramatically nationwide. Since the founding of colleges in the United States, beginning with Harvard in 1636, through the mid-1800s, most colleges mandated strict curricula. Students had little or no opportunity to select courses, and colleges emphasized the study of Latin, Greek, literature, and philosophy. Indeed, science did not hold a place of prominence in the early college curriculum.

When Salmon began teaching at Vassar in 1887, much of the student course work remained prescribed. The Vassar College catalogue for the 1899–90 school year, for example, indicated that students had a fairly substantial list of required courses; however, history was required only in the sophomore year, when students took two prescribed courses, "Greek and Roman History to the Invasion of the Barbarians" and "Medieval History." Other requirements included the study of two foreign languages. Latin was required for all, but students could choose from Greek, German, or French to fulfill the second language requirement.[67]

Nonetheless, the Vassar College curriculum permitted some electives. Salmon, a true democrat, ardently supported student choice in course selection. However, tension between the increasingly popular elective system and the traditional academic core program certainly was evident at Vassar College. The 1891–92 catalogue stated the college's position: "The curriculum has been carefully formed with regard to the conflicts between the Prescribed and Elective Systems, and with the belief that experience demonstrates the need of much careful compulsory work as a preparation for free choice."[68] Even so, the college permitted students to elect a few courses.

During Salmon's first year at Vassar, 1887–1888, as the only history professor, she was responsible for all departmental offerings. She taught to sophomores Greek and Roman history and medieval history, to juniors modern history, and to seniors English and American history and political economy.[69] When Professor Herbert Mills joined the department in 1890, Salmon did not teach the sophomore level required course in history, although, later, she shared this responsibility with departmental faculty. Mills, who later headed the economics department, taught the sophomore history courses.[70] Salmon, on the other hand, offered all the history electives to juniors and seniors. These courses included semester offerings in modern European history, English and American constitutional history, and American constitutional history. By 1893, another junior faculty member joined the department, and more courses were added to Vassar's history offerings.

The purpose of instruction in history was clearly delineated in the Vassar College course catalogue, and Salmon's ideas about the teaching of history were prominent. The 1894–95 Vassar College catalogue stated,

> The object of instruction is first, to emphasize the difference between reading history and studying history; second, to acquaint each student to independent work with the best methods of historical study; third, to show in the study of different nations the development of present from past conditions; fourth, to indicate the organic relation of history to other branches of knowledge.[71]

As noted, process rather than content-area knowledge was emphasized in Vassar's historical studies. Furthermore, Salmon's pedagogical practice of promoting independent work and methods of historical research prevailed. Later catalogues revealed similar considerations. Indeed, the "particular object" of the two courses that Salmon taught was "to give training in specific methods of historical investigation."[72] Salmon reiterated these points about the purposes of studying history in several "Suggestions for the Year's Study" that she published. These "Suggestions" were pamphlets Salmon produced at Vassar for each history class that provided guidelines and articulated the essential purposes of studying history.[73]

In 1900, after she returned from a two-year sabbatical in Europe, Salmon taught several new courses in history, as many more elective classes were added to the history department offerings. As department chair, Salmon, of course, was integral to the development of new course offerings. Generally, classes were one semester in duration. Salmon taught courses on American colonial history, the history of American political parties, the French Revolution, American constitutional history, the nature and treatment of historical material, and nineteenth-century history.[74] Obviously, Salmon's course load was substantial. She taught three classes each semester, and the range of topics was quite broad. Importantly, Salmon began her course on historical material in the 1900–01 academic year. By 1902, she extended the required course on general European history to a two-semester sequence and renamed it History 1 and 2. Eventually, most of the history department shared responsibility for teaching this course, because Salmon also promoted team teaching.

Early in the 1900s, Salmon continued to expand the range of courses that she offered. In addition to her regular courses on historical material, American colonial history, American constitutional history, and nineteenth-century history, she also taught courses on American political parties, nineteenth-century European politics, the history of the civil service in the United States, American political literature, comparative politics, and contemporary history.[75] Generally, the range and number of departmental offerings increased over time, as did the number of faculty hired to teach such a variety of courses. By the 1904–05 school year, the history department teaching staff increased to six, and seventeen history courses were offered.[76] In fact, the Vassar student body also had grown considerably. Such rapid expansion must have alarmed the college trustees. They voted in 1905 to limit the student body to 1,000 women and to continue the cap for at least five years.[77]

Throughout the early part of the century, Salmon's course offerings continued to evolve. Minor occurrences, such as a change in the title of the course on American colonial history to "American History," reflected a more modern perspective and perhaps permitted a wider range of current topics for discussion. Salmon's American history class was listed as a general elective, but her other courses were advanced or special advanced electives. Clearly, she enjoyed teaching students who demonstrated a special interest in the study of history.

In 1908 and again in 1910, Salmon added two new courses that were notable for their unusual topics of interest. These were called "The Development of Municipal Government" and "Ethnic Elements in American History." These courses underscored Salmon's commitment to the new social history, even before James Harvey Robinson wrote his seminal book on the topic in 1912. Furthermore, Salmon's interest in these courses also reflected her lifelong commitment to democracy. She sought to call attention to ethnic groups and to women and to highlight their significant, yet largely unheralded, contributions to American society.

With the exception of the addition of these two new courses, throughout the 1900s and 1910s, Lucy Salmon's courses generally remained the same. She offered some classes in alternate years only. Even when course titles remained unchanged,

Salmon continuously prepared new topics and work within each course. By 1910, Salmon was the third or fourth senior ranking member of the entire Vassar faculty (in order of appointment). Obviously, Salmon was an integral part of the institution. The regular classes she taught during the 1910s included courses on American history, contemporary history, the development of municipal government, which she alternated with a course on ethnic elements in American history, and the nature and treatment of historical material. In 1915, her name was added to the teaching staff of the European history course for the first time, although she had helped develop the syllabus, organize the course, and write the examinations long before that date.[78]

By the 1919-20 academic year, Salmon had become the most senior member of the Vassar faculty. By this time, her active teaching career was beginning to wind down. However, she did not stop working. Instead, Vassar granted Salmon a sabbatical during the fall semester so that she could complete her books on the newspaper. After the 1920-21 academic year, Salmon provided instruction in only three courses, general European history, American history, and historical material, and shared the European history course with other members of the department. In the last two years of her career, Salmon held part-time status and taught only her beloved course on historical material.

Because Salmon taught at least sixteen different history courses at Vassar during her career, all are not examined in depth here. Furthermore, the available records for each course vary in informativeness. Her favorite courses, those on historical material and American history, are examined extensively because Salmon taught these courses for a considerable period of time. She taught American history throughout the forty years she was a Vassar professor. Less information is available in her archival papers about other courses, such as those on municipal government and European history, but their subject matter is of interest, and, therefore, they are explored in the subsequent chapter.

Salmon's Course on Historical Material

Lucy Salmon's advocacy of the use of historical sources became the cornerstone of her life's work and was a remarkably progressive method of teaching history in the late 1800s and early 1900s. Indeed, she planned for her "magnum opus" a book on the subject of historical material.[79] Although the work was never completed during her lifetime, friends and colleagues at Vassar published her unfinished manuscript in 1933 as *Historical Material*. The book explored the vast forms of historical records that were available to the historian. The course outline followed the book but had more components.[80]

Salmon first taught her course on historical material for advanced students during the 1900–01 school year. The formal title was "The Nature and Treatment of Historical Material," and the class was intended to include a study of the "nature, treatment and classification of historical material, and of the laws of historical criticism."[81] By the 1906–07 school year, the purpose of the class was expanded to include imparting an understanding of the aim of the historian and the nature of the record on which history was based.[82] Twenty years later, the course description remained essentially the same, except that the catalogue noted that the course was intended for those students who planned to teach history, to undertake graduate studies in history, to enter library work, or to become curators of historical museums.[83]

Salmon provided a published pamphlet for students at the beginning of the semester for almost every history course she taught. These pamphlets were entitled "Suggestions for the Year's Study." She authored each of these pamphlets. She began the "Suggestions" with several quotations, a writing style Salmon frequently employed. The first quotation instructed students to "Take these hints as suggestions, not as instructions, and improve on them as you grow in experience."[84] True to her democratic philosophy, Salmon incorporated students' ideas and revisions into subsequent editions of "Suggestions."

"Suggestions" for each of Salmon's courses included a description of what students were expected to have learned from previous historical study and what they should gain from her course. After completing the course, students should have developed the ability "to understand the process of historical investigation, to discriminate in the use of books, to make newspaper clippings with judgment, to draw conclusions" and to be more independent and accurate in their work.[85] Salmon's "Suggestions" also included a diagram of the library in which books related to the subject could be located. The numerous recommended books for the class included a textbook, secondary works, collections of sources, an almanac, guides to literature, biographies, travel guides, and illustrative materials. Salmon also advised students to purchase a tin tray that contained library cards and guide cards for making bibliographies, a camera for taking photos of points of historic interest, post cards depicting subjects studied, and a subscription to a good daily newspaper.[86]

After indicating various forms of historical material available to students, Salmon's "Suggestions" described the anticipated course work for the year. Course work included finding a topic on which to write, reading a brief account of the topic, making a list of questions about the topic, creating a bibliography, familiarizing oneself with terminology related to the topic, finding corresponding newspaper clippings, taking notes, writing a report that was a "miniature chapter of a book,"[87] and presenting the topic orally. Salmon noted that she would provide each student the opportunity for personal conferences as often as possible. "Suggestions" also included a general outline of the subject studied and a chart depicting how all the courses in the Vassar College history department related to each other.⁸⁸ At the end of the "Suggestions," Salmon attached an original document. For example, the "Suggestions" written for her American history class contained a copy of the federal Constitution.⁸⁹

In addition to writing on a historical topic, students in the class on historical material were assigned to study their hometown in depth. They had to describe the circumstances of the settlement of the town, the nationality of early settlers, the causes of settlement, and the reasons for the growth of the town. Students also were instructed to list the monumental and literary primary sources of material available for the study of the town and to describe any efforts, or lack thereof, to preserve this material. Finally, students had to explain how this material could be used in the local elementary and secondary schools in the town.⁹⁰

Clearly, Salmon expected students to be serious and diligent. She invested considerable effort into the development of courses that enabled students to learn history in an innovative, nontraditional manner. Salmon wanted students to discover the wide variety of sources of historical material and to engage in independent projects. Reading several secondary sources on a particular subject was important but not sufficient. Students must also discover history. Take photographs. Collect postcards. Go to the sources. Locate monuments and buildings. Clip articles from newspapers. Read original documents. Analyze information. Use imagination. Experience history. Write history.

The examination held at the end of the year in Salmon's course on historical material tested students' ability to analyze, make judgments, locate sources of historical information, discern relations, and promote an interest in history. For example, questions from the May 1911 examination asked students to

1. Show what historical material can be found in (a) your back yard (b) the house in which you live.
2. Examine the text book assigned and write a report on it to the superintendent of public instruction in your home community with reference to
   (a) the authoritativeness of the text
   (b) its usefulness for classroom purposes.
3. What can be done in your home community to promote an interest in historical study?⁹¹

A particularly unique question from the May 1912 examination required students to show how the city of Poughkeepsie could be used as historical material if all literary records of the place were to perish.⁹² Salmon hoped students would discover that history was all around them, part of the present, and that infinite forms of historical records existed everywhere in life. Salmon's philosophical perspective on teaching history permeated every course she taught, regardless of the topic.

Salmon's Course on American History

Salmon's course on American history, similar to her course on historical material, stimulated student interest in social history, fostered independent research, and created a context for understanding the relationship between past and present. Salmon's American history course followed the framework, published in "Suggestions," that she created for several of her courses, no matter that the subject matter differed. The general outline of the American history course included several topics such as the first settlers, the frontier, separation from England, the establishment of the Constitution, political parties, and the chronological development of national history since 1789.[93] Problems Salmon posed for students included questions such as "Who is an American?" and "What is patriotism?"[94]

Students either chose topics to research or were assigned topics by Salmon. In the archival folder with Salmon's American history papers are several envelopes containing topics handwritten by Salmon on notecards. Subjects ranged from "ethics of the frontier" to "food," "roads," and "domestic occupations."[95] Next to each topic, Salmon inscribed a student's name. Students chose a topic, researched it in depth, wrote a chapter, and presented the topic orally. In addition, Salmon created various related assignments for students to complete. For example, Salmon gave handwritten notecards to her American history students that presented various problems for the students to solve. She gave to a Miss Cain the following conditions:

> Place. Chicago. Seven young women employed in Marshall Fields store for ten years. Fourteen days vacation given and expenses paid by employers. Problem: To plan a trip from Chicago to Charleston, SC, showing places of historic interest in the development of America since 1789. To suggest suitable books to read before, during and after the trip.[96]

She posed for a Miss Connor a different set of circumstances:

> Place. Tenafly, NJ. Commission as consulting expert from Superintendent of Schools. Problem: To outline a course of study in America history for public schools.[97]

Each of these assignments encouraged students to learn the subject matter of American history. They also fostered creativity and independent thinking. Other assignments had practical applications, as well. For example, a student, M. Connell, was told to

> Plan a course in American history for a club of boys and girls in Omaha, assuming their ages range from 15 to 18, that their fathers are in the packing home industry,

that they have left school and are employed in factories. Recommend books in American history not to exceed in value $50 to become the property of the club. How can you promote the interest of history in Omaha?[98]

Salmon clearly wanted her students to be prepared to teach history, a common profession for Vassar graduates to enter after they earned their degrees. In addition, she wanted students to be aware of practical restraints, such as the monetary limits placed on curriculum materials, while earnestly promoting historical studies.

Examinations also stimulated student thought and revealed Salmon's tremendous creativity in developing questions. Questions varied from year to year, and topics were similarly disparate, but all required students to demonstrate their knowledge of subject matter, use their imaginations, understand historical methods of research, and use their faculty of judgment. Students were asked to demonstrate their knowledge of a wide range of topics, such as biography, original source documents, and current events, as well as past history and politics.

Selected questions from Salmon's American history examinations follow.[99]

[January 1897]
1. What are the characteristics of a good biography? What personal influence was exercised on the colonies by
   a. John Smith
   b. Charles I
   c. Thomas Hooker
   d. William Penn
   e. George III

[January 1898]
1. Sources may be used in college work to reconstruct, or to illustrate history. Which is the better method? Why?
2. Describe and give one illustration of Colonial Archives, Statutes, Monographs, Historical Society Collections.

[January 1909]
1. Make out a set of ten questions that will best illustrate the work of the semester. The questions should have logical sequence and express one central idea; they may be framed a single, or as a group of questions; it is not necessary to consider the length of time or the preparation required to answer them; the text-book may be consulted in preparing the questions.
2. Why is this an examination?

[January 1915]
1. Give in outline form a plan for comparing the Revolutionary War and the present European War.
2. Select from any source in the library such facts as will illustrate the points enumerated in the plan.

[May 1912]
1. What can be said for and against the election of the president by direct vote of the people?
2. Who is an American?

Many of the questions on Salmon's examinations could be asked in contemporary American history courses. Furthermore, Salmon's questions required students to reveal their understanding of history, rather than simply to recall information as is required for typical multiple-choice questions on current standardized examinations.

Salmon's progressive philosophical beliefs about the teaching of history were consistent with the manner in which she taught history courses. She believed in an age-appropriate history curriculum. Furthermore, her work on the Committee of Seven led her to support a balanced approach to history instruction at the secondary level. At the collegiate and university levels, however, Salmon favored a progressive approach that encouraged independent research and the exercise of judgment and imagination. Courses on both historical material and American history provided Salmon the opportunity to employ such innovative methods. She encouraged students to realize that history was part of the present, all around them, in the backyard and on the main street. Indeed, historical records abounded and certainly were not limited to written forms. Salmon taught many other history courses, several of which are examined in the context of Salmon's teaching methods. The following chapter explores in detail the pedagogy Salmon employed to convey her understanding and beliefs about the nature of history.

CHAPTER 7

Lucy Salmon's Pedagogical Practices and Mentoring of Students

> *Froude informs the Scottish youth*
> *That parsons do not care for truth.*
> *The Reverend Canon Kingsley cries*
> *History is a pack of lies.*
> *What cause for judgments so malign?*
> *A brief reflection solves the mystery—*
> *Froude believes Kingsley a divine,*
> *And Kingsley goes to Froude for history.*
> BISHOP WILLIAM STUBBS,
> *Letter to J. R. Green, 17 December 1871,*
> Letters of Stubbs *(1904), p. 162*

What was it like to take a class from Lucy Salmon? Salmon's Vassar classroom at the turn of the twentieth century, in many respects, would bear little resemblance to a modern-day classroom. Indeed, one can imagine twelve young women, clad in long, full dresses with high collars, sitting around a long wooden table in a small classroom on the Vassar campus or, perhaps, gathered in Salmon's cluttered study, discussing issues of historical interest. Salmon may have begun the class session by distributing a quotation for students to ponder. She loved quotations, and they frequently headed examinations, essays, and books that she wrote. When Salmon began to teach at Vassar, cars, airplanes, radio, and movies were not current realities. Even electrically wired homes were a recent development, and not every home in Poughkeepsie enjoyed this modern convenience. During her career, however, these inventions became commonplace. As the world around Salmon changed, she sought to change the manner in which history was taught in school and college classrooms throughout the country. In many ways, she used her own classroom as the laboratory in which she tested and evolved her ideas about the teaching of history.

Lucy Salmon employed myriad innovative methods to stimulate student interest in history. She never stopped trying new techniques, nor did her mind ever retire from its relentless mode of inquiry. Salmon's classroom methods included discussion, oral presentations, evaluation of original source documents, researching and writing of history, essay examinations, and visits to historic sites and to more ordinary places, such as her kitchen. Her overriding pedagogic purpose was to immerse her students in history.

Students responded. On the whole, they worked prodigiously, and their relationship with Salmon was not unlike that of disciple and master. Students produced stellar research in her class that often reflected a newly discovered interest in social history. After they completed Salmon's courses, many students continued their work in history by attending graduate school. Others chose teaching, library work, or marriage. Regardless of their future paths, a significant number of her former students maintained relationships with Salmon through correspondence in order to inform her of their work and their continued interest in history. In many ways, Salmon's students constituted her extended family, and their work in history served as her principal legacy.

Of course, not all Vassar students were devotees of Lucy Salmon, nor did all history teachers and professors of the time promote her methodologies. In the late 1800s and early 1900s, many teachers criticized or at a minimum remained skeptical of pedagogy that differed from the traditional memorization of historical facts. Intellectually, Salmon welcomed differences of opinion, however much she personally disliked confrontation. Nonetheless, Salmon pursued a progressive pedagogy because she believed it benefited both students and the field of history.

One common criticism of progressive educational methods like those employed by Salmon was that students were not adequately intellectually challenged. This criticism simply did not apply to Salmon's courses. Her demands were quite rigorous. She dedicated tremendous energy to her profession, and she expected a reciprocal investment from her students. Very early in Salmon's career, the large amount of study that she required of students came to the attention of the Vassar president. Indeed, one Vassar official wrote Salmon to inform her that her students were spending too much time preparing for her history class and that he intended to pass this information on to President Taylor. The colleague explained, "If they remain for a few moments beyond the 9:35 bell they can not be ready for bed at 10:00."[1]

Of course, most students at Vassar were gifted, well educated, and likely diligent, even before they entered Salmon's classroom. First, in order to attend Vassar, candidates had to pass an entrance examination in history that would challenge many present-day practicing historians. Those examinations tested not only students' historical knowledge but also their secondary school preparation in history coursework and their ability to think, analyze, and form judgments. These examinations contained difficult essay questions, not multiple-choice questions, in which students manifested their historical knowledge, critical thinking skills, and writing ability. Students generally had the freedom to select from a range of questions, but occasionally they faced compulsory questions assigned to the entire group. Sample questions from Vassar's history entrance examinations during the Salmon era illustrate their rigor:[2]

[Selected questions: June 1894]
1. To gain a knowledge of the history of Greece from the chief contemporary sources what writers must be studied? State the character of the works of each author, and the century in which he wrote.
2. Compare the social, intellectual and political life of the Athenians and the Spartans.

[Selected questions: June 1897]
1. Name four important events in the history of the United States between 1789 and 1812.
2. Show how the following illustrate the struggle between the North and South:
   a. Virginia and Kentucky Resolutions
   b. Missouri Compromise
   c. Compromise of 1850
   d. Kansas and Nebraska Act
3. Name three questions in the present foreign policy of the United States. Describe the attitude of the government in any one of them.

[Selected questions: September 1902]
1. Describe your preparation in ancient history. Mention your text book, give an account of collateral reading topics, compositions on historical subjects, use of maps, etc.
2. Describe your preparation in mediaeval and modern history. Mention text books and give an account of collateral reading, topics, compositions on historical subjects use of maps, etc.
3. Point out three events in the life of Luther which are of great historical importance.

[Selected questions: September 1911]
1. What were the most important influences of the Egyptians and the Phoenicians on later civilization?

2. What kinds of material, other than literary, are used by the historian?
3. What are primary sources? Give five concrete examples.

Clearly, to pass such challenging examinations, entering Vassar students had to have substantial historical knowledge. Salmon helped to enhance students' understanding by using teaching methods employed by practicing historians and by encouraging students' independent thinking. Indeed, if a student's written work did not meet the standards that Salmon expected, she did not hesitate to return it and to require that the student rewrite it. For example, one former student received her returned paper with a note from Salmon that asked, "Have you expressed yourself in the best way in this paper? Will you not rewrite the paper and return it to me at your early convenience, and return this note with it."[3]

Not only did most Vassar students enter the college with solid academic preparation, but most had taken several history courses at the college before they came to Salmon's courses. Most of the courses Salmon taught were advanced electives, offerings designed for upper-division students. These gifted students enabled Salmon to exercise many different and innovative methods of teaching history.

The "Long Table," Discussion, and Other Teaching Methods

In addition to being rigorous, Salmon's courses stimulated vibrant discussion. When she began her Vassar career, Salmon taught juniors and seniors, and she believed that discussion was necessary in order to foster ideas and to promote independent thinking. Salmon broke with the traditional method of teaching history in which the teacher disseminated information and students learned history by memorization. In order to create a comfortable atmosphere for discussion to flow freely, Salmon frequently invited students to the library in her living quarters. There, she and her students gathered around a "long table."

The "long table" became a trademark for which Miss Salmon was well known.[4] For example, a former student, Blanche A. Jones, Vassar College 1896, recalled formal and informal discussions around the long table on topics such as "the sources of the Constitution of the United States."[5] One year after graduation, writing from Gregory, South Dakota, Mary Anderson, another former student, noted, "I am often with you inspired over the Table Long and the schedules."[6] In her memorial tribute to Salmon, another former student, Amy Reed, recalled, "I remember the excited buzz in the hall outside my door when Miss Salmon's senior class in American History came trooping up after two hours of discussion in the evening around the long table in her room."[7] The senior class of 1889 had such fond memories of evenings together at "the table long" that they broke school regulations and collectively left Salmon a gift on her doorstep with a note that read,

"In cordial remembrance of our many happy evenings at the 'Table Long' from The Senior Class."[8] Concerned about receiving a gift because the Board of Trustees had passed a regulation that prohibited an officer of the school from accepting a gift from a company of students, Salmon wrote about this circumstance to President Taylor of Vassar. He responded by granting Salmon permission to accept the gift.[9]

Salmon's pedagogical beliefs convinced her that discussion was an appropriate methodology to employ in the classroom. Discussion fostered active student learning. Salmon was keenly aware that discussion was not a dominant practice in many college history departments. Indeed, a former student, Sophia Chen, while completing graduate work in history at the University of Chicago, wrote to Salmon,

> I don't like the passivity of mind that everything here [at the University of Chicago] seems to encourage the student to acquire: there is no class discussion nor oral quiz but lecture and lecture and lecture until one becomes afraid that one's mind would become rusty and burst open with too much poured-in ideas; there is no open shelf library, and consequently, no roaming ground for mental adventure among the books. For this reason, I feel very grateful for the training that I had at Vassar.[10]

In 1920, Chen became professor of European history and English literature and the only woman faculty member at the University of Peking in China.[11]

After Chen's graduation from Vassar, Salmon served as her mentor. E-Tu Zen Sun, a professor of Chinese history at Pennsylvania State University, whose mother, Sophia Chen (Zen), Vassar College 1913, took courses from Lucy Salmon, remembered that her mother generally thought Salmon was a wonderful teacher.[12] Certainly, Sophia Chen's letters conveyed glowing admiration and respect for Lucy Salmon. Throughout Salmon's later years, Chen continually sought Salmon's advice and guidance, particularly on matters of mutual historical interest. Chen hoped to bring Salmon's methodology and knowledge of history to Chinese students. She acknowledged that the common Chinese practice was for students to remain "passive listeners" but added that she, at least, wanted to encourage thinking.[13] Never overly dogmatic in her beliefs, however, Salmon responded to Chen that she should consider the positive aspects of the lecture method.[14]

Another unusual teaching method that Lucy Salmon commonly employed was to bring students to her house in Poughkeepsie to show them her kitchen in order that they might discover the history there. Salmon displayed a photograph of a colonial kitchen in her own late-nineteenth and early twentieth-century kitchen in order that students might see the relations between the past and the present. Clearly, this activity made quite an impression upon Salmon's history students. Decades later, the visit to Salmon's kitchen continues as part of a remembered oral tradition passed down to daughters of women who enrolled in her classes.[15]

Salmon, of course, was very interested in domestic artifacts. Her books *Domestic Service* and *Progress in the Household* reflected this concern. She wanted her students to determine what history was revealed by their examination of kitchen implements, such as utensils and machinery. Certainly, Salmon's pedagogical approach reminded students that history was present even in the seemingly ordinary aspects of living, and it revealed her keen interest in cultural and social history. Undoubtedly, the field trip experience to Salmon's kitchen made a deeper impression than merely reading a text about the history of kitchens.

Salmon sporadically directed field trips for students to discover history. One excursion that took considerable planning was a visit to the New York City Post Office. In 1905, for example, Salmon arranged with the postmaster for him to meet with her class on a Saturday morning in order for students to learn about the operations of the post office and to discover its history.[16] A more common experiential learning activity in her class was for students to take a trolley ride along the main street of Poughkeepsie to observe its history. Another excursion was for students to visit Salmon's backyard. Salmon described in two essays the main street and backyard endeavors, as well as the history that students could learn by their examination of these ordinary surroundings.[17]

Salmon did not want students simply to take field trips. She encouraged students "to make use of observational sources in the laboratory world off campus, to feed and shape their views and incorporate such materials in their discussion and writing."[18] She required students in her historical material course to investigate the history of their hometowns. One student, Rebecca Lawrence Lowrie, Class of 1913, described to Salmon the fascinating history she had learned about her hometown of Galesburg, Illinois. While ascertaining Galesburg's history, Lowrie had met an elderly gentleman who as a young child had driven a wagon of runaway slaves covered with straw. This man recalled that Galesburg had been an active center of the Underground Railroad.[19]

Students in Salmon's historical material class learned that objects and items in ordinary everyday life could be seen as historical records. Almost ten years after she graduated from Vassar, one former student, Elsie Rushmore, Vassar College 1906, sent Salmon a clipping from a newspaper that she titled, "The joke as historical material!"[20]

At the Front (From the *Cleveland Plain Dealer*)
"Yes, I saw Chawlie Chippendale at the front."
"Good old Chawlie. I suppose he was waving his sword in the sunlight and shouting, 'Come on, lads, come on!'"
"Well, no, he wasn't. He was waving a spade and yelling 'Dig, you Tommies, dig!'"

Evidently, Salmon's methods of teaching history taught students that they learned history not only by reading books but also by their close observation of the world around them.

Salmon's pedagogy embraced discussion, experiential activities, observation, and analysis. Her creative approach to teaching history, moreover, was influential because of the strong and devoted relationships that Salmon cultivated with her students. During her tenure at Vassar, Salmon received thousands of letters from students. This correspondence revealed her former students' appreciation of her profound ability to mentor and guide them.

Mentoring of Students

Salmon's teaching methods were popular and gained her a large and loyal following of students. At times Salmon's students may have acted a bit cliquish, but they insisted "on spreading her fame to all unfortunates who did not have direct contact with her."[21] One former student recalled that she was shocked when a classmate remarked that Miss Salmon had no humor. "I didn't even take that idea into consideration. Indeed, I didn't care whether she had or hadn't that particular quality.... Who would wish to improve on the sunlight?"[22]

Students did not simply admire Salmon. They sought advice from her. Even after they had graduated, many students continued to request her guidance, opinion, and knowledge. Sophia Chen wrote, "One of my joys is that I could always regard my former teachers as teachers. It gives me encouragement and inspiration to have such an everlasting resource for the growth of my intellectual life."[23]

Chen frequently requested history book recommendations from Salmon, as did other former students, including Rebecca Lawrence Lowrie, Mary Berkemeier, and dozens of others.

Students also sought guidance from Salmon about how to proceed with their careers after college. Because of Salmon's nationwide connections to historians and Vassar alumni, she often was able to help students in their postcollege pursuits. For example, after assisting a history professor at Knox College for one year, Rebecca Lawrence Lowrie asked Lucy Salmon for a letter of recommendation for graduate school in history at Radcliffe and sought Salmon's opinion on what courses she should take there.[24] Salmon wrote to the Harvard historians Albert Bushnell Hart (with whom she had worked on the Committee of Seven) and Charles Homer Haskins, dean of the Harvard Graduate School, to endorse her former student. Henry Morse Stephens, professor of history at Cornell University and, later, at the University of California, claimed that his best graduate students came from Lucy Salmon's classes.[25] Mary Berkemeier, Vassar class of 1913, attended graduate school in history at the University of Wisconsin along with two other Vassar alumnae.[26] Berkemeier wrote to Salmon that she was anxious to begin teaching and sought Salmon's advice.[27] When one of Berkemeier's high school history students asserted that history was a "chronological narration of events," Berkemeier boasted that she asked students to describe what historical material they would use to write an account of Plattsburgh if the history books were to disappear.[28] Berkemeier's question to her students was remarkably similar to the kind of question Salmon posed to her pupils.

Obviously, the relationship between Salmon and her students did not end with the granting of diplomas. To many former students, she willingly gave advice throughout her life. Amy Reed remarked, "Her advice on the conduct of life was considered valuable by all her friends, and if she had not been so great a teacher of history, she would have been a wonderful head for a bureau of vocational guidance."[29]

Former students also were able to return favors to Salmon. Many students sent her newspaper clippings to add to her ever-expanding collection, which ultimately contributed to her two books on newspapers.[30] Occasionally, graduates were able to extend job openings to students Salmon recommended. For example, after attending graduate school at Radcliffe, Rebecca Lawrence Lowrie worked at the Macmillan Publishing Company, Harper Brothers, and Yale University Press before she became editor of the *Vassar Quarterly*.[31] When Lowrie worked at Harper's, she inquired whether Salmon had any students who would want to work in the summer months on a twelve-volume history of the war that was to be published in the fall of 1919.[32] Salmon later wrote to Lowrie to have some of her history manuscripts published. Elsie Rushmore, Vassar College 1906, mentioned to Salmon a vacancy on the staff of the American Red Cross when she was employed there.[33] Because Salmon was respected and maintained such strong relationships with many students, she established a large network of connections to the career world.

Years after graduation, Salmon's former students sent her tokens of appreciation. They gave her vases, handkerchiefs, paintings, dried flowers, and many other presents. Mary Berkemeier sent Salmon the following poem:[34]

To L.M.S.

Ideas—assembling, penetrating, unifying
Thoughts—generating, creating, reliving
These have been yours
In fashioning your gift of mind for us
So that we,
Blessed
May see

> Visions—clarifying, revealing, redeeming
> And dream
> Dreams—of that tomorrow, whose claim of
> parentage is this today and you.

Undoubtedly, Salmon had a profound impact on many of her students who, long after they left her classroom, remembered lessons she had taught and who appreciated her selfless devotion to them.

Certainly, some Vassar students did not favor Salmon's methods. She was very popular, however, with the vast majority of students, particularly early in her career when she was one of the few faculty members in the history department. Still, a few students found Salmon a bit unusual and did not prefer her teaching methods. For example, Ruth Adams, Vassar College 1904, daughter of a Yale historian, George B. Adams, wrote that she was cross because her teachers were making her work terribly hard and hand in written work each time "à la Miss Salmon." She continued,

> I had a conference with Miss Salmon yesterday and certainly she is a peculiar specimen. One of the questions she asked me was whether I was going to follow my father's profession, "or your mother's, shall we say, Miss Adams?" I wanted to tell her that I would follow my mother's if I could get a man, and my father's if I had to, but I didn't. Then she told me by heredity and by early training and influence !!! I should be the leader and shining light for the others!! But nothing practical does she give you, except that in a general way she is satisfied with your work.[35]

Adams also complained that Salmon was overly carping about petty details but did not provide general criticism of one's manner of working. Salmon had marked Adams's paper where she had abbreviated a man's name and indicated where Adams's right margin was not straight.[36] Although Salmon's career counseling and teaching style were not effective for Ruth Adams, Adams's letters suggest that she was not the most conscientious student. In another letter to her father, Adams wrote,

> Everybody is advising us to begin reviewing now for exams. It is such a bore. I wish I knew whether Cooley is going to flunk me in Physics. I should be terribly provoked if he does.... And on Friday I handed in a paper with "not prepared'" on it. It is such a nuisance to make such things up.[37]

Adams seems to have been struggling in her academic career, and perhaps Salmon initiated the conference out of concern. Nevertheless, Salmon's advice fell on deaf ears. Perhaps Adams eventually appreciated Salmon's teaching, for she contributed to the research fund established in Salmon's honor in the late 1920s.

Although Adams's sentiments about Salmon appear to be those of the minority, a certain partiality exists in the evidence that serves as testimony about Salmon's teaching. Undoubtedly, only students who admired Salmon took the time to write her letters. Therefore, the archival evidence necessarily biases the picture painted of Salmon's teaching. Nonetheless, students likely would not have gone to such lengths to show their gratitude had she been a less dynamic professor.

Toward the end of her career, Salmon seems to have concentrated a bit more on her professional writing than she did in earlier years and, consequently, enjoyed contact with fewer students. Thus, she did not have as large a following as she did earlier, although she remained liked and respected. Colleagues, students, and friends all noted her tremendous generosity. She made herself available to students and was often concerned with what they did after their graduation.[38]

Examinations

Salmon's examinations were another unique and progressive feature of her teaching methods. They reflected her creativity and clearly sought to stimulate students' historical thinking in a manner far beyond traditional examinations, which required only description or explanation of a particular historical phenomenon. Many of the distinctive questions she asked her students could be employed in history courses today. For example, in an examination in her American history class, she asked students to "state in detail what you would do to test the accuracy of the statements of the Declaration of Independence."[39] In another assignment, Salmon asked a student to "plan a course in American history for a club of American women resident in a Chinese city."[40] Such thought-provoking questions are as applicable today as they were when they were written.

Salmon held passionate opinions about the nature of the examination process and about how exams should be written. For example, she wrote,

> The department of History at Vassar College has always stood for a type of examination that is not "a corkscrew process of extracting information." . . . We have always believed that the examination paper should be not so much a test of what the student knows as a test of what he can do; that it should show the ability of the pupil or student to handle historical material, to solve simple historical problems, and to interpret historical situations; that it should test the pupil or student in regard to his mental independence, his intellectual curiosity, his powers of observation, his reconstructive imagination.[41]

Salmon did not favor standardized examinations that tested recall of factual information. Ironically, she worked on a committee to write some of the first common college entrance examinations in history.[42] Although Salmon's commitment to progressive methods of examination may appear to be in contradiction to her work on the Committee of Seven, this appearance may be somewhat false. First, the Committee of Seven was devoted largely to making recommendations for the national secondary course of historical study. Second, a need for a common course of study existed, as colleges faced the challenge of entering students with widely disparate learning experiences. Third, Salmon believed that college entrance examinations could be written in a progressive manner that encouraged thinking, similar to the style she employed in her own classroom. Finally, Salmon could not have anticipated the widespread use of multiple-choice, fill-in-the-bubble questions that dominate current college entrance examinations such as the SAT and the ACT. She had compromised with members of the Committee of Seven with respect to specific details of the report, but surely she would be dismayed by current standardized tests.

In her own courses, her examinations were composed only of essay questions.[43] Certainly, some questions required more thought than did others, but all called upon students to demonstrate their knowledge. Obviously, questions in which students were asked to define a historical event or to describe a historical individual demanded primarily recall of historical information. However, these types of questions never dominated Salmon's tests. All examinations included several questions in which students were called upon to exercise independent thinking, judgment, analysis, and creativity. A sampling of some of Salmon's examinations in selected courses follows.

History 1—European History[44]
[Sophomore-level required course that was team taught by the history department faculty.]

[January 1899]
Bibliography:
1. Give the authors and titles of five general works on medieval history, excluding text books.

The influence of Rome:
2. Explain how the Roman law grew up as a system of justice and how it was finally given permanent form.

[January 1907]
1. Sources of Church History: Enumerate primary sources dealing with any three of the questions you have answered.
2. Bibliography: Give characteristics of three historical works.

[June 1910]
1. What can be derived from the following documents as to social, economic, political, religious and intellectual conditions?

History O—The Development of Municipal Government[45]
[Junior/senior-level advanced elective]

[January 1913]
"The ideal college education seems to me to be the one where a student learns things he is not going to use in after life by methods that he is going to use. The former element gives the breadth, the latter element gives the training." President Hadley, cited by President Lowell in his Inaugural Address, October 6, 1909.

1. Write a series of letters to one of your local papers advocating
    a. the employment of an expert city planner,
    b. the establishment of a bureau of municipal research,
    c. a budget exhibit,
    d. a social survey
2. Show how the work in History O could be more vitally connected with the City of Poughkeepsie.

History S—Historical Material[46]
[Junior/senior advanced elective]

[May 1911]
1. Records
   Show what historical material can be found in
   a. your back yard,
   b. the house in which you live.

[Exam May 1912]
1. Show how the city of Poughkeepsie could be used as historical material if all literary records of the place had perished.
2. What can you do in your immediate home locality to promote an interest in history?

[June 1917]
1. How far is the scientific collection of historical material promoted by
   a. the moving picture
   b. the historical pageant
   c. the historical museum

2. What are the comparative advantages of writing history through the medium of
   a. printing
   b. painting
   c. sculpture

History A, AA—American History[47]
[General elective]

[January 1898]
1. Sources may be used in college work to reconstruct, or to illustrate history. Which is the better method? Why?
2. Describe and give one illustration of Colonial Archives, Statutes, Monographs, Historical Society Collections.

[January 1914]
I. The text-book.
1. Give in bibliographical form the name of the text-book used.
2. State what principles can be applied to test the authoritativeness of any text-book.
II. Apply these tests to the text-book used.
1. Why is the study of the text-book the first step in the study of any period of history?
2. What classes of materials are needed to supplement the text-book in the study of
   a. frontier life
   b. the stamp act
   c. the Philadelphia Convention.

Several unique features of Salmon's examinations were common to many of her tests. First, she asked students to demonstrate a knowledge of bibliography. She wanted students not only to know how to use proper bibliographic formatting (essential to writing history) but also to know the practical skill of being able to locate historical material in the library. Second, she wanted her students to reveal a knowledge of collateral readings and materials. The textbook alone did not suffice in Salmon's courses. In addition, she required that students reveal their understanding of how source documents illuminated historical inquiry.

A third common feature of Lucy Salmon's examinations was the placement of quotations about history that she wanted students to consider. Sometimes Salmon placed the quotation at the top of the test to read, while on other tests she provided quotations and asked students to interpret and analyze the statements contained therein. Fourth, Salmon typically asked questions that had practical applications.

Students could apply what they had learned in a real-life situation. For example, students could actually write to their hometown papers about using a city planner. Another test asked students to develop an idea that could help the city of Poughkeepsie, where Vassar was located. Salmon understood that academicians sometimes criticized practical applications of knowledge. Nevertheless, she seemed to strive to discover real-life connections between history and contemporary issues for her students. Understanding connections, she believed, would help students realize that history was alive.

The Legacy of Salmon's Students: Their Work in Her Classes

Evidence of Salmon's inventive methods of teaching history was reflected in the work of her Vassar students. Student papers, correspondence, notecards, historical material, research topics, and examinations all constitute a part of the record of Salmon's work and testify to the nature of her teaching methods. Salmon valued student opinions and incorporated their ideas for improving history courses. In general, she provided a variety of methods for students to demonstrate their talents. Much of the students' work in Salmon's courses was exemplary.

Salmon prodded students to think beyond factual recall of information. She wanted students to consider the essence of history. In her course on modern history, Salmon asked students to respond to the question "What is modern history?" Most students' answers revealed careful thought. For example, Marjorie M. Kendig's response stated,

> For some it means the period from the overthrow of Napoleon in 1815 and the subsequent reconstruction and development of Europe, and the world down to the present day.... It is the many who feel that the history of the last 100 years is the only history worth knowing about.... It includes the developments in science and commerce which made the Industrial Revolution possible.... The last hundred years have seen the growth of the intense emphasis on nationality; the extraordinary rise and development of the German empire; the alternate waves of liberal revolution, and reaction, with the final triumph of liberal conception.... No epoch in history can be separated from the rest because it has grown out of it, the 16th century is the fruit of the 15th, the 20th of all the preceding epochs whose conditions, customs, modes of thought and institutions last over into the next, and the next mold their forms. The past is always with us, and to me there is no Modern History.[48]

Of course, not every student was diligent, and some responses were not as well written as Marjorie Kendig's or were more cursory than were others. Helen Prescott's entire response comprised one sentence, "All History is modern in so far as it is necessary to know it in order to understand present conditions."[49] Salmon also asked her students to provide a date when they thought modern history began. Lalitha Folks wrote,

> To use a term in history to mark a certain definite period is always impossible. It is like marking the beginning of a great movement like the Renaissance, or its end. It forgets that history is the working out of forces inherent in human development that have no beginning or ending. As a term to designate approximately a certain part of the expression of these forces "modern history" may mean relatively recent life, but as attempting to designate a particular kind of history, definitely set off from all others, it is an impossible term.[50]

Undoubtedly, Salmon made plain to students the influence of the past upon the present such that they realized that dates were artificial boundaries.

Salmon also developed creative ways for students to reveal their understanding of the nature of history. For example, in a study of unwritten historical material, Salmon encouraged students to research "What may be learned of the history of Poughkeepsie from a study of Main Street?" Salmon's pupil G. L. Fletcher Chase wrote in her notecards, which she made in preparation for a term paper, that history was revealed on a trolley ride along Main Street, where the architecture of the buildings reflected Dutch and colonial influence, that signs and symbols were traditions handed down from a time when the public generally was illiterate, and that names of the shops and residents revealed the influence of newcomers to America of German, Dutch, Chinese, Italian, French, Irish, and Jewish descent.[51] In History "R," a course on ethnic elements in American history, another student examined the contributions of foreigners to American music.

Student research topics included conventional military and political events, as well as more unusual topics such as the indentured servant in the Middle Colonies, the farming frontier in Massachusetts, and a comparison of the politics, fashion, transportation, and fads in 1897 and 1907 through an examination of issues of *Life* magazine for both years.[52] Salmon also constructed unusual examinations that encouraged students to use their powers of reasoning, imagination, analysis, and judgment.[53] Clearly, Salmon encouraged students not only to study and to research both traditional and unusual topics but also to pursue innovative methods for gathering historical information. In these pursuits, her own work served as a model.

In addition, Salmon required students to find original source documents. She wanted pupils to comprehend how vital historical material was to historians' work. One student, Ruth Chandler, worked on a research topic in Salmon's class entitled "Forces Working for Authenticity of the News: One Source of Authentic War Information—The State Councils of Defense."[54] Included in her research were press releases from the Connecticut Council of Defense, Committee on Publicity. Chandler had worked during the summer as a manager of the clipping bureau and therefore was able to obtain many press releases. One of the press release documents she saved for her work in Salmon's class discussed the need for lightless nights. In the notecards Chandler prepared for her research, she wrote that the records she collected should be "valuable to the future historian as a means of showing how public sentiment was fashioned and war news was spread by the government during this war [World War I]."[55] Today, these documents provide relevant details about how the state governments handled the dissemination of information during World War I.

Another notable aspect of Salmon's pedagogy was that she valued student opinion. Typically, she solicited students to figure out how courses could be improved, and she incorporated their ideas into her curriculum development. For example, Salmon asked her History I students to write short essays with suggestions for improving the course. E. Lillian Hutchinson opined that more time should be spent on modern history and that more original source documents, in addition to Robinson's *Readings*, ought to be utilized in order to prepare students for advanced history courses.[56] Two other students, Gladys S. Esten, and Marion S. Tallant, reiterated Hutchinson's sentiments.[57] Salmon carefully considered students' ideas. In Salmon's "Suggestions for the Year's Study," she acknowledged members of her 1911–12 American history class "for the many helpful ideas given for the revision of 'Suggestions.' Nearly all of these have been incorporated in the pamphlet and subsequent classes will profit by them."[58] In a later version of "Suggestions," Salmon requested that ideas for improvements be passed on to officers of the History Department.[59]

Despite Salmon's success in mentoring students, not all colleagues supported her progressive methods of teaching history. Indeed, in the early 1900s, much controversy remained over the use of source documents in the teaching of secondary school history.

Criticism of Salmon's Methods

For all her successes, Salmon found that her methods of teaching history attracted significant criticism. Particularly targeted for attack was her advocacy of the use of original source documents in the teaching of history. Despite Salmon's recommendations that a balanced approach be utilized when teaching secondary and elementary history, one that combined the textbook and source documents, her suggestions were often misinterpreted and viewed as radical or extreme by other academics. Many historians and secondary history teachers in the early 1900s believed that the use of sources should be extremely limited or nonexistent in the secondary and elementary classroom. Although Salmon's perspective about the teaching of history gained credibility over time, opposition remained prevalent, especially in the elementary and secondary schools.

Throughout its first five volumes, *The History Teacher's Magazine* published dozens of articles each year about the use of sources in the classroom. Most of these articles lauded the use of source documents and expressed the notion that progressive teachers at the forefront of their discipline utilized source documents in history instruction. For example, W. L. Westermann wrote,

> There is no argument to be advanced against the statement that the teacher of history will be the better teacher the more complete is his acquaintance with the original sources of information in the field of his teaching. These are the real springs of inspiration. It is best to drink from them when one can.[60]

Nevertheless, opposition to the use of sources was not silenced in *The History Teacher's Magazine*. These dissenting perspectives contributed to the lively debate about history instruction during the first decades of the twentieth century. Several authors either opposed outright the use of sources or thought that their use should be limited strictly in secondary and elementary classrooms. For example, Henry Elson argued that some teachers who used source documents tended to emphasize historical method above the acquisition of information.

> The new method simply means that history should be taught largely if not chiefly through the sources; that is, by constantly taking a class back to the sources. The historian must go to the fountains, it is true, and college classes should be led to them frequently; but high school classes only occasionally.[61]

Others agreed with Elson that the use of source documents retarded instructional progress and, over a given period of time, that students would learn less history. Some opponents also questioned students' ability to exercise discriminating judgment in their appraisal of the value of historical sources. They believed that students were immature and "undeveloped mentally."[62] Indeed, Elson even doubted most teachers' ability to evaluate sources. He cautioned,

> Let the teacher of the secondary school remember that a great majority of pupils will never get a higher education, that their time should be employed to the best possible advantage, and that one great historic truth of world-wide significance, properly impressed on their minds, is worth far more than all they can gain by months of plodding research among sources.[63]

Certainly, opponents did not advocate the complete abandonment of sources in history teaching. They held that relatively few documents, such as the Declaration of Independence and Lincoln's Gettysburg Address, were especially important, near sacred, and should be read by all students.[64] These opponents, however, believed that sources should be used in an extremely limited manner and should not be used at the expense of routine class work.[65] The aim of the history teacher, Fling wrote, should be not to inculcate students with "the methodological search for the truth"[66] but to introduce students to the domain of history. Charles Fay explained that "the only place for the 'Sources' is in the hands of the teacher and not in those of the pupils. I do not believe in the so-called 'Source-Method' of history teaching in secondary schools; it is unsuited to the mental capacity of the pupils."[67]

The nature of the debate about the use of sources in subsequent volumes of *The History Teacher's Magazine* gradually changed. The number of articles that opposed the use of sources in history teaching declined as interest in implementation of the use of sources increased. Although one author cautioned against assigning extensive collateral reading on all historical periods because "many a high school student can hardly paraphrase accurately a few pages of simple prose," most articles on the topic accepted the legitimacy of the use of source documents.[68] Furthermore, they advanced various ways of accommodating sources into classroom instruction.[69] In addition, earlier claims that students were mentally incapable almost entirely disappeared from articles published subsequently.

Despite the decline in opposition to the use of source documents in *The History Teacher's Magazine,* many of Salmon's colleagues, such as James Baldwin and her former adviser, Woodrow Wilson, remained strong proponents of the lecture method of historical instruction. Salmon firmly supported a more progressive approach that encouraged students' active participation. Similar ideological and philosophical differences about history instruction are prevalent today.

Salmon's pedagogical practices included discussion, experiential field trips, thought-provoking essay examinations, and historical research using source documents, to mention a few. Despite criticism of Salmon's methodological approaches to history instruction, in reality, the relationships she developed with students were more significant than the history material learned. Although students remembered activities in her classroom long after they graduated, as they indicated in their letters to her, students cherished her continued advice and guidance long after they completed her classes on American history or historical material. Salmon valued student opinions, and her concern for her students' welfare forged familial bonds between teacher and pupil.

CHAPTER 8

Lucy Salmon's Legacy

> *Some of the most interesting as well as the most important side lights on the past are furnished by the homely records of everyday life. The cook book, the fashion magazine, the printed laundry list, the family almanac, all unconsciously record the changing interests of the home and the external influences that affect them.*
> LUCY SALMON *in printed sheet*
> *"The Family Cook Book."*
> *Salmon Papers, box 31, folder 7*

Lucy Salmon remained an advocate of a progressive history curriculum throughout her career. She clearly dismissed the notion that memory by itself was a primary value of history learning. She also rejected the legitimation of studying history solely for patriotic purposes. She insisted that historical studies should cover a broad range of topics and that critical thinking skills and independent research should be encouraged for mature as well as young students. Salmon's beliefs about the nature of history and her pedagogical practices constitute an important aspect of her legacy.

Salmon's scholarly writings and research about the history of newspapers are a meaningful part of her legacy. According to Salmon, newspapers not only were useful to the historian but were consequential as a source of information about people. She understood that newspapers reflected the society in which they were produced. Toward the end of her teaching career, during World War I, Salmon found newspapers to be an especially important source of war information. Although Salmon had been teaching at Vassar for almost thirty years when the European war began, she found the Great War to be a "present" "historical" event that could engage students and inspire their development of an interest in history. Never one to rely on yellow and aged lecture notes and true to her pedagogical principles, Salmon encouraged her students to research and study the Great War.

World War I

Although she nurtured student interest in the war, Salmon was an avowed pacifist. Despite her opposition to war, she did not permit her ideological beliefs to conflict with her desire to foster students' interest in studying about the war. Indeed, Salmon organized informal talks on the war at Vassar at which history department members presented information on different phases of what was then called "the European War."[1] One of Salmon's early speeches about the war, entitled "The Press and the War," reflected her ongoing fascination with newspapers and their coverage of the war. Later, she delivered a 1917 war speech that discussed the more general issue of modern history.[2] In Salmon's classroom, students engaged in independent research projects related to the war, such as Ruth Chandler's study of authentic war information, in which she employed press releases from the Connecticut Council of Defense.[3] Salmon's students also kept updated on the war's progress through careful reading of newspapers and other popular, public literature.

Nonetheless, Salmon remained committed to her pacifist position. She objected to studying history simply to enhance patriotism, but her opinions lacked widespread collegial support. Indeed, to assist the war effort, the historian J. Franklin Jameson established the National Board for Historic Service (NBHS), which included, among others, the historians Frederick Jackson Turner, Albert McKinley (editor of *The History Teacher's Magazine*), Andrew C. McLaughlin (chair of the Committee of Seven), and Carl Russell Fish. The NBHS employed these scholars essentially to produce war propaganda.[4] Salmon associated with many of these historians as they were part of the large group of colleagues with whom she communicated.

However, Salmon did not let her professional associations govern her personal opinions. In fact, she informed many colleagues of her opposition both to the war and to the work of the National Board for Historic Service. Joseph Schafer, chair of the NBHS Committee on History and Education for Citizenship in the Schools, wrote to Salmon that he thought the fundamental difference of opinion between Salmon and his committee hinged upon differing definitions of citizenship.[5] Unlike the NBHS, Salmon did not equate citizenship with patriotism. Although Schafer agreed with Salmon's expressed statement that schools should have "far better equipped teachers than we have, better salaries, more independence and self-reliance, and less government," he maintained that the work of the NBHS committee would be valuable in providing an outline of the war for teachers and districts to use.[6] Salmon respectfully disagreed.

In fact, Salmon particularly was disturbed about how the war effort manifested itself domestically. She even put aside her disdain for President Wilson and wrote a letter to him in which she related evidence of discrimination against a local-area German American doctor, J. H. N. A. Von Tiling, whom she knew personally and whom she believed had been unjustly accused of violating the law by advancing German propaganda and spying.[7] Salmon was concerned that false charges of disloyalty and "blanket criticism given all persons bearing German names and the failure to discriminate between the true and false recoils against the critics and brings discredit on themselves."[8]

On a personal level, Salmon became distressed by incidents of jingoistic propaganda and xenophobia. As a historian, she was committed to accurate portrayals of events and people. She feared that the war had distorted perceptions and had promoted discrimination. According to the historian Preserved Smith, Salmon "yielded not an inch to the fierce blast of hatred and defamation directed against the Germans, but kept a cool head and an unwavering pacifism to the end."[9] Salmon's defense of German Americans reflected her commitment to pluralism in America and to her desire that history include the study of all peoples. In retrospect, especially in light of the widespread discrimination against German-Americans during World War I, Salmon's concerns seem warranted. Indeed, Salmon's concerns, if addressed during the first World War, might have prevented discrimination against German Americans and the far worse travesty of Japanese internment during World War II.

Close of Salmon's Professional Career

Toward the end of her career, Salmon received well-deserved national recognition for her academic accomplishments. The recipient of several honors, Salmon obtained awards and honorary degrees that symbolized the culmination of a successful career dedicated to education. Because Salmon was extremely modest, however, she hesitated to accept such academic distinctions. Perhaps as a means of giving back for a career that brought her academic acclaim, Salmon helped facilitate fellowships for students.

Always loyal to her undergraduate alma matter, Salmon served on a committee that raised funds for a fellowship for students at the University of Michigan. The committee noted that other renowned colleges such as Harvard and Johns Hopkins had such fellowships, and its members considered such awards important for the University of Michigan at Ann Arbor.[10] After Salmon's committee raised funds, the fellowship was named in honor of a former University of Michigan philosophy professor, George S. Morris.[11]

Salmon also maintained her connection to Michigan by attending Class of 1876 reunions. She kept banquet tickets, menus, class updates, and invitations to each of the reunions she attended. In 1926, Salmon journeyed to Ann Arbor for the fiftieth reunion of her class, although making the trip must have required considerable effort inasmuch as she was in her early seventies and her health was failing. She obviously had fond memories of Michigan. Salmon spent two weeks in Ann Arbor and was proud but humble when the University of Michigan conferred upon her the honorary degree of Doctor of Letters.[12] A former Vassar student who worked at Michigan and spent time with Salmon during her visit remembered that she remained impressed by the youthful and progressive nature of Salmon's educational perspective after so many years of teaching.

When Salmon attended Michigan, the university did not issue letter grades. Salmon's lifelong dislike of academic distinctions probably originated during her undergraduate years. Indeed, Salmon declined her election as a graduate to membership in Phi Beta Kappa when a chapter opened at Michigan in the early 1900s.[13] In 1926, she even hesitated to accept the honorary University of Michigan degree. In the end, however, Salmon differentiated honorary degrees from rewards for academic excellence. She did not support academic incentives because she believed that such distinctions were undemocratic and that they discouraged learning as its own reward. On the other hand, honorary degrees were not incentive laden and typically were offered in recognition of lifelong accomplishments.

Salmon accepted her first honorary degree, Doctor of Humane Letters, in 1912, from Colgate University.[14] The Colgate degree had special meaning for Salmon because the president of Colgate University, Elmer Burritt Bryan, who had been her student when she taught in the Midwest, conferred it on her. Colgate's alumni magazine noted that President Bryan beamed with pride as he extended the diploma to Salmon. The honorary degree from Michigan held similar sentimental importance.

In 1923, as she approached her seventieth birthday, Salmon faced the prospect of mandatory retirement from Vassar College. Vassar president Henry MacCracken wrote to her that he hoped to find a way by which she could continue because he thought she was a remarkable teacher.[15] Happily, he later reported to her that the Board of Trustees had voted to suspend the college's retirement requirement for her "as a cordial recognition of the completion of your recent works of research and your continued success as a teacher, and of the position which you hold in the Faculty of Vassar College and in the world of American scholarship."[16]

Although Salmon did not retire, she reduced her teaching load to half-time in 1925. Recognizing that she was aging, Salmon's Vassar students wanted to express their gratitude toward her. In February 1926, the class of 1888 decided to make its reunion gift a tribute to Lucy Salmon.[17] The idea of honoring Salmon spread and became popular with alumnae from other classes, as well. After several conferences with President MacCracken and administration officials, friends and former students established the Lucy Maynard Salmon Fund in order to provide an endowment that would enable her to pursue research on historical material while she continued to teach a course on the topic.[18] The fund committee sought to express to Salmon that the offering was "prompted by our admiration and affection; in all humility, knowing how inadequate it is, we ask you to accept it in token of your belief in our friendship for you."[19]

The committee initially notified 1,500 former students of Salmon's about the proposed research fund and solicited donations. A few friends were also contacted. During commencement week of 1926, the committee informed Salmon of the fund, which totaled approximately $31,000. Salmon's pleasure was evident when she told the committee chairman, "I still have something that I want to pass on. I may never be able to do it, but if my friends believe that I can, that is my incentive."[20] Salmon was to receive income from the fund during her lifetime, and after her death, the money was to be used annually by a member of the Vassar faculty for research purposes.[21] By 1927, nearly 1,000 students had contributed more than $33,000 dollars to the fund. Salmon received the first payments from the fund in January 1927, although she had become seriously ill by that time and was hospitalized.

Salmon taught and wrote until her death, from a stroke, on Valentine's Day, February 14, 1927. The official cause of death was cerebral apoplexy. Even after she died, however, the Lucy Maynard Salmon Fund furthered Salmon's work. The fund underwrote the posthumous publication of two of her manuscripts, *Why Is History Rewritten?* (1929) and *Historical Material* (1933). In the early 1950s, Vassar officials compiled a list of all the publications that had been assisted by the fund. The list included fifty-eight books on various topics by more than fifty authors. The Lucy Maynard Salmon Fund continues to provide research assistance to Vassar faculty today.

At Salmon's memorial service, held at Vassar College on March 6, 1927, she was fondly eulogized.[22] Henry Osborn Taylor noted that

> Among the broadminded teachers of history in our universities and colleges the name of Lucy M. Salmon deserves a prominent and lasting place. For her the past was a universal web of all things, and of all things as inter-related and working upon each other.[23]

In her tribute to Salmon, the former Vassar librarian Amy Reed remarked that Salmon's books and pamphlets, which numbered perhaps one hundred items, revealed an astonishing range in variety, in soundness, and in human interest. Reed also commented about Salmon's novel and dedicated approach to teaching.

> She was always interested in teaching, and her emphasis from the first was on the use of source material and on the method of independent investigation even for the very young student. In this respect she was among the pioneers.[24]

Salmon had even spent one academic year offering a course in historical methods to a group of interested Vassar professors. Clearly, her teaching talents were well respected among Vassar faculty. Vassar president MacCracken credited Salmon with the initiation of the college's academic convocation and with fostering among the faculty an intense interest in its philosophy of education, which prompted Vassar policy to be the object of study by other institutions.[25]

Salmon also received memorial tributes from individuals and groups outside Vassar College. They included one from the Daughters of the American Republic. She had served as a Regent of the local chapter in Poughkeepsie, and under her guidance the chapter had established a playground, a restoration fund, and a historical exhibit.[26] Of course, many of the other historical organizations and academic associations in which Salmon had actively participated also printed memorial tributes in her honor.[27]

More than twenty years after her death, Salmon's impact on Vassar College was still remembered. In 1949, for example, Salmon was honored when Vassar College established the Lucy Maynard Salmon Endowed Chair in History.[28] The Vassar president remarked, "Her work during the forty years remains as perhaps the most substantial contribution to education made by a single teacher in this college."[29]

Perhaps the most significant tribute to Salmon was the 1943 publication of a biography of Salmon by her former colleague, Louise Fargo Brown, titled *Apostle of Democracy*.[30] Brown's sentimental account of Salmon's life emphasized that Salmon pursued democratic principles with conviction in all her teaching and civic actions.

Salmon's Significance to Education

Salmon firmly believed that the principal value to be derived from studying history was to "practice the understanding in pronouncing judgments."[31] Her position attracted ample support from advocates of the new social history. Still, Salmon's methodology and ideology highlighted the division that existed among historians in the late nineteenth and early twentieth centuries about the nature of their discipline.[32] The first professional historians turned to science in order to search for laws of historical development. They believed that the past could be reconstructed in a strictly factual manner. Lucy Salmon and other advocates of the new social history challenged this strictly scientific approach to history. They encouraged an interpretive history that emphasized all aspects of human development (such as domestic service and newspapers), embraced methods employed by the social sciences (e.g., surveys), and accentuated the relationship between the past and the present. Moreover, Salmon implemented innovative pedagogy in her classroom, where she carefully cultivated lifelong relationships with students.

Salmon's central ideas are still debated today, most commonly without attribution. Purposes and methods of studying history remain disputed. The methods she implemented stimulated thoughtful historical discussion, called upon students' use of imagination, and encouraged the recognition that history was all around. History did not have to be relegated to the study of meaningless, uninteresting facts, or confined to the achievements of elites. Salmon understood that people existed in the midst of history. History was and is omnipresent.

Salmon's viewpoint was distinctive, especially during her times, in the depth of her commitment to democratic ideals. She focused attention on people typically overlooked, specifically women and immigrant groups; still, her tone was never strident. She included women in the pages of her written history, worked for suffrage, and promoted women for leadership positions. Notably, she personally advanced to leadership roles within the male-dominated historical profession and received acclaim for her work, particularly her writings about newspapers and the teaching of history. She worked to obtain career paths for her Vassar students through her academic connections. She founded the Association of History Teachers of the Middle States and Maryland (which later became the Middle States Council for the Social Studies), an organization that brought historians and history teachers together and worked to improve education for all children and youth.

Salmon's legacy remains complex, yet relevant in many ways. In her leadership in the historical profession and in the suffrage movement, she paved the way for women who followed her. Those women benefited from increased opportunities and fewer closed doors. No longer would female history professors, for example, teach about "The Appointing Power of the President" without having the right to vote. Because of Salmon, and other early pioneers in women's higher education, women today enjoy the same educational prospects as men. However, much work lies ahead for women with respect to leadership roles in many of the professions. Tenured professorships, college administration posts, and university presidencies are still positions occupied largely by men.

In other ways, Salmon's advocacy of the new social history opened entirely new fields of research. Prior to Salmon's inquiry, no American scholar had examined the history of domestic service, because historians viewed it as ordinary and as lacking scholarly significance. Furthermore, Salmon's historical investigation of domestic service demonstrated her concern for women's issues and contributed to the legitimization of a new area of study—home economics. Salmon thought that the ordinary, everyday aspects of life merited examination. To Salmon, newspapers, main streets, and backyards constituted the pageantry of contemporary life. Thus, she touted them as useful and valid sources for historical study. Finally, many of her recommendations for history instruction remain timeless, yet basic, such as her familiar advice to students: "Go to the sources." Despite the dominance of the textbook, particularly at the secondary school level, Salmon's methodology now has been advocated for more than one hundred years.

Salmon's work in the suffrage movement, her fields of research, and her progressive methods of teaching history reflected her commitment to democratic principles, which included civic education for Americans regardless of gender or social status. Throughout her career, however, Salmon made teaching students her first priority. The extensive correspondence she maintained with former pupils and their accolades about her teaching testify to her remarkable abilities.[33]

In many ways, Salmon's interests and activities reflected Progressive era concerns. Not only did she maintain relationships with other progressive leaders; she also remained committed to the movement's ideals. She worked to improve the community through lectures at the YMCA, through writings in the academic literature, as well as in the local newspaper, and by dedicating her life to education.

Salmon's accomplishments and teaching merit recognition and careful examination. In the present educational climate, where standardized testing is lauded as a means for marking student achievement, Salmon's work stands as an example of alternative methodologies that provide truly rigorous learning opportunities. In addition, her legacy should remind educators that teaching is largely a profession where human relationships remain paramount.

Photographs

Adelaide Underhill, life long friend and housemate of Lucy Salmon. Special Collections, Vassar College Library. Ref. 3.952

Woman suffrage parade on the Vassar campus in the 1910s. Special Collections, Vassar College Library. Ref. 3.602

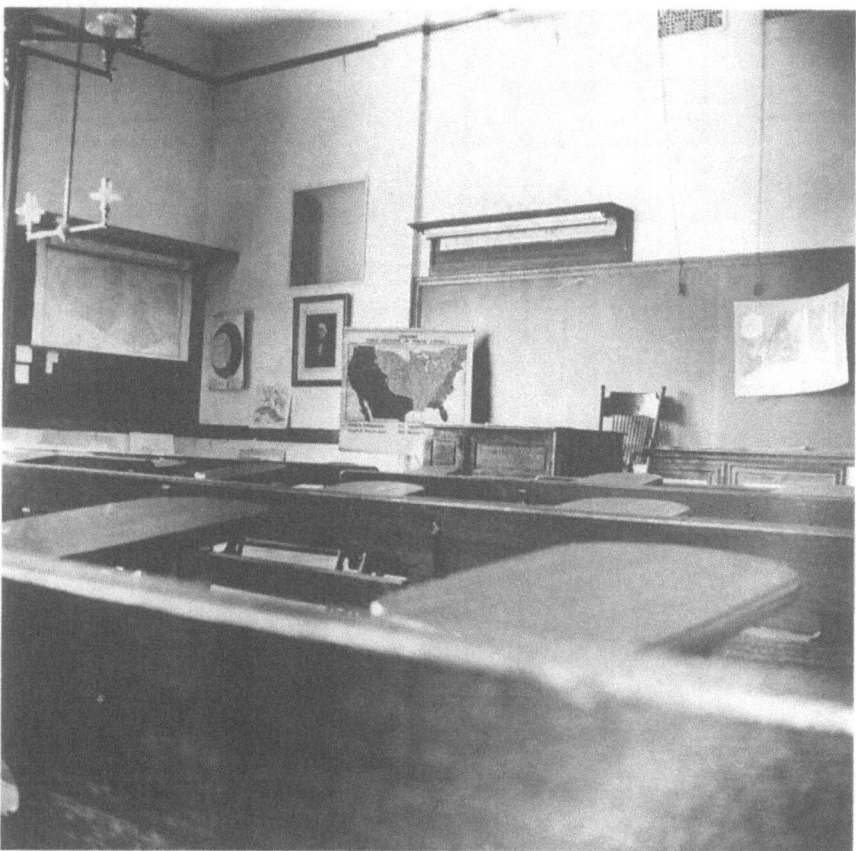

Lucy Salmon's classroom at Vassar College. The view presented is from a student's perspective. Special Collections, Vassar College Library. Ref. 3.1235

Lucy Salmon's childhood home in Fulton, New York. Special Collections, Vassar College Library. Ref. 3.1437

Photographs • 123

Lucy Salmon during her student years. Salmon, on the far right, is seated with a group of Bryn Mawr students. Special Collections, Vassar College Library. Ref. 3.1436

Lucy Salmon seated at the head of the "Long Table" with her students at Vassar College. Special Collections, Vassar College Library. Ref. 3.1438

Lucy Salmon's kitchen at her Mill Street home in Poughkeepsie, New York. Students took field trips to the kitchen to discover history. Special Collections, Vassar College Library. Ref. 3.1238

VASSAR COLLEGE

HISTORY S

MAY, 1911

"The ideal college education seems to me to be the one where a student learns things he is not going to use in after life by methods that he is going to use. The former element gives the breath, the latter element gives the training."—President Hadley, cited by President Lowell in his Inaugural Address, October 6, 1909.

1. **Records.**

    Show what historical records can be found in
    a. your back yard,
    b. the house in which you live.

2. **Text books.**

    Examine the text book assigned and write a report on it to the superintendent of public instruction in your home community with reference to
    a. the authoritativeness of the text,
    b. its usefulness for classroom purposes.

3. **Conduct.**

    What can you do in your home community to promote an interest in historical study?

Lucy Salmon's examination in History S given in 1911. One of her favorite quotations is presented near the top of the page. Special Collections, Vassar College Library. Box 59, folder 23.

Lucy Salmon as a young woman and student. Special Collections, Vassar College Library. Ref. 3.624

Lucy Salmon in 1898, eleven years after she began her career as a history professor at Vassar College. Special Collections, Vassar College Library. Ref. 4.229

Notes

Chapter 1

1. See Jackie M. Blount, *Destined to Rule the Schools: Women and the Superintendency, 1873–1995* (Albany: State University of New York Press, 1998); Ruth Bordin, *Alice Freeman Palmer: The Evolution of a New Woman* (Ann Arbor: University of Michigan Press, 1993); Alan R. Sadnovnik and Susan F. Semel (eds.), *Founding Mothers and Others: Women Educational Leaders During the Progressive Era* (New York: Palgrave, 2002); Kathleen Weiler and Sue Middleton (eds.), *Telling Women's Lives: Narrative Inquiries in the History of Women's Education* (Philadelphia: Open University Press, 1999).
2. Nicholas Adams and Bonnie G. Smith (eds.), *Lucy Maynard Salmon: History and the Texture of Modern Life* (Philadelphia: University of Pennsylvania Press, 2001).
3. Salmon's extensive papers occupy twenty-six cubic feet of shelf space at the Vassar College Libraries Special Collections department.
4. Christopher Lucas, *American Higher Education: A History* (New York: St. Martin's Griffin, 1994), 139–141; Laurence Veysey, *The Emergence of the American University* (Chicago: University of Chicago Press, 1965), 264.
5. Frederick Rudolph, *The American College and University* (Athens: University of Georgia Press, 1962, 1990), 269; Veysey, *The Emergence of the American University*, 158.
6. Veysey, *The Emergence of the American University*, 264.
7. Julie A. Reuben, "Beyond Politics: Community Civics and the Redefinition of Citizenship in the Progressive Era," *History of Education Quarterly* (winter 1997): 399.
8. Adams and Smith, *Lucy Maynard Salmon*, 1–26.
9. Nancy MacKechnie, Vassar College Archivist, Interview with author, October 23, 1997, Poughkeepsie, New York.
10. *Microsoft Encarta Dictionary* (New York: St. Martin's Press, 2001).
11. Nancy F. Cott, *The Bonds of Womanhood: "Women's Sphere" in New England, 1780–1835* (New Haven: Yale University Press, 1977), 5–9; Leslie Miller-Bernal, *Separate by Degree: Women Students' Experiences in Single-Sex and Coeducational Colleges* (New York: Peter Lang, 2000), 11–35.

12. Bordin, *Alice Freeman Palmer*, 2.
13. Nancy Woloch, *Women and the American Experience* (New York: Knopf, 1984), v.
14. Nancy F. Cott and Elizabeth H. Pleck, *A Heritage of Her Own: Toward a New Social History of American Women* (New York: Simon and Schuster, 1979), 9–10.
15. Cott, *The Bonds of Womanhood*, 5–9.
16. Carroll Smith-Rosenberg, "The Female World of Love and Ritual: Relations Between Women in Nineteenth-Century America," *Signs: Journal of Women in Culture and Society* 1 (autumn 1975):1–29. This same study was also published in Smith-Rosenberg's book, *Disorderly Conduct: Visions of Gender in Victorian America* (New York: A. A. Knopf, 1985), and in Cott and Pleck's edited book, *A Heritage of Her Own: Toward a New Social History of American Women*.
17. Miller-Bernal, *Separate by Degree*, 3–4.
18. Diane Ravitch, *What Do Our 17-Year-Olds Know?* (New York: Harper and Row, 1987).
19. President Hadley, cited by President Lowell in his Inaugural Address, October 6, 1909, quotation located in examination for Salmon course "The Development of Municipal Government," Lucy Maynard Salmon Papers, Special Collections, Vassar College Libraries, Poughkeepsie, New York, box 59, folder 17. Hereafter cited as Salmon Papers.
20. Sadnovnik and Semel, *Founding Mothers and Others*, 2.
21. Linda Eisenmann, "Reconsidering a Classic: Assessing the History of Women's Higher Education a Dozen Years After Barbara Solomon," *Harvard Educational Review* 16 (winter 1997): 710.
22. Mary Ann Dzuback, "Gender and the Politics of Knowledge," *History of Education Quarterly* 43 (summer 2003): 174.
23. Eisenmann, "Reconsidering a Classic," 710.

Chapter 2

1. Standard Certificate of Death for Lucy Maynard Salmon, Register of Deaths in the City of Poughkeepsie, County of Dutchess, State of New York.
2. Louise Fargo Brown, *Apostle of Democracy: The Life of Lucy Maynard Salmon* (New York: Harper and Brothers, 1943), 19–20.
3. Brown, *Apostle of Democracy*, 3.
4. Anon, "Three Hundred Students of Falley Seminary are Back," *Oswego Daily Times*, 1 June 1922.
5. The University of Michigan was founded in 1817, yet its first commencement was not held until 1845.
6. Transcripts of Lucy Maynard Salmon, University of Michigan, A.M. 1883, A.B. 1876, Office of the Registrar, Ann Arbor, MI; Date of school seal reads 1817; Lucas, *American Higher Education*, 117, Brown, *Apostle of Democracy*, 45.
7. Frederick Brubaker, *Higher Education in Transition* (New York: Harper and Row, 1958), 101–104.
8. Brubaker, *Higher Education in Transition*, 104; Brown, *Apostle of Democracy*, 46.
9. Lucas, *American Higher Education*, 132.
10. Brubaker, *Higher Education in Transition*, 107.
11. James B. Angell, *Selected Addresses* (New York: Longmans, Green, 1912), 7, 27.
12. Veysey, *The Emergence of the American University*, 101.
13. Lucy Salmon to James B. Angell, 12 September 1889, 23 November 1891, 29 April 1896, 18 May 1896, 9 June 1899, James B. Angell Papers, Bentley Historical Library, box 3, folder

106, box 4, folders 125, 155, 156, box 5, folder 174; James B. Angell to Lucy Salmon, 2 June 1886, 13 June 1887, 27 January 1896, 29 October 1900, 22 January 1903, Salmon Papers, box 20, folder 2.
14. Frederick Rudolph, *The American College and University* (Athens: University of Georgia Press, 1962, 1990), 214; Lucas, *American Higher Education*, 139.
15. Brubaker, *Higher Education in Transition*, 139.
16. Lucas, *American Higher Education*, 140.
17. Rudolph, *The American College and University*, 3, 486.
18. Barbara Solomon, *In the Company of Educated Women* (New Haven: Yale University Press, 1985), 44; Patricia Smith Butcher, *Education for Equality: Women's Rights Periodicals and Women's Higher Education, 1849–1920* (New York: Greenwood Press, 1989), 33–34.
19. Patricia Ann Palmieri, *In Adamless Eden: The Community of Women Faculty at Wellesley* (New Haven: Yale University Press, 1995), 22; Butcher, *Education for Equality*, 37.
20. Solomon, *In the Company*, 62.
21. Palmieri, *In Adamless Eden*, 22; Ruth Bordin, *Alice Freeman Palmer* (Ann Arbor: University of Michigan Press, 1993), 2.
22. Butcher, *Education for Equality*, x–xi.
23. Butcher, *Education for Equality*, 16.
24. Butcher, *Education for Equality*, 35.
25. Lynn D. Gordon, *Gender and Higher Education in the Progressive Era* (New Haven: Yale University Press, 1990), 21.
26. Butcher, *Education for Equality*, 45.
27. Gordon, *Gender and Higher Education in the Progressive Era*, 22.
28. Transcripts of Lucy Maynard Salmon, University of Michigan, A.M. 1883, A.B. 1876, Office of the Registrar, Ann Arbor, MI; "Charles Kendall Adams," in Robert McHenry and Frank Calvillo (eds.), *Webster's New Biographical Dictionary* (Springfield, MA: Merriam-Webster, 1983), 11.
29. Charles K. Adams, "The Relations of Higher Education to National Prosperity," in C. S. Northrup, W. C. Lane, and J. C. Schwab (eds.), *Representative Phi Beta Kappa Orations* (Boston, 1915), 160–161, cited in Veysey, *The Emergence of the American University*, 4, and Lucas, *American Higher Education*, 143.
30. Veysey, *The Emergence of the American University*, 102–103.
31. Transcripts of Lucy Maynard Salmon, University of Michigan.
32. Lucas, *American Higher Education*, 170.
33. Lucy Salmon to Pomeroy Salmon, 17 January 1876, Salmon Papers, box 2, folder 1.
34. Lucy Salmon to Pomeroy Salmon, 31 January 1876, Salmon Papers, box 2, folder 1.
35. Transcripts of Lucy Maynard Salmon, University of Michigan.
36. Lucy Salmon to Pomeroy Salmon, 17 January 1876, Salmon Papers, box 2, folder 1.
37. Lucy Salmon to Pomeroy Salmon, 17 January 1876, Salmon Papers, box 2, folder 1.
38. Necrology file, Lucy Maynard Salmon, Bentley Historical Library, University of Michigan, Alumni Association Information Form.
39. Brown, *Apostle of Democracy*, 50–51.
40. Brown, *Apostle of Democracy*, 45.
41. Lucy Salmon, "What Influence in College Life Has Proved of Most Force in My Later Life?—Opinions of Michigan Alumni," *Michigan Alumnus* 9 (1902): 408–409.
42. Solomon, *In the Company*, 128; Lucy Salmon to Emily Balch, cited in Mercedes Randall, *Improper Bostonian: Emily Greene Balch, Nobel Peace Laureate* (New York: Twayne, 1964).
43. Col. E. Hofer, "School Days in Iowa," *The Lariat* (February 1925): 85.
44. Lucy Salmon to Pomeroy Salmon, 2 Nov 1876, Salmon Papers, box 2, folder 1.
45. Brown, *Apostle of Democracy*, 87.

46. McGregor High School Materials, Literary Society Entertainment, Programme, 29 March 1878; Catalog of the Works of Art of Students, 24–25 January 1879; McGregor High School Concert, May 7, 1880; Salmon Papers, box 31, folder 3.
47. Brown, *Apostle of Democracy*, 88. Brown does not explain the criteria used to determine McGregor High School's ranking, nor does she explain precisely what the rank meant.
48. Brown, *Apostle of Democracy*, 90.
49. Brown, *Apostle of Democracy*, 87–92.
50. Transcripts of Lucy Maynard Salmon, University of Michigan, A.M. 1883, A.B. 1876, Office of the Registrar, Ann Arbor, MI.
51. Lucy Salmon, "History of the Appointing Power of the President," *Papers of the American Historical Association* 1 (New York: G. P. Putnam's Sons, 1886).
52. A. C. Howland, "Lucy Maynard Salmon, First President of the Association," *Thirtieth Anniversary, 1904–1933, Middle States Association of History Teachers Proceedings*, 31 (Philadelphia Meeting, May 5–6, 1933), 19, Salmon Papers, box 32, folder 8.
53. Transcripts of Lucy Maynard Salmon, University of Michigan, A.M. 1883, A.B. 1876, Office of the Registrar, Ann Arbor, MI.
54. Catalogue of State Normal School, Terre Haute, Indiana, 1886–1887 (Indianapolis: W. B. Burford, Contractor for State Printing, 1887), 52, Salmon Papers, box 31, folder 4.
55. Catalogue of State Normal School, Terre Haute, Indiana, 1886–1887, 26.
56. Catalogue of State Normal School, Terre Haute, Indiana, 1886–1887, 26.
57. Catalogue of State Normal School, Terre Haute, Indiana, 1886–1887, 36.
58. Lucy Salmon letter as cited in Brown, *Apostle of Democracy*, 95.
59. Lucy Salmon, "Education in Michigan During the Territorial Period," *Education* 5 (September 1884–July 1885): 12–33.
60. Lucy Salmon, "Education in Michigan," 12, 19.
61. Lucy Salmon, "Education in Michigan," 33.
62. Lucy Salmon to H. B. Adams, 30 March 1885, Herbert Baxter Adams Papers, Special Collections, Milton S. Eisenhower Library, Johns Hopkins University, ms4.
63. Lucy Salmon to H. B. Adams, 30 March 1885, Herbert Baxter Adams Papers, Special Collections, Milton S. Eisenhower Library, Johns Hopkins University, ms4.
64. Alice E. Freeman (Palmer) to Lucy Salmon, 9 March 1886, Salmon Papers, box 47, folder 14.
65. Lucy Salmon to Edith Rickert '91, 22 June 1910, Salmon Papers, box 4, folder 3.
66. James B. Angell to Lucy Salmon, 2 June 1886, Salmon Papers, box 20, folder 2.
67. Alice E. Freeman (Palmer) to Lucy Salmon, 14 August 1890, 5 August 1890, 22 July 1890, Salmon Papers, box 47, folder 14.
68. Dumas Malone (ed.), "Lucy Maynard Salmon," *Dictionary of American Biography*, Vol. 8 (New York: Charles Scribner's Sons, 1963), 312.
69. William A. DeGregorio, *The Complete Book of U.S. Presidents* (New York: Debner Books, 1989), 409; Marc Frey and Todd Davis, *The New Big Book of U.S. Presidents* (Philadelphia: Courage Books, 2000), 36.
70. Henry W. Bragdon, *Woodrow Wilson: The Academic Years* (Cambridge, MA: Belknap Press of Harvard University Press, 1967), 143.
71. Louise Fargo Brown, *Apostle of Democracy*, 100–101.
72. Liva Baker, *I'm Radcliffe! Fly Me! The Seven Sisters and the Failure of Women's Education* (New York: Macmillan, 1976), 1–2.
73. Gordon, *Gender and Higher Education in the Progressive Era*, 26.
74. Miller-Bernal, *Separate by Degree*, 204–205.
75. Solomon, *In the Company of Educated Women*, 80; Gordon, *Gender and Higher Education in the Progressive Era*, 27; Miller-Bernal, *Separate by Degree*, 204–205.
76. Solomon, *In the Company of Educated Women*, 47, 80.

77. "From the Minutes of the Seminary of Historical and Political Science," in Arthur S. Link (ed.), *The Papers of Woodrow Wilson*, Vol. 4 (Princeton: Princeton University Press, 1977), 336–337.
78. Woodrow Wilson to Lucy Salmon, 8 September 1886, in Link, *Papers of Woodrow Wilson*, Vol. 5, 347–348.
79. John M. Mulder, *Woodrow Wilson: the Years of Preparation* (Princeton, NJ: Princeton University Press, 1978), 92; Bragdon, *Woodrow Wilson*, 148.
80. Wilson's review of his course work at Bryn Mawr, c. June 1, 1887, Papers of Woodrow Wilson, 512–513.
81. Woodrow Wilson "An Old Master," *New Princeton Review*, in Donald Day (ed.), *Woodrow Wilson's Own Story* (Boston: Little, Brown, 1952), 37; c. February 1, 1887, in Link, *Papers of Woodrow Wilson*, 445.
82. Bragdon, *Woodrow Wilson*, 149.
83. Bragdon, *Woodrow Wilson*, 150.
84. Woodrow Wilson diary, October 20, 1887, Woodrow Wilson Papers, Library of Congress, quoted in Bragdon, *Woodrow Wilson*, 143.
85. Lucy Salmon to R. S. Baker, 6 January 1926, 15 January 1926, Container 115 Ray Stannard Baker Collection (hereafter cited as RSB Coll.), Library of Congress (hereafter cited as LOC); Arthur S. Link, "Editorial Note," in Link, *Papers of Woodrow Wilson*, Vol. 5, 350; Bragdon, *Woodrow Wilson*, 152–153.
86. Woodrow Wilson to Ellen Axson Wilson, 4 October 1887, in Link, *Papers of Woodrow Wilson*, Vol. 5, 605.
87. Corneila Meigs, *What Makes a College? A History of Bryn Mawr* (New York: Macmillan, 1956), 41.
88. Wilson to E. A. Wilson, 605.
89. Wilson to E. A. Wilson, 605.
90. Brown, *Apostle of Democracy,* 101–102; Lynn Gordon, "Vassar College, 1865-1920: Women with Missions," in Gordon, *Gender and Higher Education in the Progressive Era*, 131.
91. Salmon to R. S. Baker, 6 January 1926, RSB Coll., LOC; R. S. Baker, *Woodrow Wilson Life and Letters, Youth 1856–1890* (Garden City, NY: Doubleday, Page, 1927), 290.
92. Bragdon, *Woodrow Wilson*, 152–153; Woodrow Wilson to Lucy Salmon, 25 February 1887, in Link, *Papers of Woodrow Wilson*, Vol. 5, 464. In this letter Wilson apologizes for not lecturing on account of a headache.
93. Lucy Salmon, "Wilson as an Autophotographer," in Salmon, *History and the Texture of Modern Life*, 218.
94. Preserved Smith, "Tribute to Lucy Maynard Salmon," Memorial Address, Salmon Papers, box 51, folder 15, 2–3.
95. A Neutral, "Woodrow Wilson: The President's Policies Analyzed in the Lights of his Natural Inhibitions and Past Record," *The Nation*, Vol. 103, No. 2672, 14 September 1916, 258; Brown, *Apostle of Democracy,* 226. The Brown biography states that Salmon wrote the article about Woodrow Wilson that was featured in *The Nation*. A copy of the article is located in the Salmon Papers, Hollinger Box 2.
96. Mulder, *Woodrow Wilson*, 111; Bragdon, *Woodrow Wilson*, 205–206.
97. Bragdon, *Woodrow Wilson*, 206.
98. Bragdon, *Woodrow Wilson*, 306–308.
99. See e.g., Woodrow Wilson, *Congressional Government: A Study in American Politics* (Boston: Houghton, Mifflin, 1885); W. Wilson, *The State: Elements of Historical and Practical Politics* (Boston: D. C. Heath, 1889); W. Wilson, *George Washington* (New York: Harper and Brothers, c1896); W. Wilson, *An Old Master and Other Political Essays* (New York: Scribner and Sons, 1893); W. Wilson, *A History of the American People* (New York: Harper and Brothers, 1902).

100. Salmon to R. S. Baker, 6 January 1926, RSB Coll., LOC.
101. Dorothy Plum and George B. Dowell, *The Great Experiment: A Chronicle of Vassar College* (Poughkeepsie, NY: Vassar College, 1961), 23, 27.
102. Bragdon, *Woodrow Wilson*, 152.
103. Gordon, "Vassar College," 121; Matthew Vassar, *Communications to the Board of Trustees*, quoted in Dorothy Plum and George Dowell, *The Magnificent Enterprise: A Chronicle of Vassar College*, ed. Constance Ellis (Poughkeepsie, NY: Vassar College, 1961), 5.
104. Miller-Bernal, *Separate by Degree*, 203.
105. Gordon, "Vassar College," 124, 127, 129.
106. Baker, *I'm Radcliffe! Fly Me!*, 6.
107. Miller-Bernal, *Separate by Degree*, 3.
108. Jackie M. Blount, *Destined to Rule the Schools: Women and the Superintendency, 1873–1995* (Albany: State University of New York Press, 1998), 6.
109. Solomon, *In the Company of Educated Women*, 47; Palmieri, *In Adamless Eden*, xiii.
110. Gordon, "Vassar College," 136–137.
111. Robert McHenry (ed.), "Maria Mitchell," in *Webster's New Biographical Dictionary* (Springfield, MA: Merriam-Webster, 1983), 693.
112. See for ex. *What Is Modern History?* (Poughkeepsie, NY: Vassar College, 1917); *Why Is History Rewritten?* (New York: Oxford University Press, 1933), published posthumously; *Historical Material* (New York: Oxford University Press, 1933), published posthumously; "Some Principles in Teaching History," in Manfred Holmes (ed.), *National Society for the Scientific Study of Education* (Chicago: University of Chicago Press, 1908), 11–60; "History in Elementary Schools," *Education Review* 1 (January–May 1891): 439–452; "Does the College Curriculum Promote Scholarship?" in *Addresses and Proceedings of the Sixtieth Annual Meeting of the National Education Association*, 60 (Washington, DC: National Education Association, 1922), 737–745.

Chapter 3

1. Adams and Smith, *Lucy Maynard Salmon*, 1.
2. Blount, *Destined to Rule the School*, 2.
3. Charles H. Haskins to Lucy Salmon, 31 October 1902, Salmon Papers, box 47, folder 12. Haskins, Corresponding Secretary of the AHA, was trying to increase membership and included in his letter to Salmon a pamphlet with the history of the AHA.
4. Herbert B. Adams, *Report of the Organization and Proceedings of the American Historical Association 1* (New York: G. P. Putnam's Sons, 1885). Lucy Salmon's name first appears in the list of members in 1885.
5. Murry Nelson, "Lucy Maynard Salmon (1853–1927): Pioneering Views in Teaching History," *Social Studies* 87 (January–February 1996): 8.
6. David Van Tassel, "From Learned Society to Professional Organization: The American Historical Association, 1884–1900," *American Historical Review* 89 (October 1984): 952.
7. Herbert B. Adams, *Report of the Organization and Proceedings of the American Historical Association, 1887,* membership list; Receipt for life membership, 1887, Salmon Papers, box 57, folder 14.
8. Van Tassel, "From Learned Society," 951.
9. Herbert B. Adams to George B. Adams, January 7, 1897, George Burton Adams Papers, Manuscripts and Archives, Yale University Library.
10. Arthur Link, "The American Historical Association, 1884–1984: Retrospect and Prospect," *American Historical Review* 90 (February 1985): 5.

11. *Report of the Organization and Proceedings of the American Historical Association, 1884–1891* (New York: G. P. Putnam's Sons, 1885–1891); "The Miscellaneous Documents of the Senate of the U.S.," *Report of the Organization and Proceedings of the American Historical Association,* 1892–1919 (Washington, DC: Government Printing Office, 1892–1919). The list of officers of the AHA was examined in the annual reports of the AHA from 1884 to 1919. Lucy Salmon was the first woman listed. Typically, officers hailed from elite institutions, such as Harvard and Yale, many of which were single-sex, all-male colleges.
12. Louise Fargo Brown to Salmon, December 20, 1915, Salmon Papers, box 6, folder 1.
13. A. C. McLaughlin to Lucy Salmon, 3 January 1916, Salmon Papers, box 47, folder 13.
14. Waldo Leland to Lucy Salmon, 30 December 1915, Salmon Papers, box 57, folder 14; Ray A. Billington, "Tempest in Clio's Teapot: The American Historical Rebellion of 1915," *American Historical Review* (April 1973): 368–369. An original ballot is in the Salmon Papers, box 57, folder 14, and the printed ballots for this election are also in the Frederick Jackson Turner Papers, Henry E. Huntington Library and Art Gallery, TU box 59.
15. NOW staff, "Augusta National Golf Club Announces Plans to Continue Discrimination Against Women," November 12, 2002, available on-line at *www.now.org/issues/wfw/111202augusta.html,* accessed February 28, 2003.
16. Clarence Bowen to Lucy Salmon, 11 August 1916, Salmon Papers, box 57, folder 14.
17. Lucy Salmon to William Dunning, 22 November 1916, Salmon Papers, box 57, folder 14.
18. Lucy Salmon to William Dunning, 22 November 1916, Salmon Papers, box 57, folder 14.
19. William Dunning to Evarts B. Greene, 18 September 1916, 24 October 1916; Evarts B. Greene to William Dunning, 18 October 1916, Records of the American Historical Association, Library of Congress, series A, box 251.
20. William Dunning to Evarts B. Greene, 18 September 1916, Records of the American Historical Association, Library of Congress, series A, box 251.
21. William Dunning to Lucy Salmon, 24 November 1916, Salmon Papers, box 57, folder 14.
22. Evarts B. Greene to Clarence Bowen, 12 October 1917, Records of the American Historical Association, Library of Congress, series A, box 251.
23. Edward Channing to Evarts B. Greene, 25 October 1917, Records of the American Historical Association, Library of Congress, series A, box 251.
24. George Burr to Evarts B. Greene, 23 October 1917, Records of the American Historical Association, Library of Congress, series A, box 251.
25. Evarts B. Greene to Clarence Bowen, 12 October 1917; Evarts B. Greene to Voting Members of the Council, 22 October 1917, Records of the American Historical Association, Library of Congress, series A, box 251.
26. Lucy Salmon to Evarts B. Greene, 6 October 1917, Records of the American Historical Association, Library of Congress, series A, box 251.
27. Louise Fargo Brown to Salmon, November 19, 1917, Salmon Papers, box 6, folder 2. Louise Fargo Brown was working with J. Franklin Jameson in Washington, DC, in 1917 and conveyed sentiments about Salmon that Jameson had expressed to her.
28. Lucy Salmon to Evarts B. Greene, 16 December 1916, American Historical Association Records, Library of Congress, series A, box 251.
29. Lucy Salmon to Evarts B. Greene, 25 November 1919, American Historical Association Records, Library of Congress, series A, box 9.
30. Lucy Salmon to Evarts B. Greene, 16 December 1916, American Historical Association Records, Library of Congress, series A, box 251.
31. Elizabeth Gilman, "An Un-Tired Radical," *The Advance,* 29 July 1927. In this article, written after Salmon's death, Elizabeth Gilman, daughter of the first president of Johns Hopkins University, recalls meeting with Salmon and explaining that she was a radical. Salmon responded, "My dear, I have been a revolutionist all my life."

32. Pamphlet from 2nd Meeting in Saratoga, NY, September 8–10, 1885, indicates that Salmon was on the program. Also, Salmon was invited to present at a session at the New Orleans meeting in 1903. William Dunning to Lucy Salmon, 8 August 1903, Salmon Papers, box 57, folder 14.
33. Jessie Evans to Lucy Salmon, 16 November 1917, Salmon Papers, box 57, folder 14.
34. Lucy Salmon to Florence Cushing, 28 September 1914, Salmon Papers, box 3, folder 1. Amy L. Reed had been a former student of Salmon. She later taught at Vassar College in the English department and subsequently became the Vassar librarian.
35. Lucy Salmon to Edith Rickert '91, June 26, 1906, Salmon Papers, box 4, folder 1.
36. Elizabeth A. Daniels, *Bridges to the World: Henry Noble McCracken and Vassar College* (Clinton Corners, NY: College Avenue Press, 1994), 78.
37. Much of Salmon's correspondence with fellow historians includes notes in which she extended invitations to guest lecture; they thanked her for the opportunity and vice versa. See, e.g., Edward Channing to Lucy Salmon, 26 January 1895, Edward Cheyney to Lucy Salmon, 13 October 1916, Salmon Papers, box 47, folder 11; Albert Bushnell Hart to Lucy Salmon, 15 February 1891, 19 April 1891, 10 May 1891, Salmon Papers, box 47, folder 12; James H. Robinson to Lucy Salmon, 22 January 1905; H. Morse Stephens to Lucy Salmon, 25 February 1995; Moses Coit Tyler to Lucy Salmon, 29 November 1991, Salmon Papers, box 47, folder 13.
38. Henry C. Adams to Lucy Salmon, 3 April 1897; Charles A. Beard to Lucy Salmon, 27 February 1919; George Lincoln Burr to Lucy Salmon, 11 November 1921, Salmon Papers, box 47, folder 11. Adams thanked Salmon for a copy of *Domestic Service* in the first letter. Beard thanked Salmon for a reprint in the second, and Burr thanked Salmon for a copy of "What Is Modern History?" in the third.
39. William R. Thayer to Lucy Salmon, Salmon Papers, January 1, 1918, Hollinger box 47, folder 13 and Frederick Jackson Turner to Lucy Salmon, Salmon Papers, November 11, 1910, Hollinger box 47, folder 13.
40. *American Heritage* began publication in 1954 and was founded by former editors at *Life* who were "fired with the conviction that history belongs to the people and not just to scholars." Information on *American Heritage* found on its homepage on the web at www.americanheritage.com.
41. Brown, *Apostle of Democracy,* 140.
42. Lucy Salmon to Adelaide Underhill, 18 January 1896, Salmon Papers, box 45, folder 13.
43. Dorothy Plum and George B. Dowell, *The Great Experiment: A Chronicle of Vassar College* (Poughkeepsie, NY: Vassar College, 1961), 25. Brown's *Apostle of Democracy* reports that the invitations for the reunion were dated February 21, 1896. Presumably, the reunion lasted a couple days.
44. Herbert B. Adams to Lucy Salmon, 19 October 1900, Salmon Papers, box 47, folder 11.
45. Henry Bourne to Lucy Salmon, 25 February 1904, Salmon Papers, box 47, folder 11.
46. James H. Robinson to Lucy Salmon, 21 October 1901, 8 November 1901, Salmon Papers, box 47, folder 13.
47. H. Morse Stephens to Lucy Salmon, 20 October 1900, Salmon Papers, box 47, folder 13. Stephens wrote that he appreciated Salmon's desire to organize the history teachers.
48. Association of History Teachers of Middle States and Maryland printed literature, Salmon Papers, box 48, folder 5.
49. Association of History Teachers of Middle States and Maryland printed literature, Salmon Papers, box 48, folder 5.
50. Minutes of Association of History Teachers of Middle States and Maryland, First Annual Meeting, Friday and Saturday, March 13–14, 1903, Salmon Papers, box 48, folder 5.

51. Anon, "In Memory of Lucy Maynard Salmon," *Proceedings of the Association of History Teachers of the Middle States and Maryland* 25 (November 26, 1927, Atlantic City Meeting): 106-108, Salmon Papers, box 32, folder 7; A. C. Howland, "Lucy Maynard Salmon, First President of the Association," *Thirtieth Anniversary, 1904-1933 Middle States Association of History Teachers Proceedings* 31 (Philadelphia meeting, May 5-6, 1933), 18-19 Salmon Papers, box 32, folder 8.
52. Anon, "To Officers and Members of the AAUW," pamphlet of the American Association of University Women, Salmon Papers, box 48, folder 13.
53. H. W. Tyler, printed literature of American Association of University Professors, January 1919, Salmon Papers, box 48, folder 15.
54. H.W. Tyler to Lucy Salmon, 5 February 1917, Salmon Papers, box 48, folder 15.
55. H.W. Tyler to Lucy Salmon, 22 January 1919, Salmon Papers, box 48, folder 15.
56. Albert McKinley to Lucy Salmon, 3 April 1917; Robert Ford to Lucy Salmon, 6 April 1917; Arthur Lovejoy to Lucy Salmon, 22 January 1920, Salmon Papers, box 48, folder 15.
57. Margaret Smith Crocco, "The Road to the Vote," *Social Education* 59 (September 1995): 257.
58. George B. Tindall, *America: A Narrative History* (New York: W. W. Norton, 1988), 524.
59. Woloch, *Women and the American Experience*, 326.
60. Lucy Salmon to Adelaide Underhill, 22 July 1897, Salmon Papers, box 45, folder 13.
61. Address by Professor Lucy M. Salmon, Thirty-Eighth Annual Convention of the National American Suffrage Association, February 7-13, 1906, Baltimore, MD, Salmon Papers, box 56.
62. Nancy Woloch, *Women and the American Experience*, 325.
63. Nancy Woloch, *Women and the American Experience*, 326.
64. See Harriot Stanton Blatch to Lucy Salmon, April 20, n.d., March 17, 1897, March 22, 1897, October 25, n.d., January 22, 1925, Salmon Papers, box 47, folder 14; Crocco, "The Road to the Vote," 257-264.
65. Harriot Stanton Blatch to Lucy Salmon, 17 March 1897, Salmon Papers, box 47, folder 14.
66. Harriot Stanton Blatch to Lucy Salmon, 20 April n.d., Salmon Papers, box 47, folder 14.
67. Harriot Stanton Blatch to Lucy Salmon, 25 October n.d., 22 January 1925, Salmon Papers, box 47, folder 14.
68. Harriot Stanton Blatch to Lucy Salmon, 26 January 1908, Salmon Papers, box 51, folder 9.
69. Alice Paul to Lucy Salmon, August 3, 1914; Mary Blackford to Lucy Salmon, December 15, 1916, January 10, 1917; Mrs. Henry Wade Rogers to Lucy Salmon, December 28, 1916, January 8, 1917, Salmon Papers, box 51, folder 9.
70. Henry Holt to Lucy Salmon, 16 March 1916, Salmon Papers, box 47, folder 16.
71. Caroline Atwater to Lucy Salmon, 18 November 1909, Salmon Papers, box 51, folder 9.
72. Debbie Cottrell, *Pioneer Woman Educator: The Progressive Spirit of Annie Webb Blanton* (College Station: Texas A & M Press, 1993), 52; Daniels, *Bridges to the World*, 65.
73. Lucy Salmon to Frances Davenport, November 18, 1906, Salmon Papers, box 3, folder 2.
74. Anna Howard Shaw to Lucy Salmon, September 14, 1911, Salmon Papers, box 51, folder 9; "The Suffrage Meeting," *Eagle,* September 8, 1911, Salmon Papers, box 51, folder 9.
75. "To Punish Girl Suffragists," *New York Herald,* June 10, 1908; "Vassar Meets in Graveyard," *The Woman's Journal,* Boston, Saturday, 13 June 1908. Clippings in the James M. Taylor Papers, Special Collections, Vassar College Libraries, Poughkeepsie, New York, box 1, folder 15; clippings also in the Woman Suffrage Materials, box 5, folder 23, Special Collections, Vassar College Libraries, Poughkeepsie, New York. See also Vassar College history on Vassar website: http://vassun.vassar.edu/~daniels/1905_1914.html.
76. Daniels, *Bridges to the World,* 67; Cottrell, *Pioneer Woman Educator,* 52.

77. Gordon, *Gender and Higher Education in the Progressive Era*, 136–137.
78. M. Carey Thomas to Lucy Salmon, 13 January 1906, Salmon Papers, box 51, folder 9.
79. Mabel Caldwell Willard to Lucy Salmon, 3 May 1907, Salmon Papers, box 51, folder 9.
80. M. Carey Thomas to Lucy Salmon, 10 May 1910; Lucy Salmon to M. Carey Thomas, 10 April 1912, Salmon Papers, box 51, folder 9.
81. Helena Hill to Lucy Salmon, 11 November 1915, Salmon Papers, box 51, folder 9.
82. M. Carey Thomas to Lucy Salmon, 25 February 1916, Salmon Papers, box 51, folder 9.
83. M. Carey Thomas, "Notice to the Leagues and Chapters of the National College Equal Suffrage League," n.d., 1, Salmon Papers, box 51, folder 9.
84. Thomas, "Notice to the Leagues," 3.

Chapter 4

1. John H. Raymond, *Vassar College: A Sketch of Its Foundation, Aims, and Resources, and of the Development of Its Scheme of Instruction to the Present Time* (New York: S. W. Green, 1873), reprinted in David J. Rothman and Sheila M. Rothman (eds.), *Women and Children First: The Dangers of Education, Sexism and the Origins of Women's Colleges* (New York: Garland, 1987), 38.
2. Raymond, *Vassar College: A Sketch of its Foundation*, 31; *Annual Catalogue of Vassar College, 1906–1907* (Poughkeepsie, NY: A.V. Haight, 1906), 18.
3. Alice Freeman Palmer, "A Review of the Higher Education of Women," in Anna C. Brackett (ed.), *Woman and Higher Education* (New York: Harper Brothers, 1893), 103–130.
4. Palmer, "A Review of the Higher Education," 117.
5. Palmer, "A Review of the Higher Education," 119.
6. Palmer, "A Review of the Higher Education," 125.
7. Palmer's article was published in 1893, and the founding date of Radcliffe, for example, was 1894 (see Katherine S. Mangan, "Radcliffe College Will Merge into Harvard," *The Chronicle of Higher Education*, 30 April 1999, A39, for information on the merging of Radcliffe into Harvard or Solomon's *In the Company of Educated Women*, 55, for information about the founding of Radcliffe). Obviously, the "annexes" were still in the founding stages in the late 1800s.
8. Mangan, "Radcliffe College Will Merge into Harvard," A39.
9. Edward R. Linner, *Vassar, the Remarkable Growth of a Man and His College*, ed. Elizabeth A. Daniels (Poughkeepsie, NY: Vassar College, 1984), 46–47.
10. Linner, *Vassar*, 137.
11. Raymond, *Vassar College: A Sketch of Its Foundation, Aims, and Resources*, 15.
12. Gordon, "Vassar College," 122.
13. Gordon, "Vassar College," 131.
14. Gordon, "Vassar College," 132.
15. Lucy Salmon, "College Government," *The Vassar Miscellany* 24 (January 1895): 149–160.
16. Salmon, "College Government," 156.
17. Salmon, "College Government," 157.
18. Lucy Salmon to Henry Noble MacCracken, 22 February 1915, Salmon Papers, box 7, folder 7.
19. Lucy Salmon to Henry Noble MacCracken, 1 October 1918, Henry Noble MacCracken Papers, box III, folder 34.
20. Lucy Salmon to Alumnae Council, September 28, 1914, Salmon Papers, box 3, folder 1.
21. A Near Professor (Lucy Salmon), "The Next College President," *The Popular Science Monthly* (September 1913).

22. Daniels, *Bridges to the World*, 17.
23. Daniels, *Bridges to the World*, 91.
24. Brown, *Apostle of Democracy*, jacket cover.
25. Theodore Clark Smith, "Book Review," *American Historical Review* 49 (January 1944): 266.
26. Palmieri, *In Adamless Eden*, 261-262. Palmieri claimed that a 1915 faculty insurrection led by Salmon forced Taylor to resign. Actually, Taylor retired in February 1914, so the controversy occurred at least one year earlier than Palmieri stated.
27. Daniels, *Bridges to the World*, 88.
28. Lucy Salmon to Frances Davenport, 27 September 1906, Salmon Papers, box 3, folder 2.
29. Daniels, *Bridges to the World*, 60.
30. Lucy Salmon to Davenport, 27 September 1906.
31. Lucy Salmon to James Monroe Taylor, 6, 12 December 1906, Salmon Papers, box 3, folder 4, Salmon Papers. Salmon wrote several versions of a letter to Taylor in which she denied making an ultimatum. Some were unsigned and certainly not sent to him.
32. Daniels, *Bridges to the World*, 59.
33. Lucy Salmon to Frances Davenport, 15 March 1907, Salmon Papers, box 3, folder 2.
34. Evalyn Clark, Former History Department Chair, Vassar College, Oral History Interview with author, October 23, 1997. Tape deposited at the Oral History in Education Collection, College of Education, University of Texas at Austin.
35. Gordon, "Vassar College," 133.
36. Daniels, *Bridges to the World*, 79.
37. Lucy Salmon, "Vassar College Introductory Course in History," *The History Teacher's Magazine* 1 (March 1910): 145.
38. Correspondence of James Baldwin to Lucy Maynard Salmon, Salmon Papers, box 5, folder 10.
39. Correspondence of Louise Fargo Brown to Lucy Salmon, Salmon Papers, box 6, folders 1-8; Correspondence of Eloise Ellery to Lucy Salmon, Salmon Papers, box 6, folders 9-12 and box 7, folders 1-5.
40. Daniels, *Bridges to the World*, 88.
41. Daniels, *Bridges to the World*, 150.
42. Louise Fargo Brown to Lucy Salmon, 20 December 1915, Salmon Papers, box 6, folder 1.
43. Louise Fargo Brown to Lucy Salmon, 19 November 1917, Salmon Papers, box 6, folder 2; Lucy Salmon to Frances Davenport, 9 September 1906, Salmon Papers, box 3, folder 2. In Salmon's letter to Davenport, she mentions her friend Edith Rickert, Vassar College 1891.
44. Louise Fargo Brown to Lucy Salmon, 30 May 1919, Salmon Papers, box 6, folder 4.
45. Eloise Ellery to Lucy Salmon, 3 August 1921, Salmon Papers, box 7, folder 2; Eloise Ellery to Lucy Salmon, 1 September 1923, 6 September 1923, 11 September 1923, 6 December 1923, 18 December 1923, Salmon Papers, box 7, folder 3.
46. Eloise Ellery to Lucy Salmon, 15 January 1925, Salmon Papers, box 7, folder 4.
47. Lucy Salmon to Henry Noble MacCracken and Henry Noble MacCracken to Lucy Salmon, Salmon Papers, box 3, folder 3 and box 7, folders 7-14; Lucy Salmon to James Monroe Taylor and James Monroe Taylor to Lucy Salmon, Salmon Papers, box 3, folder 4; box 8, folders 6-12; box 9, folders 1-14; box 10, folders 1-9; box 11, folders 1-3. The number of letters accounted for include only those preserved in the Salmon Papers and not the correspondence retained in the presidential papers.
48. Henry Noble MacCracken to Lucy Salmon, 25 September 1915, 9 December 1915, Salmon Papers, box 7, folder 7; Lucy Salmon to James Monroe Taylor, 28 October 1907, 23 September 1908, 8 February 1909, Salmon Papers, box 3, folder 4.
49. Lucy Salmon to Henry Noble MacCracken, 19 February 1915, Salmon Papers, box 3, folder 3.
50. Daniels, *Bridges to the World*, 97.

51. Gordon, "Vassar College," 130.
52. Correspondence of Students and Alumnae to Lucy Salmon, Salmon Papers, boxes 13–19, and portions of 45 and 57.
53. Brown, *Apostle of Democracy*, "Tributes from Students—Classes of 1896, 1897," 278.
54. Confidential Letter from Elizabeth Updegraff '95 to Friends and Former Students of Lucy Maynard Salmon, April 1926, Salmon Papers, box 45, folder 9.
55. Mrs. William Harrington, Class Day Speech, 11 June 1938, Salmon Papers, box 51, folder 15.
56. Lucy Salmon to Edith Rickert '91, 26 June 1906, Salmon Papers, box 4, folder 1.
57. Lucy Salmon to Edith Rickert '91, 8 June 1909, Salmon Papers, box 4, folder 2.
58. Elsie M. Rushmore, "In Memory of Lucy Maynard Salmon," reprinted from *Vassar Quarterly* (July 1932), Salmon Papers, box 51, folder 15.
59. Brown, *Apostle of Democracy*, 110.
60. Gordon, "Vassar College," 132; Brown, *Apostle of Democracy*, 110.
61. Margaret (Peggy) Shipp '05 to May Louise (Mamie) Shipp, 26 January 1905, box 16, Vassar Student Letters Collection, 1865–1935; Gordon, "Vassar College," 133.
62. Mrs. William Harrington, Class Day Speech, 11 June 1938, Salmon Papers, box 51, folder 15.
63. Report of the Committee in Charge of the Lucy Maynard Salmon Fund for Research, 6 April 1927, Salmon Papers, box 45, folder 9.
64. Brown, *Apostle of Democracy*, 140.
65. Brown, *Apostle of Democracy*, 140–141, 181.
66. See, for ex., Cottrell, *Pioneer Woman Educator;* Susan Ware, *Partner and I: Molly Dewson, Feminism, and New Deal Politics* (New Haven: Yale University Press, 1987); Nelson, "Lucy Maynard Salmon."
67. Nelson, "Lucy Maynard Salmon," 12.
68. Smith-Rosenberg, "The Female World of Love and Ritual," 27; and Carroll Smith-Rosenberg, "Book Review: *Independent Women: Work and Community for Single Women, 1850–1920*, by Martha Vicinus," *Signs*, Vol. 13 (spring 1988): 648.
69. Palmieri, *In Adamless Eden*, 137.
70. Palmieri, *In Adamless Eden*, 138.
71. Clark, Interview with author, 23 October 1997.
72. Will of Lucy Maynard Salmon, Salmon Papers, box 47, folder 9.
73. See Louise Fargo Brown to Lucy Salmon, July 29, 1915, Salmon Papers, box 6, folder 1; Louise Fargo Brown to Lucy Salmon, November 19, 1917, Salmon Papers, box 6, folder 2; Lucy Salmon to Edith Rickert, July 29, 1907 and June 8, 1909, Salmon Papers, box 4, folder 2; Lucy Salmon, "Remember the Library," *Vassar Quarterly*, Vol. 8 (November 1922): 55.
74. Lucy Salmon to Adelaide Underhill, May 17, 1894, Salmon Papers, box 45, folder 13.
75. Brown, *Apostle of Democracy*, 140–141.
76. See, for ex., Lucy Salmon, "Vacation Reading," *Public Libraries* 19 (June 1914): 233–238; Lucy Salmon, "College Library," *Libraries* 31 (July 1926): 322–325; Lucy Salmon, "Instruction in the Use of a College Library," *Bulletin of the American Library Association* 7 (July 1913): 301–309.
77. Lucy Salmon to James Monroe Taylor, 28 October 1907, 23 September 1908, 8 February 1909, Salmon Papers, box 3, folder 4; Lucy Salmon to Henry Noble MacCracken, 19 February 1915, 9 April 1926, Salmon Papers, box 3, folder 3.
78. Brown, *Apostle of Democracy*, 141.

Chapter 5

1. Carol S. Gruber, *Mars and Minerva: World War I and the Uses of Higher Learning in America* (Baton Rouge: Louisiana State University Press, 1975), 39.
2. James H. Robinson, *The New History: Essays Illustrating the Modern Historical Outlook* (New York: Macmillan, 1912).
3. Lucy Salmon, *Why Is History Rewritten?* (New York: Oxford University Press, 1929), 68.
4. James H. Robinson to Lucy Salmon, 6 February 1921, Salmon Papers, box 47, folder 13.
5. Lucy Salmon, "The Sources of Robinson's *History of Western Europe*" (with chart), *The Text-Book Bulletin for High Schools and Colleges* 4 (New York: Ginn, 1904).
6. James H. Robinson to Lucy Salmon, 21 October 1901, 8 November 1901, 12 May 1904, Salmon Papers, box 47, folder 13.
7. James H. Robinson to Lucy Salmon, 22 January 1905, Salmon Papers, box 47, folder 13.
8. Frederick Jackson Turner to Lucy Salmon, 2 December 1909, Salmon Papers, box 47, folder 13.
9. Salmon, *Why Is History Rewritten?* 94.
10. See Letters from Fellow Historians, Salmon Papers, box 47, folders 11–13.
11. Lucy Salmon, "On a Certain Indefiniteness in History," *Eighth Annual Convention of the Association of History Teachers of the Middle States and Maryland* (New York: March 11–12, 1910), 6–12.
12. Lucy Salmon, *Historical Material* (New York: Oxford University Press, 1933), 1–10.
13. Salmon, *Why Is History Rewritten?* 105.
14. Lucy Salmon, *What Is Modern History?* (Poughkeepsie, NY: Vassar College, 1917), 6.
15. Salmon, *Historical Material*, 7.
16. Salmon, *Historical Material*, 11–12.
17. Salmon, *Historical Material*, 14.
18. Salmon, *Historical Material*, 16.
19. Salmon, *What Is Modern History?* 68–69.
20. Bibliography of Lectures and Addresses not found in Print, Salmon Papers, box 55, folder 1.
21. Salmon, *What Is Modern History?* 24.
22. Salmon, *Why Is History Rewritten?* 92–93.
23. Salmon, *What Is Modern History?* 20.
24. Salmon, *What Is Modern History?* 24.
25. Salmon, *Why Is History Rewritten?* 28.
26. Salmon, *What Is Modern History?* 28–29.
27. Salmon, *Why Is History Rewritten?* 23.
28. Salmon, *What Is Modern History?* 33.
29. Kirkpatrick Sale, *The Conquest of Paradise: Christopher Columbus and the Columbian Legacy* (New York: Knopf, 1990).
30. Lucy Salmon, *Why Is History Rewritten?* 105.
31. William R. Thayer to Lucy Salmon, 1 January 1918; Frederick Jackson Turner to Lucy Salmon, 11 November 1910, Salmon Papers, box 47, folder 13; Lucy Salmon to Evarts B. Greene, 10 December 1918, Evarts B. Greene to Lucy Salmon, 4 January 1919, American Historical Association Records, series A, box 254, Library of Congress.
32. Turner to Lucy Salmon, 11 November 1910.
33. Thayer to Lucy Salmon, 1 January 1918.
34. Salmon, *Why Is History Rewritten?* 82.
35. Salmon, *Why Is History Rewritten?* 2.
36. Salmon, *Why Is History Rewritten?* 10–11.
37. Salmon, *Why Is History Rewritten?* 16.

38. Salmon, *Why Is History Rewritten?* 117.
39. Salmon, *Why Is History Rewritten?* 30.
40. Jeanette Hopkins, Interview with author, November 3, 1998, telephone.
41. Lucy Salmon, *Domestic Service* (New York: Macmillan, 1897).
42. Dorothy Ross, *The Origins of American Social Science* (Cambridge: Cambridge University Press, 1991), 158.
43. Ross, *The Origins of American Social Science*, 62.
44. Salmon, *Domestic Service*, xii.
45. Salmon, *Domestic Service*, 3.
46. Salmon, *Domestic Service*, 9.
47. Salmon, *Domestic Service*, 54–55.
48. Salmon, *Domestic Service*, 72.
49. Salmon, *Domestic Service*, 103.
50. Salmon, *Domestic Service*, 165.
51. Salmon, *Domestic Service*, 213.
52. Salmon, *Domestic Service*, 219.
53. Salmon, *Domestic Service*, 236.
54. Salmon, *Domestic Service*, 259.
55. Salmon, *Domestic Service*, 272.
56. Anon, "Review," *Chicago Tribune*, 26 March 1897, Salmon Papers, box 49, folder 8.
57. Nancy Huston Banks, "A Very Practical Book," *The Daily Tribune*, 21 February 1897, Salmon Papers, box 49, folder 8.
58. Lucy Salmon, "Some Historical Aspects of Domestic Service," *New England Magazine* 8 (April 1893): 175–184.
59. Anon, "Review," *The Churchman*, 13 July 1901, Salmon Papers, box 49, folder 8.
60. Anon, "Review," *New York Communal Advertiser*, 24–27 August, n.d., Salmon Papers, box 49, folder 8.
61. Anon, "Review," *London Quarterly Review*, July 1901, Salmon Papers, box 49, folder 8.
62. Anon, "The Insoluble Problem," *Daily Chronicle*, 25 May 1897, Salmon Papers, box 49, folder 8.
63. Lucy Salmon to Adelaide Underhill, November 11, 1898, Salmon Papers, box 45, folder 13.
64. Jane Bernard Powers, *The 'Girl Question' in Education: Vocational Education for Young Women in the Progressive Era* (London: Falmer Press, 1992), 12.
65. See, as current examples, Arlie Russell Hochschild, *The Time Bind: When Work Becomes Home and Home Becomes Work* (New York: Metropolitan Books, 1997); Ruth Schwartz Cowan, *Household Technology from the Open Hearth to the Microwave* (New York: Basic Books, 1983).
66. Lucy Salmon, *Progress in the Household* (New York: Houghton, Mifflin, 1906).
67. Brown, *Apostle of Democracy*, 244.
68. Vassar College Catalogues, 1900–1927 (Poughkeepsie, NY: A. V. Haight, 1900–1927).
69. Henry Noble MacCracken to Lucy Salmon, June 7, 1918, Salmon Papers, box 7, folder 10.
70. Michael Schudson, *Discovering the News: A Social History of American Newspapers* (New York: Basic Books, 1978), 99.
71. Schudson, *Discovering the News*, 99.
72. Lucy Salmon, "The Development of the Newspaper," *The Vassar Quarterly* 5 (July 1920): 244–252.
73. Lucy Salmon, *The Newspaper and the Historian* (New York: Oxford University Press, 1923), 469.
74. Salmon, *The Newspaper and the Historian*, 470.
75. Salmon, *The Newspaper and the Historian*, 475.

76. Salmon, *The Newspaper and the Historian*, 482.
77. Lucy Salmon, *The Newspaper and Authority* (New York: Oxford University Press, 1923), v; see Robert Nozick, *Anarchy, State and Utopia* (New York: Basic Books, 1974) for contemporary discussion of the nature of the state and its legitimate functions and justifications.
78. Salmon, *The Newspaper and Authority*, 2-4.
79. Salmon, *The Newspaper and Authority*, 15.
80. Salmon, *The Newspaper and Authority*, 16.
81. Salmon, *The Newspaper and Authority*, 117.
82. Salmon, *The Newspaper and Authority*, 182.
83. Salmon, *The Newspaper and Authority*, 252.
84. Salmon, *The Newspaper and Authority*, 385-386.
85. Salmon, *The Newspaper and Authority*, 447.
86. Salmon, *The Newspaper and Authority*, 466-467.
87. Anon, "Book Review," *American Historical Review* 30 (October 1925): 146-147.
88. Brown, *Apostle of Democracy*, 245.
89. Mary Ross, "Review of *The Newspaper and the Historian*," *The Vassar Quarterly* 9 (November 1923): 244.

Chapter 6

1. Lucy Salmon, "The Teaching of History in Academies and Colleges," *The Academy: A Journal of Secondary Education* 5 (September 1890): 285.
2. Salmon, "The Teaching of History," 285.
3. Lucy Salmon, "Some Principles in the Teaching of History," *Publications of the National Society for the Scientific Study of Education 1902-1906* (Chicago: University of Chicago Press, 1908), 1-61.
4. Salmon, "Some Principles in the Teaching of History," 31.
5. Marcy Driscoll, *Psychology of Learning for Instruction* (Boston: Allyn and Bacon, 1994), 176. Driscoll provides an excellent summary of Piaget's stages of cognitive development.
6. Salmon, "Some Principles," 35.
7. Lucy Salmon, "History in the Elementary Schools," *Education Review* 1 (January-May 1891): 439, 442.
8. Salmon, "Some Principles," 45.
9. Salmon, "The Teaching of History," 289; Salmon, "History in Elementary Schools," 446.
10. Ross, "Review of," 244. Salmon's course outlines, readings lists, and examples of students' work are contained in the Salmon Papers, box 14, folder 5-23. Further examples of student work, such as notecards, papers, and examinations, are part of the Vassar College Student Collection. Salmon also published an article, "Vassar College Introductory Course in History," in *The History Teacher's Magazine* 1 (March 1910): 145-148, which describes methods used in the introductory history course.
11. Salmon, "Some Principles in the Teaching of History," 48.
12. Nelson, "Lucy Maynard Salmon," 8.
13. American Historical Association, *The Study of History in Schools: Report to the American Historical Association by The Committee of Seven* (New York: Macmillan, 1899), v. Hereafter cited as The Committee of Seven.
14. National Education Association, *Report of the Committee on Secondary School Studies* (Washington, DC: GPO, 1893). Hereafter cited as The Committee of Ten. American Historical Association, *The Study of History in Schools: Report of the Committee of Five* (New

York: Macmillan, 1899). Hereafter cited as the The Committee of Five. American Historical Association, *The Study of History in the Elementary Schools: Report to the American Historical Association by The Committee of Eight* (New York: Charles Scribner's Sons, 1912). Hereafter cited as The Committee of Eight.

15. See Chara Haeussler Bohan, "Early Vanguards of Progressive Education: The Committee of Ten, The Committee of Seven, and Social Education," in Woyshner, Watras, and Crocco (eds.), *Social Education in the Twentieth Century: Curriculum and Context for Citizenship* (New York: Peter Lang) (in press).

16. See Henry Johnson, *Teaching of History in Elementary and Secondary Schools* (New York: Macmillan, 1917); Herbert Kliebard, *The Struggle for the American Curriculum, 1893–1958* (New York: Routledge and Kegan Paul, 1987); Edward Krug, *The Shaping of the American High School* (New York: Harper and Row, 1964); Michael Whelan, "A Particularly Lucid Lens: The Committee of Ten and the Social Studies Committee in Historical Context," *The Journal of Curriculum and Supervision* 12 (spring 1997): 256–268; David Warren Saxe, *Social Studies in Schools: A History of the Early Years* (Albany: State University of New York Press, 1991); Diane Ravitch, *The Schools We Deserve* (New York: Basic Books, 1985).

17. The Committee of Ten, 8–11.

18. The Committee of Ten, 11.

19. Johnson, *Teaching of History*, 134.

20. Chara Haeussler Bohan, "Early Vanguards of Progressive Education: The Committee of Ten, The Committee of Seven, and Social Education," *Journal of Curriculum and Supervision*. (Fall 2003): 73–94.

21. Saxe, *Social Studies in Schools*, 53–54; Howard Boozer, *The American Historical Association and the Schools, 1884–1956*, Ph.D. diss., Washington University, 1960, 51, 55.

22. The Committee of Seven, 3–4.

23. The Committee of Seven, iii; see also Chara Haeussler Bohan, "Historical and International Dimensions of History Education: The Work of the Committee of Seven," in Alaric Dickinson, Peter Gordon, and Peter Lee (eds.), *Raising Standards in History Education, International Review of History Education Vol. 3* (London: Woburn Press, 2001), 56–72.

24. Michael Whelan, "Albert Bushnell Hart and the Origins of Social Studies Education," *Theory and Research in Social Education* 22 (fall 1994): 423–440.

25. Whelan, "A Particularly Lucid Lens," 260.

26. Boozer, "The American Historical Association and the Schools," 53; The Committee of Seven, v.

27. The Committee of Seven, 34–35.

28. Bohan, "Historical and International Dimensions of History Education: The Work of the Committee of Seven" in Dickinson, Gordon, and Lee, *Raising Standards in History Education*, 57–62.

29. Dorothy Ross, *The Origins of American Social Science* (Cambridge: Cambridge University Press, 1991), 158.

30. Records of the American Historical Association, Library of Congress, Box 459, from the minutes of the Cambridge meeting, April 16–17, 1897, recorded by Albert Bushnell Hart, Secretary of the Committee of Seven.

31. Records of the American Historical Association, Library of Congress, Box 459, from the minutes of the Cambridge meeting, April 16–17, 1897.

32. The Committee of Seven, 42–44.

33. The Committee of Seven, 16–17.

34. James Sullivan, "Suggested Changes in Course of Study in History," *The History Teacher's Magazine* 2 (January 1911): 103.

35. The Committee of Seven, 101.
36. Salmon, "History in Elementary Schools," 450.
37. Lucy Salmon, "History in the German Gymnasia," The Committee of Seven, 173-198.
38. The Committee of Seven, 174.
39. Lucy Salmon to Adelaide Underhill, 15 August 1897, Salmon Papers, Hollinger box 45, file 13.
40. Lucy Salmon to Adelaide Underhill, 15 August 1897, Salmon Papers, Hollinger box 45, file 13.
41. The Committee of Seven, 243-245.
42. The Committee of Eight, vii.
43. Van Tassel, "From Learned Society," 952; Boozer, "The American Historical Association," 62-66; Michael Whelan, "History as the Core of Social Studies Curriculum," in E. Wayne Ross (ed.), *The Social Studies Curriculum: Purposes, Problems and Possibilities* (Albany: State University of New York Press, 1997), 28; Glenn Kinzie, "Historians and the Social Studies: A History and Interpretation of the Activities of the American Historical Association in the Secondary School Social Studies, 1884-1964," Ph.D. diss., University of Nebraska, 1965, 40-47.
44. Lawrence Cremin, *The Transformation of the School: Progressivism in American Education 1876-1957* (New York: Vintage Books, 1961), 22, 347-353.
45. Elisabeth Israels Perry, "The Changing Meanings of Progressive Era," *Magazine of History* 13 (spring 1999): 3.
46. Susan Semel and Alan R. Sadovnik, *"Schools of Tomorrow," Schools of Today: What Happened to Progressive Education* (New York: Peter Lang, 1999), 5.
47. Semel and Sadovnik, *"Schools of Tomorrow,"* 3-4.
48. Daniel T. Rogers, "In Search of Progressivism," *Reviews in American History* 10 (December 1982): 113-32, 122-123.
49. George Tindall, *America: A Narrative History* (New York: W. W. Norton, 1988), 940; Cremin, *The Transformation of the School*, viii-x.
50. Cremin, *The Transformation of the School*, viii-ix.
51. William Reese, "Origins of Progressive Education," *History of Education Quarterly* (spring 2001): 3.
52. Reese, "Origins of Progressive Education," 4.
53. Reese, "Origins of Progressive Education," 5-16.
54. Semel and Sadovnik, *"Schools of Tomorrow,"* 4-5; Gerald Gutek, *Historical and Philosophical Foundations of Education: A Biographical Introduction* (Upper Saddle River, NJ: Prentice Hall, 1997), 313.
55. Semel and Sadovnik, *"Schools of Tomorrow,"* 6.
56. Linda Robinson Walker, "John Dewey's Philosophical While at Michigan," *Michigan Today* (summer 1997): available on-line at http://www.umich.edu/~newsinfo/MT/97/Sum97/mtalj97.html. Accessed on February 12, 2003.
57. Linda Robinson Walker, "John Dewey at Michigan," *Michigan Today* (fall 1997): 18.
58. Lucy Salmon to Henry Noble MacCracken, 1 October 1918, MacCracken Papers, box 111, folder 34.
59. Lucy Salmon, "History in a Back Yard," reprinted in *Historical Material*, 143-157.
60. Salmon, "History in a Back Yard," 144-148.
61. Salmon, "History in a Back Yard," 154-155.
62. Salmon, "History in a Back Yard," 156-157.
63. Lucy Salmon, "Main Street," reprinted in *Historical Material*, 161-182.
64. Salmon, "Main Street," 161-162.
65. Ruth Bordin, *Women at Michigan: The "Dangerous Experiment," 1870s to the Present* (Ann Arbor: University of Michigan Press, 1999), 9.

66. Salmon, "History in Elementary Schools," 451.
67. *Annual Catalogue of Vassar College, 1891–92* (Poughkeepsie, NY: A. V. Haight, 1891), 25.
68. *Annual Catalogue of Vassar College, 1891–92*, 28.
69. Amy Louise Reed, "Miss Salmon as I Knew Her," *Addresses at the Memorial Service for Lucy Maynard Salmon* (6 March 1927, Poughkeepsie, NY), 14, Salmon Papers, Box 30, folder 2. Catalogues for the first two years Salmon taught at Vassar, 1887–88 and 1888–89, could not be located (and perhaps do not exist), so the exact courses she taught are not recorded in this official Vassar College record. However, Amy Reed, who came to Vassar in the fall of 1888 and was a student of Salmon's, recorded in her memorial tribute the courses Salmon taught that first year. Reed later taught English at Vassar and eventually became the Vassar College librarian.
70. *Annual Catalogue of Vassar College, 1890–91*, 48; *Annual Catalogue of Vassar College, 1891–92*, 50.
71. *Annual Catalogue of Vassar College, 1894–95* (Poughkeepsie, NY: A. V. Haight, 1894), 62.
72. *Annual Catalogue of Vassar College, 1895–96* (Poughkeepsie, NY: A. V. Haight, 1895), 50.
73. Pamphlets for several courses are located in Salmon Papers, box 59, folders 4–21.
74. *Annual Catalogue of Vassar College, 1900–1901* (Poughkeepsie, NY: A. V. Haight, 1900), 50–53.
75. *Annual Catalogue of Vassar College, 1890–1927*.
76. *Annual Catalogue of Vassar College, 1904–1905* (Poughkeepsie, NY: A. V. Haight, 1904), 32–36.
77. *Annual Catalogue of Vassar College, 1906–1907* (Poughkeepsie, NY: A. V. Haight, 1906), 18; Daniels, *Bridges to the World*, 100.
78. Vassar History Department Course outlines and examinations, History 1 and 2, Salmon Papers, box 59, folder 6.
79. Lucy Salmon to Frances Davenport, 9 September 1909, Salmon Papers, box 3, folder 2.
80. Course Outline, Historical Material, located with materials on course on American history rather than with papers for course on historical material, Salmon Papers, box 59, folder 8.
81. *Annual Catalogue of Vassar College, 1900–01*, 53.
82. *Annual Catalogue of Vassar College, 1906–07*, 38.
83. *Annual Catalogue of Vassar College, 1925–26* (Poughkeepsie, NY: A. V. Haight, 1925), 155.
84. Lucy Salmon, "Suggestions for the Year's Study: Vassar College" (Poughkeepsie, NY: Vassar College, 1912), Salmon Papers, box 59, folder 4.
85. Salmon, "Suggestions for the Year's Study," 7.
86. Salmon, "Suggestions for the Year's Study," 13.
87. Salmon, "Suggestions for the Year's Study," 21.
88. Salmon, "Suggestions for the Year's Study," 22, 28.
89. Salmon, "Suggestions for the Year's Study," reprinted from "Old South Leaflets," 1–20.
90. Questionnaire Sheet on Local Historical Material, n.d., Salmon Papers, box 59, folder 23.
91. History S Examination, May 1911, Historical Material, Salmon Papers, box 59, folder 18.
92. History S Examination, May 1912, Historical Material, Salmon Papers, box 59, folder 18.
93. Salmon, "Suggestions for the Year's Study," 22–27.
94. Salmon, "Suggestions for the Year's Study," 27.
95. Envelopes located in American History Folder, Salmon Papers, box 59, folder 8.
96. Salmon's handwritten notecards with problems for students to solve located in American History Folder, Salmon Papers, box 59, folder 8.
97. Salmon's notecards, Salmon Papers, box 59, folder 8.
98. Salmon's problem for M. Connell located in American History Folder, Salmon Papers, box 59, folder 8.
99. American History Examinations, Salmon Papers, box 59, folder 8.

Chapter 7

1. A. F. Goodwell to Lucy Salmon, 26 Oct 1888, Salmon Papers, box 59, folder 23.
2. Vassar College History Entrance Examinations, Salmon Papers, box 59, folder 3.
3. Lucy Salmon to Miss Dinky, 27 January 1909, Salmon Papers, box 59, folder 23.
4. Blanche A. Jones, "Recollections of Miss Salmon," December 1935, Salmon Papers, box 59, folder 23; Brown, *Apostle of Democracy,* 117–119.
5. Jones, "Recollections of Miss Salmon," Salmon Papers, box 59, folder 23.
6. Mary Anderson to Lucy Salmon, 12 April 1890, Salmon Papers, box 13, folder 3.
7. Amy Louise Reed, "Miss Salmon as I Knew Her," *Addresses at the Memorial Service for Lucy Maynard Salmon* (6 March 1927, Poughkeepsie, NY), 16, Salmon Papers, Box 30, folder 2.
8. Lucy Salmon to Miss Greer, 25 June 1889, Salmon Papers, box 59, folder 23. Salmon wrote a thank-you note to Miss Greer acknowledging receipt of the gift. She also saved the note attached to the gift.
9. James Monroe Taylor to Lucy Salmon, June 1889, Salmon Papers, box 59, folder 23.
10. Sophia Chen (Zen) to Lucy Salmon, 23 October 1919, Salmon Papers, box 16, folder 13.
11. Sophia Chen (Zen) to Lucy Salmon, 20 April 1920, 6 September 1920, Salmon Papers, box 16, folder 13.
12. E-tu Zen Sun, Interview with author, November 3, 1998. Telephone.
13. Sophia Chen (Zen) to Lucy Salmon, 23 October 1919, Salmon Papers, box 16, folder 13.
14. Sophia Chen (Zen) to Lucy Salmon, 13 November 1919, Salmon Papers, box 16, folder 13.
15. Interview with Jeannette Hopkins, Vassar College '44, November 3, 1998, telephone interview from Austin to Portsmouth, NH. Jeannette Hopkins is a literary editor/agent whose papers are housed at the Vassar College Special Collections. She attended Vassar with Lucy Salmon's niece, Elizabeth Salmon Teall. Hopkins spoke of her mother, Gladys Hull, Vassar College '13, a history major, who took several classes with Lucy Salmon and told her about the class visit to Salmon's kitchen, which clearly made quite an impression.
16. M. R. Williams, Postmaster, to Lucy Salmon, 10 November 1905, Salmon Papers, box 59, folder 23.
17. Lucy Salmon, "History in a Back Yard," reprinted in *Historical Material,* 143–157; Lucy Salmon, "Main Street," reprinted in *Historical Material,* 161–182.
18. Daniels, *Bridges to the World,* 196.
19. Rebecca Lawrence Lowrie to Lucy Salmon, 13 August 1912, Salmon Papers, box 14, folder 6.
20. Elsie M. Rushmore to Lucy Salmon, 2 February 1915, Salmon Papers, box 16, folder 1.
21. Jones, "Recollections of Miss Salmon," Salmon Papers, box 59, folder 23.
22. Jones, "Recollections of Miss Salmon," Salmon Papers, box 59, folder 23.
23. Sophia Chen (Zen) to Lucy Salmon, 19 June 1920, Salmon Papers, box 16, folder 13.
24. Rebecca Lawrence Lowrie to Lucy Salmon, 24 September 1914, Salmon Papers, box 14, folder 6.
25. H. Morse Stephens to Lucy Salmon, 19 January 1901, Salmon Papers, box 47, folder 13; Gordon, "Vassar College," 133.
26. Mary Berkemeier to Lucy Salmon, 5 October 1913, Salmon Papers, box 13, folder 9.
27. Mary Berkemeier to Lucy Salmon, 30 September 1913, 8 March 1914, Salmon Papers, box 13, folder 9.
28. Mary Berkemeier to Lucy Salmon, 22 November 1915, Salmon Papers, box 13, folder 9.
29. Amy Louise Reed, "Miss Salmon as I Knew Her," *Addresses at the Memorial Service for Lucy Maynard Salmon* (6 March 1927, Poughkeepsie, NY), 25, Salmon Papers, Box 30, folder 2.
30. Many letters from students to Salmon noted the inclusion of newspaper clippings or entire newspapers. See for example, Elsie M. Rushmore to Lucy Salmon, 2 February 1915, Salmon

Papers, box 16, folder 1; Rebecca Lawrence Lowrie to Lucy Salmon, October 1913, Salmon Papers, box 14, folder 6.
31. Rebecca Lawrence Lowrie to Lucy Salmon, 15 September 1917, 12 May 1919, 4 October 1921, 23 August 1926, Salmon Papers, box 14, folder 6.
32. Rebecca Lawrence Lowrie to Lucy Salmon, 12 May 1919, Salmon Papers, box 14, folder 6.
33. Elsie M. Rushmore to Lucy Salmon, 16 June 1919, Salmon Papers, box 16, folder 1.
34. Mary Berkemeier to Lucy Salmon, 5 October 1913, Salmon Papers, box 13, folder 9.
35. Ruth Adams to her parents, 16 January 1903, Vassar Student Letters Collection, 1865–1935, box 4; Gordon, *Gender and Higher Education in the Progressive Era*, 133.
36. Ruth Adams to her parents, 16 January 1903, Vassar Student Letters Collection, box 4.
37. Ruth Adams to George B. Adams, 12 January 1903, Vassar Student Letters Collection, box 4.
38. Jones, "Recollections of Miss Salmon," Salmon Papers, box 59, folder 23.
39. History A Examination, Salmon Papers, box 59, folder 8.
40. Lucy Salmon's handwritten assignment, Salmon Papers, box 59, folder 8.
41. Lucy Salmon to Adam Leroy Jones, 27 Oct 1922, Salmon Papers, box 59, folder 23.
42. Nelson, "Lucy Maynard Salmon," 10; Adams and Smith, "Introduction," *Lucy Maynard Salmon*, 5; Brown, *Apostle of Democracy*, 115–116, 161.
43. Hundreds of examinations for the classes Lucy Salmon taught are located in the Salmon Papers, box 59.
44. European History Examinations, Salmon Papers, box 59, folder 6.
45. The Development of Municipal Government Examinations, Salmon Papers, box 59, folder 17.
46. Historical Material Examinations, Salmon Papers, box 59, folder 18.
47. American History Examinations, Salmon Papers, box 59, folder 8.
48. Student work of Marjorie M. Kendig, Salmon Papers, box 59, folder 22.
49. Student work of Helen Prescott, Salmon Papers, box 59, folder 22.
50. Student work of Lalitha Folks, Salmon Papers, box 59, folder 22.
51. G. L. Chase Fletcher, Student Notecards 1911, box 77, Vassar College Student Collection.
52. Helen C. Cole, Student Notecards 1926, box 76; Anne Goodrich Swann, Student Notecards 1917, box 76; G. L. Chase Fletcher, Student Notecards 1911, box 77, Vassar College Student Collection.
53. Nelson, "Lucy Maynard Salmon," 10.
54. Notecards for Ruth Chandler's research, Salmon Papers, box 59, folder 22.
55. Ruth Chandler, Salmon Papers, box 59, folder 22.
56. E. Lillian Hutchinson's essay, "Suggestions for Change in History I Course," Salmon Papers, box 59, folder 22.
57. See Gladys S. Esten's essay, "Suggestions for Change in History I," and Marion S. Tallant's essay, "Suggestions for Improvement in History," Salmon Papers, box 59, folder 22.
58. Lucy Salmon, "Suggestions for the Year's Study—History A, AA" (Poughkeepsie, NY: Vassar College, 1912), preface.
59. Lucy Salmon, "Suggestions for the Year's Study—History 1–2" (Poughkeepsie, NY: Vassar College, 1921), preface.
60. W. L. Westermann, "The Teaching of Greek History: The Sources of Greek History," *The History Teacher's Magazine* 4 (November 1913): 249.
61. Henry Elson, "Use of Sources in History Teaching," *The History Teacher's Magazine* 1 (June 1910): 219.
62. Charles Fay, "Historical Sources in Public High Schools," *The History Teacher's Magazine* 1 (November 1909): 67.
63. Elson, "Use of Sources," 219.

64. See also Pauline Maier, *American Scripture: The Making of the Declaration of Independence* (New York: Knopf, 1997).
65. See, e.g., Elson,, "Use of Sources," 218–219 and Fay,, "Historical Sources in Public Schools." 67–68.
66. Fred Morrow Fling, "One Use of Sources in Teaching History," *The History Teacher's Magazine* 1 (September 1909): 5.
67. Fay, "Historical Sources in Public Schools," 68.
68. Clarence Perkins, "Reference Work in High School History Courses," *The History Teacher's Magazine* 2 (February 1911): 123.
69. See, e.g., Arthur M. Wolfson, "English History: A Series of Exercises in the Use of Sources," *The History Teacher's Magazine* 2 (December 1910): 83; Lillian W. Thompson, "Pictures in History Classes," *The History Teacher's Magazine* 2 (April 1911): 177–179; Thomas N. Hoover, "History Material and Its Keeping," *The History Teacher's Magazine* 3 (September 1911): 4–5; Westermann, "The Teaching of Greek History," 249–255; Maud Hamilton, "The Use of Illustrative Material in Secondary Schools," *The History Teacher's Magazine* 5 (March 1914): 81–86.

Chapter 8

1. Lucy Salmon, "Informal Lectures on the War," printed sheet, Vassar College Department of History, 1914, Salmon Papers, box 31, folder 7.
2. Lucy Salmon, "Informal Lectures on the War," printed sheet, Vassar College Department of History, 1917, Salmon Papers, box 31, folder 7.
3. Notecards for Ruth Chandler's research, Salmon Papers, box 59, folder 22.
4. Carol Gruber, *Mars and Minerva: World War I and the Uses of the Higher Learning in America* (Baton Rouge: Louisiana State University Press, 1975), 120.
5. Joseph Schafer to Lucy Salmon, 4 April 1919, Salmon Papers, box 57, folder 14.
6. Joseph Schafer to Lucy Salmon, 4 April 1919, Salmon Papers, box 57, folder 14.
7. Lucy Salmon to Woodrow Wilson, 1 June 1918, Salmon Papers, box 4, folder 12.
8. Lucy Salmon to Wilson, 1 June 1918.
9. Preserved Smith, "Tribute to Lucy Maynard Salmon," *Addresses at the Memorial Service for Lucy Maynard Salmon* (6 March 1927, Poughkeepsie, NY), 9, Salmon Papers, box 30, folder 2.
10. University of Michigan Printed Materials, Salmon Papers, box 31, folder 2.
11. University of Michigan Printed Materials, Salmon Papers, box 31, folder 2.
12. Brown, *Apostle of Democracy,* 263.
13. Brown, *Apostle of Democracy,* 218.
14. Anon, "The Ninety-Third Commencement," *Colgate Alumni Quarterly* 1 (July 1912): 3.
15. Henry Noble MacCracken to Lucy Salmon, February 17, 1923, Salmon Papers, box 7, folder 13.
16. Henry Noble MacCracken to Lucy Salmon, March 13, 1923, Salmon Papers, box 7, folder 14.
17. Elizabeth Updegraft, "Report of the Committee in Charge of The Lucy Maynard Salmon Fund for Research," Salmon Papers, box 45, folder 9.
18. Henry Noble MacCracken to Lucy Salmon, June 26, 1926, Salmon Papers, box 7, folder 14.
19. Updegraft, "Report of the Committee in Charge of The Lucy Maynard Salmon Fund for Research."

20. Updegraft, "Report of the Committee in Charge of The Lucy Maynard Salmon Fund for Research."
21. Brown, *Apostle of Democracy*, 262.
22. *Addresses at the Memorial Service for Lucy Maynard Salmon*, 6 March 1927, Poughkeepsie, NY, Salmon Papers, box 30, folder 2.
23. Henry Osborn Taylor, "Lucy Salmon," *Addresses at the Memorial Service for Lucy Maynard Salmon* (6 March 1927, Poughkeepsie, NY), 5, Salmon Papers, box 30, folder 2.
24. Amy Louise Reed, "Miss Salmon as I Knew Her,"*Addresses at the Memorial Service for Lucy Maynard Salmon* (6 March 1927, Poughkeepsie, NY), 23, Salmon Papers, box 30, folder 2.
25. Henry Noble MacCracken, "Lucy Maynard Salmon," *Addresses at the Memorial Service for Lucy Maynard Salmon* (6 March 1927, Poughkeepsie, NY), 29, Salmon Papers, box 30, folder 2.
26. Memorial Tributes, Salmon Papers, box 51, folder 15.
27. Anon, "In Memory of Lucy Maynard Salmon" *Proceedings of the Association of History Teachers of the Middle States and Maryland*, 25, November 26, 1927, Atlantic City Meeting, 106–108; A.C. Howland, "Lucy Maynard Salmon, First President of the Association," *Thirtieth Anniversary, 1904–1933 Middle States Association of History Teachers Proceedings*, 31, Philadelphia Meeting, May 5–6, 1933, 18–19.
28. Information on Lucy Maynard Salmon Endowed Chair in History located on Vassar College website, www.vassar.edu.
29. Updegraft, "Report of the Committee in charge of The Lucy Maynard Salmon Fund for Research."
30. Brown, *Apostle of Democracy*.
31. Lucy Salmon, "The Teaching of History in the Elementary Schools," *Educational Review* 1 (January–May 1891): 443.
32. Gruber, *Mars and Minerva*, 37–41.
33. Salmon Papers, *Finding Aid*, 19–24.

Bibliography

Archival Sources

Adams, George Burton. Papers. Yale University Library., New Haven, CT.
Adams, Herbert Baxter. Papers. Milton S. Eisenhower Library, Johns Hopkins University, Baltimore, MD.
American Historical Association. Papers. Library of Congress, Washington, D. C.
Angell, James B. Papers. Bentley Historical Library, University of Michigan, Ann Arbor, MI.
Baker, Ray Stannard. Papers. Library of Congress, Washington, D. C.
Dow, E. W. Papers. Bentley Historical Library, University of Michigan, Ann Arbor, MI.
MacCracken, Henry Noble. Papers. Special Collections, Vassar College Libraries, Poughkeepsie, NY.
Necrology File. Lucy M. Salmon. Bentley Historical Library, University of Michigan, Ann Arbor, MI.
Salmon, Lucy Maynard. Papers. Special Collections, Vassar College Libraries, Poughkeepsie, NY.
Taylor, James Monroe. Papers. Special Collections, Vassar College Libraries, Poughkeepsie, NY.
Turner, Frederick Jackson. Papers. Huntington Library and Art Gallery, Harvard University,. Cambridge, MA.
University of Michigan Alumni Association Records. Bentley Historical Library, University of Michigan, Ann Arbor, MI.
Vassar College Faculty Collection. Special Collections, Vassar College Libraries, Poughkeepsie, NY.
Vassar College Student Letters Collection. Special Collections, Vassar College Libraries, Poughkeepsie, NY.
Woman Suffrage Materials Collection. Special Collections, Vassar College Libraries, Poughkeepsie, NY.

Books

Adams, Charles K. "The Relations of Higher Education to National Prosperity." In *Representative Phi Beta Kappa Orations*, edited by C. S. Northrup, W. C. Lane, and J. C. Schwab, 160–161. Boston: Houghton Mifflin, 1915.

Adams, Nicholas, and Smith, Bonnie G., eds. *Lucy Maynard Salmon: History and the Texture of Modern Life*. Philadelphia: University of Pennsylvania Press, 2001.

Allison, Clinton. *Teachers for the South: Pedagogy and Educationists in the University of Tennessee, 1844–1995*. New York: Peter Lang, 1998.

American Historical Association. *The Study of History in Schools: Report to the American Historical Association by the Committee of Seven*. New York: Macmillan, 1899.

Angell, James B. *Selected Address*. New York: Longmans, Green, 1912.

Anon. "Charles Kendall Adams." In *Webster's New Biographical Dictionary*, edited by Robert McHenry and Frank Calvillo, 11. Springfield, MA: Merriam-Webster, 1983.

Anon. "Lucy Maynard Salmon." In *Dictionary of American Biography*, edited by Dumas Malone, 312–313. New York: Charles Scribner's Sons, 1963.

Anon. "Maria Mitchell." In *Webster's New Biographical Dictionary*, edited by Robert McHenry, 693. Springfield, MA: Merriam-Webster, 1983.

Antler, Joyce. *Lucy Sprague Mitchell: The Making of a Modern Woman*. New Haven: Yale University Press, 1987.

Baker, Liva. *I'm Radcliffe! Fly Me! The Seven Sisters and the Failure of Women's Education*. New York: Macmillan, 1976.

Baker, Ray S. *Woodrow Wilson Life and Letters, Youth 1856–1890*. Garden City: Doubleday, Page, 1927.

Blount, Jackie M. *Destined to Rule the Schools: Women and the Superintendency, 1873–1995*. Albany: State University of New York Press, 1998.

Bohan, Chara Haeussler. "Early Vanguards of Progressive Education: The Committee of Ten, the Committee of Seven, and Social Education," in Christine Woyshner, Joseph Watras, and Margaret Smith Crocco (eds.) *Social Education in the Twentieth Century: Curriculum and Context for Citizenship*. Peter Lang, New York (Spring 2004, in press).

Bohan, Chara Haeussler. "Historical and International Dimensions of History Education: The Work of the Committee of Seven," in *Raising Standards in History Education, International Review of History Education*, Vol. 3, edited by Alaric Dickinson, Peter Gordon, and Peter Lee, 56–72. London: Woburn Press, 2001.

Bohan, Chara Haeussler. "Lucy Maynard Salmon: Progressive Historian, Teacher, and Democrat," in *"Bending the Future to Their Will": Civic Women, Social Education, and Democracy*, edited by Margaret Smith Crocco and O. L. Davis Jr., 47–72. Lanham, MD: Rowman and Littlefield, 1999.

Bordin, Ruth. *Alice Freeman Palmer: The Evolution of a New Woman*. Ann Arbor: University of Michigan Press, 1993.

Bordin, Ruth. *Women at Michigan: The "Dangerous Experiment" 1870s to the Present*. Ann Arbor: University of Michigan Press, 1999.

Bragdon, Henry W. *Woodrow Wilson: The Academic Years*. Cambridge, MA: Belknap Press of Harvard University Press, 1967.

Brophy, Jere, and Bruce Van Sledright. *Teaching and Learning History in Elementary Schools*. New York: Teachers College Press, 1997.

Brown, Louise Fargo. *Apostle of Democracy: The Life of Lucy Maynard Salmon*. New York: Harper and Brothers, 1943.

Brubaker, Frederick. *The American College and University: A History*. Athens: University of Georgia Press, 1990.

Brubaker, John. *Higher Education in Transition*. New York: Harper and Row, 1958.
Butcher, Patricia Smith. *Education for Equality: Women's Rights Periodicals and Women's Higher Education, 1849-1920*. New York: Greenwood Press, 1989.
Cott, Nancy F. *The Bonds of Womanhood: "Women's Sphere" in New England, 1780-1835*. New Haven: Yale University Press, 1977.
Cott, Nancy F., and Elizabeth H. Pleck. *A Heritage of Her Own: Toward a New Social History of American Women*. New York: Simon and Schuster, 1979.
Cottrell, Debbie. *Pioneer Woman Educator: The Progressive Spirit of Annie Webb Blanton*. College Station: Texas A&M Press, 1993.
Cowan, Ruth Schwartz. *Household Technology from the Open Hearth to the Microwave*. New York: Basic Books, 1983.
Cremin, Lawrence. *American Education: The Metropolitan Experience, 1876-1980*. New York: Harper and Row, 1988.
Cremin, Lawrence. *American Education: The National Experience, 1783-1876*. New York: Harper and Row, 1980.
Cremin, Lawrence. *The Transformation of the School: Progressivism in American Education 1876-1957*. New York: Vintage Books, 1961.
Crocco, Margaret Smith, and O. L. Davis Jr., eds. *"Bending the Future to Their Will": Civic Women, Social Education and Democracy*. Lanham, MD: Rowman and Littlefield, 1999.
Daniels, Elizabeth. *Main to Mudd, An Informal History of Vassar College Buildings*. Poughkeepsie, NY: Vassar College, 1987.
Daniels, Elizabeth A. *Bridges to the World: Henry Noble MacCracken and Vassar College*. Clinton Corners, NY: College Avenue Press, 1994.
DeGregorio, William A. *The Complete Book of U.S. Presidents*. New York: Dember Books, 1989.
Driscoll, Marcy. *Psychology of Learning for Instruction*. Boston: Allyn and Bacon, 1994.
Faragher, John, and Florence Howe, eds. *Women and Higher Education in American History: Essays from the Mount Holyoke College Sesquicentennial Symposia*. New York: W. W. Norton, 1988.
Gordon, Lynn D. *Gender and Higher Education in the Progressive Era*. New Haven: Yale University Press, 1990.
Gruber, Carol S. *Mars and Minerva: World War I and the Uses of Higher Learning in America*. Baton Rouge: Louisiana State University Press, 1975.
Hochschild, Arlie Russell. *The Time Bind: When Work Becomes Home and Home Becomes Work*. New York: Metropolitan Books, 1997.
Jencks, Christopher, and David Riesman. *The Academic Revolution*. New York: Doubleday, 1968.
Johnson, Henry. *Teaching of History in Elementary and Secondary Schools*. New York: Macmillan, 1917.
Kliebard, Herbert M. *The Struggle for the American Curriculum, 1893-1958*. New York: Routledge and Kegan Paul, 1987.
Kridel, Craig. *Writing Educational Biography: Explorations in Qualitative Research*. New York: Garland, 1998.
Kridel, Craig, Jr., Robert Bullough, and Paul Shaker. *Teachers and Mentors: Profiles of Distinguished Twentieth Century Professors of Education*. New York: Garland, 1996.
Krug, Edward. *The Shaping of the American High School*. New York: Routledge and Kegan Paul, 1964.
Leinhardt, Gaea, Isabel Beck, and Catherine Stainton, eds. *Teaching and Learning in History*. Hillsdale: Lawrence Erlbaum, 1994.
Link, Arthur S., ed. *The Papers of Woodrow Wilson*, Vols. 4, 5. Princeton: Princeton University Press, 1977.
Linner, Edward R. *Vassar, the Remarkable Growth of a Man and His College*, edited by Elizabeth A. Daniels. Poughkeepsie, NY: Vassar College, 1984.

Lucas, Christopher. *American Higher Education: A History.* New York: St. Martin's Griffin, 1994.
Maier, Pauline. *American Scripture: The Making of the Declaration of Independence.* New York: Knopf, 1997.
Massialas, Byron, and Rodney Allen. *Crucial Issues in Teaching Social Studies.* New York: Wadsworth, 1996.
Meigs, Cornelia. *What Makes a College? A History of Bryn Mawr.* New York: Macmillan, 1956.
Miller-Bernal, Leslie. *Separate by Degree: Women Students' Experiences in Single-Sex and Coeducational Colleges.* New York: Peter Lang, 2000.
Mulder, John M. *Woodrow Wilson: the Years of Preparation* (Princeton, NJ: Princeton University Press, 1978.
Newcomber, Mabel. *A Century of Higher Education for American Women.* New York: Harper, 1959.
Nozick, Robert. *Anarchy, State and Utopia.* New York: Basic Books, 1974.
Palmer, Alice Freeman. "A Review of the Higher Education of Women." In *Woman and Higher Education,* edited by Anna C. Brackett, 103–130. New York: Harper Brothers, 1893.
Palmieri, Patricia Ann. *In Adamless Eden: The Community of Women Faculty at Wellesley.* New Haven: Yale University Press, 1995.
Pinar, William, William Reynolds, Patrick Slattery, and Peter Taubman. *Understanding Curriculum.* New York: Peter Lang, 1995.
Powers, Jane Bernard. *The "Girl Question" in Education: Vocational Education for Young Women in the Progressive Era.* London: Falmer Press, 1992.
Plum, Dorothy, and George B. Dowell. *The Great Experiment: A Chronicle of Vassar College.* Poughkeepsie, NY: Vassar College, 1961.
Plum, Dorothy, and George Dowell. *The Magnificent Enterprise: A Chronicle of Vassar College.* Edited by Constance Ellis. Poughkeepsie, NY: Vassar College, 1961.
Randall, Mercedes. *Improper Bostonian: Emily Greene Balch, Nobel Peace Laureate.* New York: Twayne, 1964.
Ravitch, Diane. *The Schools We Deserve.* New York: Basic Books, 1985.
Ravitch, Diane. *What Do Our 17-Year-Olds Know?* New York: Harper and Row, 1987.
Raymond, John H. "Vassar College: A Sketch of Its Foundation, Aims, and Resources, and of the Development of Its Scheme of Instruction to the Present Time." In *Women and Children First: The Dangers of Education, Sexism and the Origins of Women's Colleges,* edited by David J. Rothman and Sheila M. Rothman, 1–78. New York: Garland, 1987.
Robinson, James H. *The New History: Essays Illustrating the Modern Historical Outlook.* New York: Macmillan, 1912.
Ross, Dorothy. *The Origins of American Social Science.* Cambridge: Cambridge University Press, 1991.
Rudolph, Frederick. *The American College and University.* Athens: University of Georgia Press, 1962, 1990.
Sadovnik, Alan R., and Susan F. Semel, eds. *Founding Mothers and Others: Women Educational Leaders During the Progressive Era.* New York: Palgrave, 2002.
Sale, Kirkpatrick. *The Conquest of Paradise: Christopher Columbus and the Columbian Legacy.* New York: Knopf, 1990.
Salmon, Lucy M. *Domestic Service.* New York: Macmillan, 1897.
Salmon, Lucy M. *Historical Material.* New York: Oxford University Press, 1933.
Salmon, Lucy M. *History and the Texture of Modern Life: Selected Essays.* Nicholas Adams and Bonnie G. Smith, eds. Philadelphia: University of Pennsylvania Press, 2001.
Salmon, Lucy M. "History in a Back Yard." In *Historical Material,* 143–160. New York: Oxford University Press, 1933.
Salmon, Lucy M. "Main Street." In *Historical Material,* 161–184. New York: Oxford University Press, 1933.

Salmon, Lucy M. *The Newspaper and Authority*. New York: Oxford University Press, 1923.
Salmon, Lucy M. *The Newspaper and the Historian*. New York: Oxford University Press, 1923.
Salmon, Lucy M. *Progress in the Household*. New York: Houghton, Mifflin, 1906.
Salmon, Lucy M. "The Sources of Robinson's *History of Western Europe*." In *The Text-book Bulletin for High Schools and Colleges*. New York: Ginn, 1904.
Salmon, Lucy M. "Suggestions for the Year's Study: Vassar College." Poughkeepsie, NY: Vassar College, 1912.
Salmon, Lucy M. "The Teaching of History in Academies and Colleges." In *Woman and the Higher Education*, edited by Anna C. Brackett, 131–152. New York: Harper and Brothers, 1893.
Salmon, Lucy M. *What Is Modern History?* Poughkeepsie, NY: Vassar College, 1917.
Salmon, Lucy M. *Why Is History Rewritten?* New York: Oxford University Press, 1929.
Saxe, David Warren. *Social Studies in Schools: A History of the Early Years*. Albany: State University of New York Press, 1991.
Schudson, Michael. *Discovering the News: A Social History of American Newspapers*. New York: Basic Books, 1978.
Semel, Susan F., and Alan R. Sadnovnik, eds. *"Schools of Tomorrow," Schools of Today: What Happened to Progressive Education*. New York: Peter Lang, 1999.
Solomon, Barbara. *In the Company of Educated Women*. New Haven: Yale University Press, 1985.
Tindall, George B. *America: A Narrative History*. New York: W. W. Norton, 1988.
Urban, Wayne J. *Horace Mann Bond, 1904–1972*. Athens: University of Georgia Press, 1992.
Veysey, Laurence. *The Emergence of the American University*. Chicago: University of Chicago Press, 1965.
Ware, Susan. *Partner and I: Molly Dewson, Feminism, and New Deal Politics*. New Haven: Yale University Press, 1987.
Weiler, Kathleen, and Sue Middleton, eds. *Telling Women's Lives: Narrative Inquiries in the History of Women's Education*. Philadelphia: Open University Press, 1999.
Whelan, Michael. "History as the Core of the Social Studies Curriculum." In *The Social Studies Curriculum: Purposes, Problems and Possibilities*, edited by E. Wayne Ross, 21–37. Albany: State University of New York Press, 1997.
Wilson, Woodrow. *Congressional Government: A Study in American Politics*. Boston: Houghton, Mifflin, 1885.
Wilson, Woodrow. *George Washington*. New York: Harper and Brothers, 1896.
Wilson, Woodrow. *A History of the American People*. New York: Harper and Brothers, 1902.
Wilson, Woodrow. *An Old Master and Other Political Essays*. New York: Scribner and Sons, 1893.
Wilson, Woodrow. *The State: Elements of Historical and Practical Politics*. Boston: D. C. Heath, 1889.
Woloch, Nancy. *Women and the American Experience*. New York: Knopf, 1984.
Woody, Thomas. *A History of Women's Education in the United States*. New York: New Science Press, 1929.
Woyshner, Christine, Joseph Watras, and Margaret Smith Crocco, eds. *Social Education in the Twentieth Century: Curriculum and Context for Citizenship*. New York: Peter Lang (in press).

Dissertations and Theses

Boozer, Howard R. "The American Historical Association and the Schools, 1884–1956." Ph.D. diss., Washington University, 1960.

Kinzie, Glenn. "Historians and the Social Studies: A History and Interpretation of the Activities of the American Historical Association in the Secondary Social Studies, 1884–1964." Ph.D. diss., University of Nebraska in the Teachers College, 1965.

Official Documents/Electronic Information

Annual Catalogue of Vassar College. Poughkeepsie, NY: A. V. Haight, 1890–1927.
Catalogue of State Normal School, Terre Haute, Indiana, 1886–1887. Indianapolis, IN: W. B. Burford, Contractor for State Printing, 1887.
Standard Certificate of Death. Lucy Maynard Salmon. February 14, 1927. Register of Deaths in the City of Poughkeepsie, County of Dutchess, State of New York.
Transcripts of Grade Report. Lucy Maynard Salmon. University of Michigan, A.M. 1883, A.B. 1876, Office of the Registrar, Ann Arbor, MI.
U. S. Congress. Senate. Miscellaneous Documents of the Senate of the United States. *Report of the Organization and Proceedings of the American Historical Association,* 8–28, Washington, DC: Government Printing Office, 1892–1919.
American Heritage. Information on founding and history accessed from Internet @ www.americanheritage.com.
Michigan Today (summer 1997): Information on-line accessed at *http://www.umich.edu/~newsinfo/MT/97?Sum97/mtalj97.html.*
National Organization for Women. NOW staff, "Augusta National Golf Club Announces Plans to Continue Discrimination Against Women," November 12, 2002, Information on-line at *www.now.org/issues/wfw/111202augusta.html.*
Vassar College. Information on Lucy Maynard Salmon Endowed Chair in History accessed from Internet @ *www.vassar.edu.*

Oral History Interviews

Clark, Evalyn. Interview with author. October 23, 1997. Poughkeepsie, Tape deposited in the Oral History Collection, College of Education, University of Texas at Austin.
Hopkins, Jeanette. Interview with author. November 3, 1998. Telephone.
Sun, E-tu Zen. Interview with author. November 3, 1998. Telephone.

Periodic Literature

Adams, Herbert B. *Report of the Organization and Proceedings of the American Historical Association.* Vol. 1–7. New York: G. P. Putnam's Sons, 1885–1891.
Anon. "Book Review." *American Historical Review* 20 (October 1925): 146–147.
Anon. "In Memory of Lucy Maynard Salmon." Paper presented at the Proceedings of the Association of History Teachers of the Middle States and Maryland, Atlantic City, NJ, November 26, 1927.
Anon. "The Insoluble Problem." *Daily Chronicle,* May 25, 1897.
Anon. "The Ninety-Third Commencement." *Colgate Alumni Quarterly* 1 (July 1912): 3.
Anon. "Review of *Domestic Service.*" *The Churchman,* July 13, 1901.
Anon. "Review of *Domestic Service.*" *Chicago Tribune,* March 25, 1897.

Anon. "Review of *Domestic Service.*" *London Quarterly Review,* July 1901.
Anon. "Review of *Domestic Service.*" *New York Communal Advertiser,* August 24-27, n.d.
Anon. "The Suffrage Meeting." *Eagle,* September 8, 1911.
Anon. "Three Hundred Students of Falley Seminary Are Back." *Oswego Daily Times,* June 1, 1922.
Anon. "To Punish Girl Suffragists." *New York Herald,* June 10, 1908.
Anon. "Vassar Meets in Graveyard." *The Women's Journal,* Boston, June 13, 1908.
Banks, Nancy Huston. "A Very Practical Book." *The Daily Tribune,* February 21, 1897.
Barton, Keith. "History—It Can Be Elementary: An Overview of Elementary Students Understanding of History." *Social Education* 61 (1997): 13-16.
Billington, Ray A. "Tempest in Clio's Teapot: The American Historical Rebellion of 1915." *American Historical Review* 78 (April 1973): 348-369.
Bohan, Chara Haeussler. "Early Vanguards of Progressive Education: The Committee of Ten, the Committee of Seven, and Social Education." *Journal of Curriculum and Supervision* (fall 2003): 73-94.
Clifford, Geraldine Joncich. "'Shaking Dangerous Questions from the Crease': Gender and American Higher Education." *Feminist Issues* 2 (1983): 3-62.
Crocco, Margaret Smith. "The Road to the Vote." *Social Education* 59 (September 1995): 257-264.
Dzuback, Mary Ann. "Gender and the Politics of Knowledge." *History of Education Quarterly* 43 (summer 2003): 171-195.
Eisenmann, Linda. "Reconsidering a Classic: Assessing the History of Women's Higher Education a Dozen Years After Barbara Solomon." *Harvard Educational Review* 67 (winter 1997): 689-717.
Elson, Henry. "Use of Sources in History Teaching." *The History Teacher's Magazine* 1 (June 1910): 218-219.
Fay, Charles. "Historical Sources in Public High Schools." *The History Teacher's Magazine* 1 (November 1909): 67-68.
Fling, Fred Morrow. "One Use of Sources in Teaching History." *The History Teacher's Magazine* 1 (September 1909): 5-7.
Gilman, Elizabeth. "An Un-Tired Radical." *The Advance,* July 29, 1927.
Hamilton, Mau. "The Use of Illustrative Material in Secondary Schools." *The History Teacher's Magazine* 5 (March 1914): 81-86.
Hofer, Col. E. "School Days in Iowa." *The Lariat* (February 1925): 85-88.
Hoover, Thomas N. "History Material and Its Keeping." *The History Teacher's Magazine* 3 (September 1911): 4-5.
Howland, A. C. "Lucy Maynard Salmon, First President of the Association." Paper presented at the Thirtieth Anniversary, 1904-1933, Middle States Association of History Teachers Proceedings, Philadelphia, PA, May 5-6, 1933.
Jameson, J. Franklin. "The American Historical Association, 1884-1909." *American Historical Review* 15 (October 1909): 1-20.
Jameson, J. Franklin. "The American Historical Review, 1895-1920." *American Historical Review* 26 (October 1920): 1-17.
Jones, Blanche A. "Recollections of Miss Salmon," December 1935, Salmon Papers, box 59, folder 23.
Keels, Oliver M., Jr. "The Collegiate Influence of the Early Social Studies Curriculum: A Reassessment of the Role of Historians." *Theory and Research in Social Education* 8 (fall 1980): 105-120.
Levstik, Linda, and C. Pappas. "Exploring the Development of Historical Understanding." *Journal of Research and Development in Education* 21 (1987): 1-15.
Link, Arthur. "The American Historical Association, 1884-1984: Retrospect and Prospect." *American Historical Review* 90 (February 1985): 1-17.

MacCracken, Henry Noble. "Lucy Maynard Salmon." In *Addresses at the Memorial Service for Lucy Maynard Salmon* (6 March 1927, Poughkeepsie, NY), 29, Salmon Papers, box 30, folder 2.

Maher, Frances A. "Progressive Education and Feminist Pedagogies: Issues in Gender, Power, and Authority." *Teachers College Record* 101 (fall 1999): 35–59.

Mangan, Katherine S. "Radcliffe College Will Merge into Harvard." *Chronicle of Higher Education*, April 30, 1999, A39.

Nelson, Murry. "Lucy Maynard Salmon (1853–1927): Pioneering Views in Teaching History." *The Social Studies* 87 (January/February 1996): 7–12.

Neutral, A. (Salmon, Lucy). "Woodrow Wilson: The President's Policies Analyzed in the Lights of His Natural Inhibitions and Past Record." *The Nation*, September 14, 1916, 258.

Perkins, Clarence. "Reference Work in High School History Courses." *The History Teacher's Magazine* 2 (February 1911): 123–126.

Perry, Elisabeth Isreals. "The Changing Meanings of Progressive Era." *Magazine of History* 13 (spring 1999): 3–4.

Professor, A Near (Salmon, Lucy). "The Next College President." *The Popular Science Monthly* (September 1913).

Reed, Amy Louise. "Miss Salmon as I Knew Her." In *Addresses at the Memorial Service for Lucy Maynard Salmon* (6 March 1927, Poughkeepsie, NY), 14, Salmon Papers, Box 30, folder 2.

Rogers, Daniel T. "In Search of Progressivism." *Reviews in American History* 10 (December 1982): 113–132.

Ross, Mary. "Review of *The Newspaper and the Historian*." *Vassar Quarterly* 9 (November 1923): 244.

Rushmore, Elsie M. "In Memory of Lucy Maynard Salmon." *Vassar Quarterly* (July 1932).

Salmon, Lucy. "College Government." *The Vassar Miscellany* 24 (January 1895): 149–160.

Salmon, Lucy. "College Library." *Libraries* 31 (July 1926): 322–325.

Salmon, Lucy M. "Address by Professor Lucy M. Salmon." Paper presented at the Thirty-Eighth Annual Convention of the National American Suffrage Association, Baltimore, MD, February 7–13, 1906.

Salmon, Lucy M. "The Development of the Newspaper." *Vassar Quarterly* 5 (July 1920): 244–252.

Salmon, Lucy M. "Does the College Curriculum Promote Scholarship?" Address before the Ninth Annual Meeting of the National Association of Deans of Women, Department of National Education Association, Chicago, IL (February 24, 1922) in *Addresses and Proceedings of the Sixtieth Annual Meeting of the National Education Association* 60 (1922): 737–745.

Salmon, Lucy M. "Education in Michigan During the Territorial Period." *Education* 5 (September 1884–July 1885): 12–33.

Salmon, Lucy M. "History of the Appointing Power of the President." In *Papers of the American Historical Association*, 5–129. New York: G. P. Putnam's Sons, 1886.

Salmon, Lucy M. "Instruction in the Use of a College Library." *Bulletin of the American Library Association* 7 (July 1913): 301–309.

Salmon, Lucy M. "On a Certain Indefiniteness in History." Paper presented at the Association of History Teachers of the Middle States and Maryland, New York, NY, March 11–12, 1910.

Salmon, Lucy M. "Remember the Library." *Vassar Quarterly* 8 (November 1922): 55.

Salmon, Lucy M. "Some Historical Aspects of Domestic Service." *New England Magazine* 8 (April 1893): 175–184.

Salmon, Lucy M. "Some Principles in Teaching History." In *Publications of the National Society for the Scientific Study of Education, 1902–1906*, edited by Manfred Holmes, 1–61. Chicago: University of Chicago Press, 1908.

Salmon, Lucy M. "The Teaching of History in Academies and Colleges." *The Academy: A Journal of Secondary Education* 5 (September 1890): 283–292.

Salmon, Lucy M. "The Teaching of History in Elementary Schools." *Education Review* 1 (January–May 1891): 439–452.
Salmon, Lucy M. "Vacation Reading." *Public Libraries* 19 (June 1914): 233–238.
Salmon, Lucy M. "Vassar College Introductory Course in History." *The History Teacher's Magazine* 1 (March 1910): 145–148.
Salmon, Lucy M. "What Influence in College Life Has Proved of Most Force in My Later Life?—Opinions of Michigan Alumni." *Michigan Alumnus* 9 (1902): 408–409.
Smith, Preserved. "Tribute to Lucy Maynard Salmon." Memorial Address, Salmon Papers, box 51, folder 15, 2–3.
Smith, Theodore Clark. "Book Review of Apostle of Democracy." *American Historical Review* 49 (January 1944): 266.
Smith-Rosenberg, Caroll. "Book Review: Independent Women: Work and Community for Single Women, 1850–1920." *Signs* 13 (spring 1988): 648–651.
Smith-Rosenberg, Caroll. "The Female World of Love and Ritual: Relations Between Women in Ninteenth-Century America." *Signs: Journal of Women in Culture and Society* 1 (autumn 1975): 1–29.
Sullivan, James. "Suggested Changes in Course of Study in History." *The History Teacher's Magazine* 2 (January 1911): 103–104.
Taylor, Henry Osborn. "Lucy Salmon." In *Addresses at the Memorial Service for Lucy Maynard Salmon* (6 March 1927, Poughkeepsie, NY), 5, Salmon Papers, box 30, folder 2.
Thompson, Lillian W. "Pictures in History Classes." *The History Teacher's Magazine* 2 (April 1911): 177–179.
Updegraft, Elizabeth. "Report of the Committee in Charge of The Lucy Maynard Salmon Fund for Research," 1927, Salmon Papers, box 45, folder 9.
Van Tassel, David. "From Learned Society to Professional Organization: The American Historical Association, 1884–1900." *American Historical Review* 89 (October 1984): 929–956.
Walker, Linda Robinson. "John Dewey at Michigan, the Birth of Pragmatism: The Philosopher's Second Ann Arbor Period, 1889–1884." *Michigan Today* (fall 1997): 17–19.
Walker, Linda Robinson. "John Dewey's Philosophical Shift While at Michigan." *Michigan Today* (summer 1997) accessed on-line at *www.umich.edu/-newsinfo/MT/97/Sum97/mta1j97.html.*
Weiler, Kathleen. "Reflections on Writing a History of Women Teachers." *Harvard Educational Review* 67 (winter 1997): 635–657.
Westermann, W. L. "The Teaching of Greek History: The Sources of Greek History." *The History Teacher's Magazine* 4 (November 1913): 249–255.
Whelan, Michael. "A Particularly Lucid Lens: The Committee of Ten and the Social Studies Committee in Historical Context." *The Journal of Curriculum and Supervision* 12 (spring 1997): 256–268.
Wineburg, Sam. "Historical Problem Solving: A Study of the Cognitive Processes Use in the Evaluation of Documentary and Pictorial Evidence." *Journal of Educational Psychology* 83 (1991): 73–87.
Wolfson, Arthur M. "English History: A Series of Exercises in the Use of Sources." *The History Teacher's Magazine* 2 (December 1910): 83.
Yeager, Elizabeth, and O. L. Davis Jr. "Teaching the 'Knowing How' of History: Classroom Teachers' Thinking About Historical Topics." Paper presented at the American Educational Research Association, San Francisco, CA, 1995.

Index

Adams, C. K., 13, 16, 17, 19, 21
Adams, G. B., 27, 51, 101
Adams, H. B., 17, 26, 27, 32, 77
Adams, R., 51, 101
Addams, J., 23, 63, 78, 81
American Academy of Arts and Sciences, 24
American Academy of Medicine, 23
American Association of University Professors, 24, 33–34
American Association of University Women, xviii, 33–34
American Heritage, 31
American Historical Association, xviii, 3, 16, 17, 24, 25, 26–28, 32, 39, 48, 56, 57, 62, 66
    1916 annual banquet of, 27, 28–32
    Committee of Seven, 26, 27, 31, 73, 75, 76, 77, 78, 80, 92, 99, 103, 112
American Historical Review, 27, 45, 62, 71
American Political Science Association, 77
American Red Cross, 100
Anderson, M., 49, 96
Angell, J. B., 11, 18, 82
Anthony, S. B., 35
Antler, J., 8
Apostle of Democracy: The Life of Lucy Maynard Salmon (Brown), 1, 116
Arnold, M., 62
Association of Colleges and Preparatory Schools of the Middle States and Maryland, 33
Association of Collegiate Alumnae, 23, 34
Association of History Teachers of the Middle States and Maryland, xviii, 24, 32–33, 57, 117
Atwater, C., 37
Augusta National Golf Club, 27

Baker, L., 23
Baldwin, J., 45, 46, 47, 48, 84, 110
Bancroft, J., 29
Barker, E. C., 27
Barnard College, 19, 43
Barnard, E. F., 41
Barnes, A. H., 23
Baskus, H. H., 23
Beard, C., 57
Beard, M., 63
Benneson, C. A., 20
Benson, M. S., 5
Berkemeier, M., 99, 100
Berkheimer, M., 49
Bishop, B. B., 49
Blatch, H. S., 23, 36, 38
Blount, J., 8, 25
Bohan, C. H., xvii, xviii, xix
Bordin, R., 8
Boston marriages, 52

Bourne, H., 32
Bowen, C., 28, 29
Brown, L. F., 1, 27, 45, 48, 53, 116
Brownell, J., 33
Brubaker, J., 11
Bryan, E. B., 114
Bryn Mawr College, 12, 18, 22, 23, 26, 33, 38
Burk, M., 27
Burr, G., 29
Butcher, P., 12

Carlyle, Thomas, 62
Castle, E. H., 33
Catt, C. C., 39
Chandler, R., 107, 112
Chapin, A., 12
Chase, G. L. F., 107
Chen, S., 97, 99
Cheyney, E., 57
Chicago Tribune, 66
Clark College, 63
Clark, E., 47, 53
Colgate University, 114
Columbia University, 28, 29, 30, 33, 43, 48, 82
Columbus, C., 61
Connecticut Council of Defense, 108, 112
Congressional Union for Woman Suffrage, 34, 36
Conquest of Paradise: Christopher Columbus and the Columbian Legacy (Sale), 61
Cook County Normal School, 76
Cooke, F. J., 26
Cornell University, 13, 29, 30, 99
Cott, N., 5
Cremin, L., 81
Crocco, M. S., 8
Culbertson, E., 23

Daily Chronicle, 66
Daily Tribune, 66
Daniels, E., 46, 48
Daughters of the American Revolution, 116
Davenport, F., 37, 46, 48
Davis, J., 58
Davis, O. L., xix
Dewey, A., 82
Dewey, J., 8, 82
Dexter, E. A., 5
Dickinson College, 13
Domestic Service (Salmon), 24, 36, 56, 62–68, 98
    reviews of, 66

Dunning, W., 28
Dzuback, M. A., 8

Edmonds, F. S., 33
Education for Equality (Butcher), 12
educational philosophy, 73, 74–76
Eisenmann, L., 8
Eisner, E., 1
Eliot, C., 10
Ellery, E., 48
Elson, H., 109
Emerson, R. W., 82
Esten, G. S., 108
feminism, 5
First Yearbook of the National Society for the Scientific Study of Education (Salmon), 74
Fish, C. R., 112
Fling, F. M., 110
Folks, L., 107
Ford, G. S., 27
Ford, W. C., 29
"Founding Mothers," 26
Founding Mothers and Others: Women Educational Leaders During the Progressive Era (Semel and Sadovnik), 8
Fox, G. L., 77
Froebel, F., 82
Fulton Female Seminary, 10

Gender and Higher Education in the Progressive Era (Gordon), 49
Gillman, C. P., 37, 38
Gordon, L., 43, 49
Green, J. R., 59
Greene, E. B., 28, 29, 30, 62
Guizot, François, 62

Harding, S. B., 27
Harper Brothers, 100
Harrington, W., 50
Hart, A. B., 57, 76, 77, 99
Harvard University, 10, 19, 43, 57, 84, 99, 113
Haskins, C. H., 27, 57, 77, 99
higher education
    in the post-Civil War era, 11
    19th c. statistics on, 11
historical criticism, 62
Historical Material (Salmon), 57, 58, 87, 115
Historical Outlook, 79
history in the round, 59

History of Western Europe (Robinson), 56
History Teacher's Magazine, 79, 109, 110, 112
history, teaching of
  purpose of, 55, 63
  role of newspapers in, 24
  use of original source material, xvii, 7, 46
Holt, H., 37
Hopkins Grammar School, 77
Hull House, 23
Hutchinson, E. L., 108

In Adamless Eden (Palmieri), 45
International Congress of Arts and Science, 56
Introduction to the History of History (Shotwell), 56
Ipswich Seminar, 10

Jameson, J. F., 48, 57, 112
Johns Hopkins University, 2, 17, 18, 19, 26, 113
Jones, Miss, 96
Justice, A., 68

Kelly, F., 63, 78
Kendig, M. M., 106
Knox College, 99

Last Judgment, 58
Lathrop, J., 23
Leach, A., 38
Learning and Teaching the Ways of Knowing (Eisner), 1
Library of Congress, 48
literary quality, 62
Locke, J., 82
London Quarterly Review, 66
Lowrie, R. L., 49, 98, 99, 100
Lucy Maynard Salmon Endowed Chair in History, 116
Lucy Maynard Salmon Fund for research, 50, 51, 115
Lyon, M., 10
Lyttle, E. W., 33

Macauley, Thomas, 62
MacCracken, H. N., 24, 31, 45, 47, 49, 68, 82, 114, 115, 116
MacCracken, M. D., 47
Macmillan Publishing Company, 100
Mann, H., 8, 82
Marstin, M., 12

McKinley, A., 112
McLaughlin, A. C., 27, 77, 112
Metropolitan Club (New York), 27, 28, 29
Michaelangelo, 58
Middle Sates Council for the Social Studies, 117
Miller-Bernal, L., 8, 23
Mills, H., 47, 85
Mitchell, M., 24, 43
Modge, Mrs. J., 73
Morris, G. S., 114
Mott, L., 35, 36
Mount Holyoke College, 19, 26
Munro, D. C., 33

Nation, 22, 67
National American Women Suffrage Association, 34, 35, 36
National Board of Historical Service, 112, 113
National College Equal Suffrage League, 34, 37, 38, 39
National Education Association, 26, 76, 77
National Equal Suffrage Association, 22
National Organization of Women, 27
National Women's Party, 36
New Century Club, 59
New England Magazine, 66
New History: Essays Illustrating the Modern Historical Outlook (Robinson), 56
new social history, 6, 22, 56–57, 58, 59, 60–61, 62, 67, 73, 117
Newspaper and the Authority (Salmon), 24, 68, 70
Newspaper and the Historian (Salmon), 24, 68, 69, 71
New Woman, 5
New York Communal Advertiser, 66
New York Times, 41
Nightingale, A. F., 77

Outlook, 35

Page, C., 10
Palmieri, P., 45, 46, 52
Palmer, A. F., 12, 14, 18, 26, 42, 43
Parker, F. W., 76
Pankhursts, 36
Parkhurst, H., 26
Paul, A., 34, 36
Pestalozzi, J., 82
Philips, U. B., 27

Piaget, J., 74
Pleck, E., 5
Pratt, C., 26
Prescott, H., 106
Prescott, William, 62
Princeton University, 19, 20, 22
Progress in the Household (Salmon), 24, 67, 98
Progressive Education Movement, 8, 25, 36, 81, 94
Progressive era, 4
  women's sexual relationships and, 52
Progressivism, 81, 82
Pure Food and Drug Act, 81

Q. C., 14

Radcliffe College, 19, 43, 99, 100
Ravitch, D., 6
Raymond, J. H., 41, 43
Readings (Robinson), 108
Reed, A. L., 31, 96, 100
Reese, W., 81, 82
Revolution, 13
Reynolds, W., 8
Richert, E., 49, 50
Robinson, J. H., 33, 33, 56, 57, 108
Ross, M., 71
Rottschaefer, H. G., 49
Rousseau, J.-J., 82
Rushmore, E. M., 49, 50, 98, 100

Sachs, J., 33
Sale, K., 61
Salmon, G., 9, 10
Salmon, L. M.
  Adelaide Underhill and, 52-54
  American Historical Association and, 28-32
  as an early feminist leader, 5
  as a teacher of history, xviii, 2, 4, 84-87, 90-92, 93-96, 96-99
    progressive methods, 81-84
    purpose of history, 55, 62
    testing students, 102-106
    use of primary sources, 7, 46, 87-89
    use of the seminar, 84
  birth and childhood, 8-9
  college education, 10-15
  criticisms of her teaching, 108-110
  current relevance of, 6-8
  death of, 115
  defining history, 57-59
  developmentally appropriate historical study and, 76
  early career of, 15-18
  early Vassar College career, 23-24
  educational philosophy of, 73, 74-76
  everyday life at Vassar College, 41-42, 45-49
  desire for democratic governance at, 42-45
  relations with students, 49-51
  her significance in education, 116-118
  history in the round and, 59
  late career of, 113-116
  legacy of, 111-112, 112-113
  legacy of her students, 106-108
  literary history and, 31
  "long table" and, 96
  Louise Fargo Brown biography of, 1
  master's thesis by, 16
  mentoring of students, 93, 99-102
  new social history and, 6, 56-57, 58, 59, 60-61, 67, 117
  professional associations and, 25-26, 26-28, 32
  Progressive era and, 4
  publications by, 16, 17, 24, 56, 57, 67, 68-71, 83, 111
  sexual orientation of, 52
  significance of her work, 3-6
  suffrage activities of, 34-37
  Woodrow Wilson and, 18-23, 47
  Also see Vassar College
Salmon, M. C. M., 9, 10
Salmon, P., 13, 14, 15
Schafer, J., 112
scientific history, 61
Seamen, L. M., 49
Seminary of Historical and Political Science, 19
Seneca Falls Convention, 35
Seven Sister colleges, 19
Shakespeare, W., 55
Shaw, A. H., 36, 37, 38, 39
Shipp, M., 50
Shotwell, J. T., 56
Smith College, 19, 23
Smith, P., 71, 113
Smith-Rosenberg, C., 52

Smith, T. C., 45
Social Studies, 79
Solomon, B., 8
Spruill, J. C., 5
standardized examinations, 102–103
Stanton, E. C., 23, 35, 36
State Normal School (Indiana), 16, 17, 18
Stephens, H. M., 57, 77, 99
Stubbs, W., 93
Students' Christian Association, 14
Sun, E-T. Zen, 97

Tallant, M. S., 108
Tappan, H., 10
Taylor, H. O., 115
Taylor, J. M., 24, 37, 38, 44, 45, 46, 49, 67, 94, 97
Textor, L. E., 48
Thallon, I. C., 48
Thayer, W. R., 31, 57, 62
Thomas, M. C., 26, 38, 39
Thompson, A. B., 30
Thompson, C. M., 48
Thoreau, H. D., 82
transmission model of learning, 4
Turner, F. J., 31, 56, 57, 62, 112

Una, 12
Underground Railroad, 98
Underhill, A., 35, 46, 47, 48, 49, 51, 52–54, 67
University of California, 99
University of Chicago, 12, 27, 30, 82, 97
University of Michigan, 2, 10, 11–15, 16, 19, 20, 42, 43, 82, 113
University of Nevada, 27, 48
University of Peking, 97
University of Wisconsin, 13, 30, 57, 100
U. S. Children's Bureau, 23
Unpopular Review, 37
Updegraff, E., 49, 50

Van Tassel, D., 80
Vassar College, 2, 15, 22, 23–24, 29, 30, 34, 37, 48, 82, 91, 112, 114
    democratic governance at, 42–45
    entrance requirements, 94–96
    Also see Lucy Salmon
Vassar College Historical Association, 32
Vassar College Statute of Instruction, 45
Vassar College Suffrage Movement, 37–39
Vassar Miscellany, 44
Vassar, M., 23, 43
Vassar Quarterly, 53, 69, 100
Von Tilling, J. H. N. A., 113

Ward, L. F., 78
Washington, G., 22
Weiler, K., 8
Wellesley College, 12, 18, 20, 22, 23, 26, 42
Westermann, W. L., 109
Western Association of Collegiate Alumni, 33, 34
What Do Our 17-Year-Olds Know? (Ravitch), 6
What Is Modern History? (Salmon), 57
Why Must History Be Rewritten? (Salmon), 3, 57, 61, 115
Wilson, W., 2, 18–23, 47, 56, 81, 84, 110, 113
Woloch, N., 25, 35
Women and the American Experience (Woloch), 25
Women Suffrage Convention, 38
women's suffrage, 34–37
Wooley, M. E., 26
World Anti-Slavery Convention, 35
Wright, C., 63, 78

Yale Report of 1828
Yale University, 19, 30
Yale University Press, 100
Young, E. F., 26

Zen, S. C., 49

THIS SERIES EXPLORES THE HISTORY OF SCHOOLS AND SCHOOLING in the United States and other countries. Books in this series examine the historical development of schools and educational processes, with special emphasis on issues of educational policy, curriculum and pedagogy, as well as issues relating to race, class, gender, and ethnicity. Special emphasis will be placed on the lessons to be learned from the past for contemporary educational reform and policy. Although the series will publish books related to education in the broadest societal and cultural context, it especially seeks books on the history of specific schools and on the lives of educational leaders and school founders.

For additional information about this series or for the submission of manuscripts, please contact the general editors:

>   Alan R. Sadovnik Susan F. Semel
>   Rutgers University-Newark The City College of New York, CUNY
>   Education Dept. 138th Street and Convent Avenue
>   155 Conklin Hall NAC 5/208
>   175 University Avenue New York, NY 10031
>   Newark, NJ 07102

To order other books in this series, please contact our Customer Service Department:

> 800-770-LANG (within the U.S.)
> 212-647-7706 (outside the U.S.)
> 212-647-7707 FAX

Or browse online by series at:

> www.peterlangusa.com